Reading Jewish Religious Texts

Reading Jewish Religious Texts introduces students to a range of significant post-biblical Jewish writing. It covers diverse genres such as prayer and liturgy, biblical interpretation, religious law, philosophy, mysticism and works of ethical instruction. Each text is newly translated into English and accompanied by a detailed explanation to help clarify the concepts and arguments. The commentary situates the text within its broader historical and ideological context, giving readers an enhanced appreciation of its place in the Jewish religious experience. This volume also includes a comprehensive timeline, glossary and bibliography.

Eliezer Segal is Professor of Religious Studies at the University of Calgary, Canada. He has published extensively on rabbinic texts and Jewish biblical interpretation. His books include *Introducing Judaism* (Routledge 2008).

Reading Religious Texts series

This exciting series introduces students to the key texts from each of the major world religious traditions. It provides students with tools to engage with the texts, while helping them to understand their religious, social, cultural, historical and literary contexts. Each book addresses the issues arising from the text's interpretation and contemporary approaches and responses to these issues.

Reading the New Testament: Contemporary Approaches
James Crossley

Reading Jewish Religious Texts
Eliezer Segal

Forthcoming:
Reading Hindu Texts
Reading the Hebrew Bible
Reading the Qur'an

Reading Jewish Religious Texts

Eliezer Segal

 Routledge
Taylor & Francis Group

LONDON AND NEW YORK

First published 2012
by Routledge
2 Park Square, Milton Park, Abingdon, Oxon OX14 4RN

Simultaneously published in the USA and Canada
by Routledge
711 Third Avenue, New York, NY 10017

Routledge is an imprint of the Taylor & Francis Group, an informa business

British Library Cataloguing in Publication Data
A catalogue record for this book is available from the British Library

Library of Congress Cataloging in Publication Data
A catalog record for this book has been requested

ISBN: 978-0-415-58821-8 (hbk)
ISBN: 978-0-415-58822-5 (pbk)
ISBN: 978-0-203-80594-7 (ebk)

Typeset in Sabon
by RefineCatch Limited, Bungay, Suffolk

MIX
Paper from
responsible sources
FSC
www.fsc.org   FSC® C004839

Printed and bound in Great Britain by
CPI Antony Rowe, Chippenham, Wiltshire

Contents

Introduction   1

1   Prayers and liturgical texts   10

Daily prayer: The eighteen blessings 10
From the additional service for festivals 16
From the additional service for Rosh Hashanah 17
Various liturgical blessings 19
The Passover Haggadah 21
Piyyuṭ—*Hebrew liturgical poetry 25*
T'khinnes 32

2   Aggadah and Midrash   36

Halakhic Midrash 36
Aggadic Midrash: homiletic 43
Aggadic Midrash: exegetical 49

3   The literature of halakhic discourse   54

Passages from the Torah 54
Mishnah 55
The Babylonian Talmud 56
The Babylonian Geonim *64*
The Sephardic codes of Jewish law 68
Rashi and the medieval French and German
  commentators 71
Later halakhic authorities 80

4   Jewish bible commentaries   89

Interpreting Balak 89

5   **Philosophy and rational theology**   110

From: Saadiah Gaon's The Book of
   Doctrines and Opinions *111*
Baḥya Ibn Paquda 113
Moses Maimonides 114
Judah Halevi, Kuzari *122*
Abraham Isaac Hakohen Kook 126

6   **Esoteric, mystical and kabbalistic texts**   130

Mishnah Ḥagigah 2:1 130
Tosefta Ḥagigah 2:2 131
Babylonian Talmud Ḥagigah 131
Tosefta Ḥagigah 133
"Heikhalot" mysticism 134
*Kabbalah and the symbolism of the ten
   sefirot 137*
Abraham Abulafia 154
The Kabbalah of Rabbi Isaac Luria 157
Rabbi Joseph Caro's Maggid Meisharim *160*

7   **Moralistic and ethical writings**   162

Mishnah Avot chapter 4 162
Baḥya Ibn Paquda 165
The Book of the Pious *168*
The discourses of Rabbi Nissim ben Reuben of Gerona 171
The memoirs of Glueckel of Hameln 174
Rabbi Moses Hayyim Luzzatto, The Path of the Upright *175*
Ḥasidic stories 178
Ḥasidic teachings: Rabbi Elimelech of Lyzhansk 188

Timeline of Jewish religious texts and authors   190
Glossary   192
Notes   211
Bibliography of Jewish religious texts in English   214
Index   225

Introduction

The sanctity and authority that are attached to the Hebrew Scriptures derive from the conviction held by Jews that the contents of these works originated in a revelation from God. The process is known in Hebrew as *nevu'ah* and in English as "prophecy." The Bible is largely a record of the communications that were vouchsafed to the people of Israel, mostly through the instrument of the prophets [Hebrew: *navi* (plural: *nevi'im*)]. The prophets were depicted as proclaiming their divinely commanded messages whenever the people required it. Often this involved castigating Israelite society for their failures to maintain their commitments as required by their covenant with God; but at other times, the prophets consoled their community with reassurances of a peaceful and glorious future if they would remain faithful to their spiritual mission. The greatest of the prophets was Moses. Jewish tradition held that God revealed to him the five books of the Torah, a revelation that serves as the foundation for the covenant between God and the community of Israel. Much of the Torah consists of hundreds of commandments (613 of them, according to what was to become the standard Jewish enumeration), and this is consistent with the central role that Judaism has attached to the study and observance of laws, statutes and commandments [in Hebrew: *miṣvah* (plural: *miṣvot*) as the preeminent unit of religious virtue.

At a particular point in history, Jewish tradition held that the institution of prophecy ceased to operate. The last of the prophets to be included in the biblical canon were in fact the last to receive direct communications from the Lord. Haggai, Zechariah and Malachi operated during the early Persian era (not later than the fifth century BCE) when the Persian emperors allowed the Judeans, who had been exiled by Babylonia, to return to Jerusalem and rebuild their Temple. Jewish tradition provides no definitive explanation for the cessation of prophecy at this particular juncture, and perhaps not all Jews agreed that the process had come to a complete end—and yet this assumption underlies most of the religious literature produced by subsequent generations. In the second century BCE, the Hasmonean dynasty, for all its triumphalist confidence, issued decrees with the proviso that their authority was "pending the advent of a true prophet." The ancient authors of apocalyptic visions ascribed their revelations to figures (even minor figures) from the biblical past. And this perception that prophecy was a phenomenon of the past was the prevailing attitude among the rabbis of the Talmud and Midrash.

Whatever its reason, the cessation of prophecy meant that the canon of the Jewish scriptures was thereafter closed and could not be added to or altered. Though some works (such as Daniel or Ecclesiastes) were composed or incorporated into the body of sacred scriptures at later dates, their acceptance could be assured only by ascribing them to earlier eras. God might still convey messages to individuals in an irregular manner—through encounters with the immortal prophet Elijah or by the heavenly voice that the rabbis designated "*bat qol*"—but these were usually limited to intimate communications for particular persons, no longer the momentous messages that the prophets of old had directed to the nation, society, the political and cultic leaderships of Israel and the nations of the world.

Now that God was no longer addressing the nation directly, the people were impelled to seek out religious guidance in the prophetic messages that had been revealed to the earlier generations. It was assumed that the divinely inspired preaching that had been recorded and written in the Bible contained eternally valid truths, so it was natural that Jews should devote their energies to a meticulous examination of those ancient texts. The upshot of this process is that Judaism, as it evolved since the biblical era, is very much a religion of texts, in which the study of books—and of unwritten traditions (in keeping with the doctrines of the Pharisees and the rabbis that became the predominant interpretation of Judaism)—occupies a central position in defining Jewish religious experiences. This truism has far-reaching implications when it comes to shaping the ideals and realities of Judaism. Although it is arguable that all—or at least most—of the major world religions draw inspiration from their respective sacred scriptures, the importance of textual authority in Judaism—and this was not confined to the "rabbinic" version of Judaism—is strikingly pronounced and ubiquitous. It has a decisive impact on the determining of key religious values, such as the ideals of piety and authority, the curricula of elementary schools and seminaries, and even the qualities that are to be sought in a prospective marital partner. By assuming a correlation between virtue and literacy, however, the emphasis on textual study also had the effect of marginalizing or excluding those segments of the community (such as the women of previous generations) who do not possess the requisite knowledge, opportunities or skills to master the authoritative texts.

No doubt, the religious experiences of being Jewish cannot all be reduced to reading books or understanding oral traditions. Nonetheless, to an extraordinary extent, descriptions of the Jewish religion are contiguous with outlines of its principal texts, which of course include accounts of sacred history, beliefs, moral values and obligatory practices. Our knowledge of how Judaism was lived in earlier times is of necessity mediated by the surviving texts, and if a religious community did not transmit any texts to posterity, then it is probable that we have been left unaware of its existence. Even archeological relics are unlikely to divulge their religious significance without crucial assistance from written documents.

The present collection consists of representative texts from numerous and varied expressions of the Jewish religion as they emerged in the many eras and places where Jews have resided. For the most part, I have striven toward inclusiveness when determining which works should appear here; but the sheer magnitude of the corpus demanded that I set some limitations on the inclusion.

Though it is possible to quibble at length about the correct definition of a "Jewish religious text," I found it quite easy to come up with a simple working definition that seemed appropriate for the task at hand. For example, aside from whatever semantic arguments one might raise over the appropriateness of applying the term "Jewish" to the Hebrew Bible, the simple truth is that it is covered in a separate volume of this series. Nevertheless, the specifically Jewish approaches to reading and living with the Bible do in fact permeate almost every page in this book—not only the sections that are explicitly devoted to Midrash or biblical interpretation.

Almost all the texts selected for this volume were regarded as sacred by the Jewish community, or at least by an important segment thereof. In many cases, this led to the perception that the study of these texts constitutes a religious activity in its own right. This criterion served to exclude some important descriptions of Judaism, or documents produced by religious Jews, because those texts were not considered subjects of religious reverence or obligatory study. Accordingly, you will not find here passages from the first-century CE historian Josephus Flavius, invaluable though they might be for enriching our knowledge of Judaism in the Second Commonwealth; from his contemporary, the philosophical commentator Philo Judaeus of Alexandria; or from Moses Mendelssohn's *Jerusalem* which never, to the best of my knowledge, achieved the status of a text that was studied by Jews as a religious duty. A similar set of considerations accounts, at least in part, for the under-representation of modern non-traditionalist Jewish move-ments in the present volume, in that it is difficult to point to instances of writings authored by Liberal, Reform or Conservative spokespersons that are approached by their communities as bearing religious authority or deserving of ritualized study. It is likely that the compiler of a similar anthology a hundred years from now will include authors from the twen-tieth and twenty-first centuries after their teachings have had the time to acquire the proper aura of reverent sanctity.

In undertaking this anthologizing project, I was initially guided by a commitment to a pluralistic perspective on Jewish religious expression that should, in principle, not discriminate between orthodoxy and heresy, or between normative and sectarian streams. As the quantity of texts began to grow, I realized that this was an aspiration that could not be followed through with any consistency. Ideally, a compendium of religious law such as the Qumran *Serekh Hayyaḥad* ("Community Rule" or "Manual of Discipline") or the Karaite Anan's *Book of Commandments* have as much a right as the Mishnah to be included here. In practical terms, however, it soon became evident to me that each of the "peripheral" or "non-normative" Jewish movements—such as the Essenes, the Karaites, the Ethiopian Jews—has produced its own variegated literatures of liturgy, exegesis, theology, religious law and other genres, and that any attempt to represent them here beyond the most minimal tokenism would result in an unmanageably cumbersome tome, as well as exceeding by far my own pretensions to scholarly competence. In the end, this assortment of texts, for all its broad range and variety of genres, is restricted to religious works produced by the chief religious movements of contemporary Judaism. As such, they are all versions of "rabbinic" Judaism as the movement emerged in late antiquity and during the Middle Ages. Most of the authors did in fact bear the title "Rabbi," a title that is earned principally by virtue of the person's mastery of the texts that are held in esteem by the community.

The great majority of texts in this book were composed in the classical Jewish tongues of Hebrew and Aramaic, and I have translated them myself; as was the case with the few passages in Yiddish (Judeo-German). Some of the medieval philosophical texts were written in Judeo-Arabic. Though my proficiency in Arabic is at a much more rudimentary level, I did nonetheless attempt the task of translation on my own; though to be sure, when dealing with these works, I placed much more reliance on existing translations and commentaries in Hebrew and English. Where possible and appropriate (this was especially true when it came to liturgical texts), I tried to make use of authentic readings as preserved in manuscripts and published in academic text-critical editions. In those instances, I provided references to the sources; where no such references appear, I utilized the standard printed editions. When translating poetry, I was unable to reproduce rhymes and meters, though my comments contain descriptions of the salient formal features of the text.

Readers accustomed to the current conventions of English writing, especially in academic venues, have come to expect that sentences be formulated in a gender-neutral manner, whether by relatively inconspicuous means such as the widespread use of plurals, or by more awkward usages such as "he/she" or alternating masculine and feminine forms. Though I made some efforts in that direction in passages where it did not require intrusive tampering with the original syntax, it quickly became clear to me that imposing current standards on the older texts would involve a fundamental distortion of those documents. The languages of those texts are too conscious of grammatical gender to allow for the degrees of ambiguity or inclusiveness that are possible in English. The general rule in those languages (as it was for English prior to the 1970s) is that masculine adjectives or verbs are used with any noun that is not explicitly or entirely feminine. Accordingly, in any given instance, "he" or "him" is likely (but by no means certain) to be gender-neutral in its intention, but it would be patently misleading to reflect such concerns in a translation of an ancient or medieval work.

All of the texts selected for inclusion in this volume can be considered "religious" in the straightforward sense that they speak of God and his relationship to humans. They include explications of the divine message as it was expressed in the revealed scriptures or in the oral Torah; the words or prayers that are to be recited by the people of Israel when they address the Almighty in praise, petition or thanksgiving; systematic discussions of rational doctrine or esoteric theories about metaphysical topics; or guides to developing qualities of moral uprightness and living a life of holiness. Similar genres may be encountered in other religious literatures.

It was not possible to include examples of every kind of Jewish religious text, but I believe that I did succeed in covering the most important types. The main categories, as reflected in this book's division into sections, are:

1 Prayers and liturgical texts—including both the "official" standardized texts from the weekday and holy day prayer books, samples of literary liturgical poetry (*piyyuṭ*) and some vernacular private devotions composed in Yiddish (*T'khinnes*). The material covers a broad chronological range extending from the first century CE through to modern times.

2 Aggadah and Midrash—the chief focus here is on interpretations of the Bible produced by the rabbis during the era of the first six or seven centuries CE. These texts subdivide into the subject areas of halakhah (legal analysis) and aggadah (homiletical expositions).

3 The literature of halakhic discourse—the talmudic discipline of intensely detailed legal analysis holds a place of honor and prestige in the scale of Jewish religious scholarship. For all its centrality and importance, it is a dauntingly difficult enterprise, and the intellectual and spiritual atmospheres of talmudic study cannot easily be conveyed to outsiders who lack the requisite experience, mindset, background and erudition. In addition to the subtle arguments and discussions that fill the authoritative volumes of the Jerusalem and Babylonian Talmuds, the ongoing discourse of Jewish religious law generated specialized genres of literature that were designed to explain, expand and apply the teachings of the ancient rabbis. Most notably, the collective efforts of medieval and modern Jewish scholars produced a monumental *oeuvre* of explanatory and critical commentaries to the Talmud, systematic codifications of the laws, as well as a literature of "responsa" in which prominent rabbis answered inquiries posed to them regarding practical or theoretical questions. Rather than trying to illustrate the variegated spectrum of topics that are dealt with in rabbinic *halakhah*—encompassing areas of civil, criminal and family law, dietary and agricultural regulations, the sacrificial cult, priesthood and purity, and much more—I have chosen

instead to focus on a specific question that occupied many of the commentators and halakhic authorities over the generations; namely, the apparent contradiction between the official law and popular practice with regard to defining the earliest permissible time for reciting the "*Shema' Yisra'el*" section of the evening prayer service.[1] It is my hope that by guiding the readers through the scholarly give-and-take on this one issue, as the discussion evolved across the centuries in the numerous centers of rabbinic learning, they will achieve a better appreciation of the extraordinary intellectual and religious experiences of halakhic discourse, which occupies so prominent a position in the world of Jewish spirituality, while at the same time acquiring a taste for the various modes of literary platforms in which this discourse was recorded.

4 Jewish Bible commentaries—for this section I chose to follow a similar approach as in the previous one in focusing on a single problematic passage—Numbers 22:12–22—that confronted the exegetes with a glaring contradiction and theological quandary. The distinctive approaches and insights of the selected commentators, who span the centuries from talmudic times to the nineteenth century, will furnish us with an ideal opportunity to appreciate their learned ingenuity, as well as to recreate the experience enjoyed by the religious Jews who engage in this lively exegetical conversation as they study the pages of the traditional "Rabbinic Bibles" (where the most eminent commentaries are printed side by side) and other exegetical texts.

5 Philosophy and rational theology—as a rule, systematic and dogmatic theology have been less of a concern for Jews than for some other religious communities. Nonetheless, the encounter between Jewish thinkers and the (primarily) Greek philosophical tradition—especially in the medieval Arabic-speaking environment—generated a number of different responses from within the Jewish intellectual community. In some cases, the instruments of logical analysis were employed to bring consistency and order to the ideas and truth-claims of the classical Jewish texts or received traditions. Leading Jewish advocates of philosophy produced an impressive synthesis of traditional Judaism and rationalist doctrines, arguing not only that Judaism was the religion most compatible with rigorous rational thought, but also that the attainment of an intellectually refined understanding of metaphysics and theology should be posited as the ultimate objective of religious life. Indeed, Rabbi Judah Halevi marshaled the instruments of philosophical argument in order to prove that the traditional faith based on supernatural revelation provides a path that is superior to that of the philosophers. Passages in this section deal with various facets of the confrontation between faith and reason. Most of these texts were composed in Arabic between the tenth and thirteenth centuries. Although many of their contemporaries opposed the authors' attempts to impose Greek ideas

on the revealed truth of the Torah, the unassailable rabbinic credentials of figures such as Saadiah Gaon and Moses Maimonides made them all but impossible to dismiss, and the treatises that they authored continued to wield a powerful and lasting influence on subsequent Jewish thought. To be sure, the literature of Jewish philosophy is much broader than the sampling that is presented here; it extends from first-century Alexandria (Philo) and includes resourceful thinkers in Renaissance Italy, post-Enlightenment Germany and contemporary America and Israel. The current selection represents the most prominent figures whose writings came to be revered by the tradition, and some of the key issues that engaged their lively intellects.

6   Esoteric, mystical and kabbalistic texts—this section groups together a number of religious outlooks and schools that are often treated as expressions of a single dominant ideology, but in fact are quite varied in their approaches to religious values and Jewish tradition. The authors and devotees of these works are likely to compound this confusion when they trace the origins of their own teachings back to earlier authoritative texts that they have recast in the image of their own beliefs. The texts included here are distinguished by their claims to one or both of two main characteristics: (1) they are esoteric, cultivating a secret mode of interpreting scriptures and traditions, usually by identifying their doctrines with those of the "account of the chariot" that was singled out in the Mishnah as a subject that should not be expounded openly; (2) they are "mystical" in the sense of aspiring to a direct, intense and usually ecstatic personal encounter with the divine. (It should be noted that these two characteristics would also apply to most of the medieval rationalists of the Neoplatonic or Aristotelian schools whose works were presented in the the previous section, and that the familiar division between philosophical and other mysticisms is at times more a matter of editorial convenience than an intrinsic distinction between differing religious orientations.) Most of the works that are included in this section belong to the esoteric (but not necessarily mystical) school known as "Kabbalah" that first arose in the twelfth century in southern Europe, and introduced its distinctive theological and hermeneutical system based on the symbolism of ten divine powers—"*sefirot*"—by means of which the unknowable "*Ein Sof*" created our world, and through which humans can in turn influence the workings of the celestial realms. Selections are provided here from the earliest known kabbalistic document, the *Bahir*; from the most revered kabbalistic compendium, the *Zohar*; and from the teachings of the influential school of Rabbi Isaac Luria.

7   Moralistic and ethical writings—ever since biblical times, Jewish authors have produced works that were designed to provide guidance for leading a life of virtue and piety. Such works frequently have a special importance in the broader context of Jewish values, in light of the strong

emphasis that Jewish tradition has usually placed on the legal component of the religion, as embodied in the study and application of halakhah. Moralistic texts therefore serve to remind their readers that the technical details of ritual or legal observance should be seen as part of a coherent set of spiritual values. This section assembles sample texts from several classic works that fit this characterization, ranging chronologically from the tractate *Avot* ("Ethics of the Fathers") in the Mishnah through to Ḥasidic tales from nineteenth-century Eastern Europe. Some of these works are informed by specific theologies, such as Neoplatonic philosophy or Kabbalah, but on the whole they express a more general array of moral ideals, such as submission to God's will, overcoming physical and material temptations, a striving for altruism and purity, and the suppression of egotism.

The target audience for this book consists of intelligent adults, including university undergraduates, who have no previous familiarity with Judaism or its literature beyond an ability to locate references to an English translation of the Bible. I would hope that this collection will be useful in college courses or adult education classes about Judaism, most likely in conjunction with another textbook that would provide a more systematic presentation of the history, ideas and practices of the Jewish religion. Teachers who assign this book to students will probably do so selectively, or divide their curricula between texts that are suitable for independent study and those that would benefit from the instructor's active guidance. The sequence of chapters need not be rigidly followed, and readers or teachers might prefer to approach the material in a different order. In order to allow this flexibility, some background information is repeated in different chapters. Of course, readers will do well to avail themselves of the glossary and historical timeline that have been provided at the end of the volume.

Indeed, one feature that is likely to strike the uninitiated reader is the formidable difficulty of so many of these texts. There is scarcely a passage that can be understood on its own without an extensive commentary. In some cases, as in the standard daily prayers or popular Bible commentaries, the explanations may involve no more than filling in background information that would be familiar to an "insider," a member of the Jewish community who was brought up on the Bible and other fundamental traditions that define standard literacy. Similarly, with regard to some of the philosophical texts, it is necessary to provide background to the doctrines of arcane schools of rational thought, medieval versions of Neoplatonism or Aristotelianism that were once standard subjects of the academic curriculum. It is probably not surprising that the technical discourse of religious law, which makes up the bulk of talmudic literature, requires extensive explanations to follow its intricate legalistic argumentation—though many will be surprised, and perhaps even dismayed, by the realization of how such prosaic academic dialectic (which our society often dismisses cynically as obscurantist casuistry fit only for lawyers) came to occupy a central position in the Jewish hierarchy of valued religious activities.

Analogous degrees of difficulty and intellectual complexity apply also to genres where we would not normally expect to meet with them, such as liturgical poetry, homiletics and especially in the esoteric literature that is often characterized as "mystical." Here we might reasonably have anticipated that the authors would be addressing their messages to a broader audience and to the shared yearnings of the human spirit. And yet, as we shall see, the masterpieces of *piyyuṭ* seem to presuppose an encyclopedic familiarity with the full text of the Bible and midrashic literature; and the mythic symbolism of Lurianic Kabbalah is built on such an intricate mapping of the divine *sefirot* and their subsidiary configurations, that it is scarcely possible to convey a coherent explanation to an uninitiated reader.

This degree of scholarly obscurity or "bookishness" that typifies Jewish religious discourse can doubtless be accounted for in a number of ways, but for purposes of this introductory anthology it is most important to accept them as a given. It is to be hoped that a combination of my own detailed explanations and the reader's patience and determination will result in a satisfactory understanding of the texts, and of a satisfying appreciation of the profound religious outlooks that they express.

1   Prayers and liturgical texts

Daily prayer: The eighteen blessings

The "Eighteen Blessings" is first attested in rabbinic traditions from the first century CE as a prayer that is to be recited three times every day (with additional recitations on special occasions). The title aptly describes its formal structure: it is a sequence of "blessings," that is to say, passages containing the formula "Blessed are you, O Lord." The Talmud provides considerable detail as to the themes of the blessings, but does not prescribe specific texts; and scholars are in disagreement about whether a specific text of the prayer actually existed in ancient times. The Talmud traces the choice of themes and their sequence to biblical sources, and though some of those explanations are quite plausible, it is not possible to fully reconstruct the prayer's origins.

The prayer is worded so that the worshipper's perspective is always expressed in the plural ("we," "us") form, and this is consistent with the communal nature of its content. There are few references to individual concerns and needs. Rather, most of the blessings consist of petitions and hopes on behalf of the entire community or nation, including several eschatological themes. The link between the idealized past and future is evident in many passages.

According to Jewish law, the obligation to recite this prayer applies whether or not one is in a communal setting, though congregational worship is preferred. When recited communally, a prayer leader ("representative of the congregation") repeats the prayer after the worshippers have recited it individually in a quiet tone. This practice originated in ancient times when the texts of the prayers were categorized as part of the "oral Torah" that could not be written down, and hence it could not be presumed that everyone was capable of reciting all the prayers from memory. There are certain portions of this prayer that may only be recited in full in a congregational setting.

The following text is compiled from manuscripts in the Cairo Genizah and represents versions of the Palestinian rite as it was recorded in the early medieval era. Though its content (if we ignore the many stylistic differences) is quite similar to the standard versions that are in use among traditionalist Jewish communities today, there are nevertheless some significant differences as well. Most prominent among these is probably the fact that this version is actually composed of eighteen blessings, as its ancient name should imply. The Babylonian version that has now been adopted universally contains nineteen blessings, because the two topics of the fourteenth blessing—the restoration of the Davidic dynasty and of Jerusalem—were divided up into two separate blessings.

In most respects, the meaning of this prayer is quite straightforward and understandable, and consequently it can be understood without an extensive explanation. The headings that appear before each blessing are not part of the actual text, but are based on the terminology used in the Talmud.

The eighteen blessings:[1]

1 The forefathers

> Blessed are you O Lord, our God and God of our forefathers
> The God of Abraham, the God of Isaac and the God of Jacob,
> The great God, the mighty and awesome, the supreme God
> who bestows lovingkindness.
> He is the master of all
> and he remembers the gracious deeds of the forefathers
> and brings a redeemer to their children's children
> for the sake of his great name, in love.
> King, savior and protector.
> Blessed are you, O Lord, shield of Abraham.

2 God's power

> You are mighty forever, O Lord
> resurrecting the dead, you are great to redeem.
> [He who causes the wind to blow and the dew to fall,]
> He who apportions life graciously,
> who resurrects the dead with great compassion,
> who supports those who are falling and frees those who are confined
>   and keeps his faith with those who sleep in the dust.
> Who is like unto you, the powerful one?
> And who resembles you,
> the one who causes death and life?
> And you are faithful to revive the dead.
> Blessed are you, O Lord, who revives the dead.

Comments

Note how a declaration of belief in the resurrection of the dead was given a central place in this blessing which is supposed to speak in general terms of

God's great power. This harks back to the era of the Second Temple when belief in resurrection was a distinctive doctrine of the Pharisee sect and was denied by their rivals the Sadducees.

The focus on rainfall reflects the crucial importance of seasonal rain in the land of Israel (and it is the main theme of blessing 9 below). For Jewish peasants, the prospect of abundant, life-giving rainfall at the conclusion of the dry summer months was comparable to the miraculous restoration of life to the dead.

3 Sanctification of God's name

> You are holy and your name is holy
> and the holy ones each day praise you, Selah.
> Blessed are you, the holy God.

Comments

"the holy ones" refers to the angels.

"selah" a Hebrew word, probably some sort of musical direction, that is inserted for emphasis in biblical poetry.

When recited with the prayer leader in a congregational setting, a more elaborate version of this blessing is used. The leader and the congregation responsively reenact the prophetic visions of the angels praising God, incorporating mystically charged verses such as "Holy, holy, holy is the Lord of hosts; the whole earth is full of his glory" (Isaiah 6:3) and "Blessed be the glory of the Lord from his abode" (Ezekiel 3:12).

4 Knowledge

> You bestow knowledge on humans
> and instruct people in understanding.
> Bestow upon us knowledge and understanding.
> Blessed are you, O Lord who bestows wisdom.

5 Repentance

> Cause us to return, our father, to your Torah,
> and bring us near, our king, to your worship.
> And draw us back in complete repentance before you.
> Blessed are you, O Lord, who desires repentance.

6 Forgiveness

> Forgive us, our father, for we have sinned.
> Absolve us, our king, for we have transgressed.

Blessed are you, O Lord, the compassionate who is abundant in forgiveness

7 *Redemption*

Behold our affliction and fight our battles.
Redeem us speedily for the sake of your name.
Blessed are you, O Lord, the redeemer of Israel.

8 *Healing*

Heal us, Lord, that we may be healed
and bring upon us a full healing for all our wounds.
For you are God, the merciful healer.
Blessed are you, O Lord, who heals the sick of his people Israel.

9 *The Seasons*

Bless for us, Lord our God, this year for good and all the varieties of its grain.
And give dew and rain on the face of the earth
for your name's sake.
And satisfy the whole world from the blessings of your goodness.
And moisten the face of the universe with the richness of the gifts of your hands.
And preserve and rescue, O Lord our God, this year from all kinds of destruction and all kinds of punishment.
Have care and compassion, and be merciful toward us and toward all its fruits.
And may we enjoy abundance and peace and blessing for its outcome as the blessing of the good years.
And instill a blessing in the work of our hands.
For you are the God who is good and does good.
Blessed are you, O Lord, who blesses the years.

Comments

Different versions of this blessing are recited in the winter (that is, the rainy season) and in the summer. In the former case, the prayer is for rain and in the latter, it is for dew.

10 *Ingathering of the exiles*

Sound the trumpet for our liberation
and raise up a banner for the ingathering of our exiles.

Blessed are you, O Lord, who gathers the dispersed of his people Israel.

11 Justice

Restore our judges as at first,
and our counsellors as in the beginning,
and remove from us agony and sighing,
and reign over us you alone
in mercy and righteousness and justice.
Blessed are you, O Lord, the king who loves righteousness and justice.

12 Heretics

May the apostates have no hope,
and may the malicious empire be speedily uprooted,
and may it be destroyed in our days.
Blessed are you, O Lord, who destroys the wicked and vanquishes the infidels.

Comments

To the extent that this paragraph can properly be designated a "blessing," it blesses or thanks God for eventually eradicating assorted enemies of Judaism and of the Jewish people. The list of enemies varies considerably in different rites, reflecting changing historical and cultural circumstances.

Our text refers to "apostates" (people who abandoned their Judaism) and to the "malicious empire" (Rome). Some medieval versions also mention "Nazarenes" (Christians), most likely originating in ancient times when the nascent Christian community was still viewed as a heresy within Judaism.

The versions of the blessing that are in current use (according to the Babylonian rite) contain very few of those explicit references. They tend to be worded in very generic terms, referring to "your enemies," "slanderers" (or informers), "wickedness" (or "the kingdom of wickedness") and the like.

13 Support of the righteous

Upon the righteous and the pious
and upon the righteous proselytes
may your mercies be stirred, O Lord our God.
And give a good reward to all those who trust in your name in truth.
And place our portion among them.
And we shall not be shamed

for we have trusted in your great name.
Blessed are you, O Lord, the stay and trust of the righteous.

14 *David and Jerusalem*

Have mercy, O Lord our God, upon us
in your abundant mercies
upon Israel your people
upon Jerusalem your city
and on your sanctuary and your Temple
and your abode
and on Zion the dwelling-place of your glory
on the kingdom of the house of David your anointed.
Build your house and complete your sanctuary.
Blessed are you, O Lord, the God of David and the builder of
Jerusalem.

15 *Hearer of prayer*

Harken unto our voices, O Lord our God, have concern and take pity
and be merciful for us.
And accept our prayer, with compassion and willingness.
For you are the God who harkens unto our prayer and our supplications,
and you will not turn us away empty-handed from before your
presence.
Be responsive, our sovereign, to our prayer, and listen to our sobbing
even as you listened to the sobbing of our ancestors.
Blessed are you, O Lord, who harkens unto prayer.

16 *Worship service*

Accept, O Lord our God, your people Israel and their prayers,
and restore the worship service to the sanctuary of your house.
Speedily with love accept willingly the burnt offerings of Israel and their
prayers,
and may the worship service of your people Israel always be found
acceptable.
And may our eyes witness your return to Zion in mercy as in earlier
times.
Blessed are you, O Lord, who restores his presence to Zion.

17 *Thanksgiving*

We acknowledge our gratitude to you
who are the Lord our God and the God of our ancestors for all eternity,

for our lives that are entrusted to your hands
and for our souls that are in your keeping
and for your miracles that are with us each day
and for your wonders that are at all times, evening and morning
—for all these things may your name be blessed and exalted, our king,
forever.
All living creatures will thank you.
Blessed are you, O Lord, whose name is good and to whom it is fitting
to offer thanks.

18 Peace

Establish peace, goodness and blessing, lovingkindness and compassion
upon us and upon Israel your people.
And bless us all as one in the light of your countenance.
For from the light of your countenance you have bestowed upon us,
O Lord our God,
the Torah of life and the love of kindness, righteousness, mercy, blessing
and peace.
And it is proper in your eyes to bless your people Israel at all times.
Blessed are you, O Lord, who blesses his people Israel with peace.

Comments

In the congregational version of this blessing, when it is repeated by the
prayer leader, it includes the text of the "priestly blessing" as found in
Numbers 6:24–26: "The Lord bless you and keep you. The Lord make His
face shine upon you, and be gracious to you. The Lord lift up His countenance upon you, and give you peace."

It became paradigmatic to conclude prayers, ceremonial texts and formal
letters with blessings of peace (*shalom*).

From the Additional Service for Festivals (according to the prayer book of Saadiah Gaon)[2]

God and God of our Fathers, on account of our sins we were exiled
from our land and sent far from our native soil, so that we cannot go up
to be seen and to bow down before you in your chosen sanctuary in the
great and holy house that is called by your name; because of the destruction that has been inflicted on your Temple.

May it be your will, O Lord our God, merciful father, king of Jacob,
that you will return and have mercy upon it and upon us in your abundant mercies, and swiftly rebuild it and increase its glory.

Our father, our king, quickly reveal your sovereignty over us, manifest yourself and be exalted before the eyes of all living creatures. Gather

in our scattered ones from among the nations and assemble our dispersed ones from the ends of the earth, and bring us to Zion in joyous song, and to Jerusalem your city in eternal happiness. And we shall prepare before you our obligatory sacrifices as you have written for us in your Torah through your servant Moses.

Comments

The Additional Services [Hebrew: *Musaf*] of prayer on the Sabbath and holy days were ordained to parallel the additional sacrifices that were offered up in the Jerusalem Temple on those occasions. The text of the prayers stresses that the recitation of verbal prayers is a very incomplete substitute for sacrificial worship which has been discontinued because of the destruction of the Jerusalem Temple, which is the only place in which it is permitted to offer sacrifices. This section restates the biblical conception that the Temple was destroyed and the people exiled from Jerusalem as a punishment for Israel's sins. The prayer implores God to redeem Israel, restore them to their homeland and rebuild the sanctuary so that they may reinstate the proper worship as set out in the Torah.

"**as you have written for us in your Torah . . .**" At this point the relevant verses from the Torah are read outlining the sacrifices that are ordained for the respective holidays.

From the Additional Service for Rosh Hashanah (according to the prayer book of Saadiah Ga'on)

It is our duty to praise the master of all things, to magnify the first creator.

For he did not make us like the nations of the earth and did not set us as the other tribes of the land.

He did not place our portion among them, or make our fate like all their multitudes.

For they bow down to vanity and unreality and pray to a deity that cannot save them.

Whereas we bow down to the king of kings of kings, may he be blessed,

who spreads out the heavens and establishes the earth.

The seat of his glory is in the heavens above and the presence of his might is in the most elevated heights.

He is our God and there is no other.

As it is written (Deuteronomy 4:39): "Therefore know this day, and consider it in your heart, that the Lord himself is God in heaven above and on the earth beneath; there is no other."

Therefore we look to you, Lord our God, that we may swiftly behold the glory of your might,

to remove abominations from the land, and the idols will be utterly
   cut off;
to establish the world under the sovereignty of the Almighty.
And all creatures of flesh shall call upon your name
that the wicked of the earth will be turned toward you.
May all the denizens of the earth know and acknowledge that it is to
   you that every knee must bend, and every tongue must swear before
   you, Lord our God.
Let them kneel and fall, and offer acclaim in honor of your great name.
And let them all accept upon themselves the yoke of your dominion,
   and you shall reign over them for all eternity.
For sovereignty is yours and you shall rule in glory for all eternity.
As it is written in your Torah.

Comments

According to the Talmud, the Additional Service (*Musaf*) for Rosh Hashanah
has three principal themes:

* *Zikhronot*: God's recalling the deeds of his creatures
* *Malkhuyyot*: Divine kingship
* *Shofarot*: Trumpets (divine revelation by means of the shofar, the ram's
  horn).

Each of the three sections includes a reading of ten verses from the Bible
dealing with the designated theme.

This selection is taken from the introduction to the *Malkhuyyot* section, and
expresses the acceptance of God's sovereignty as the unrivaled ruler of the
universe. It serves as an introduction to the recitation of the scriptural texts.

The prayer declares Israel's commitment to the exclusive authority of the
unique and all-powerful God, which is contrasted to the folly of other
nations of the world who continue to stray after false and ineffectual idols.

The language and attitudes that find expression in this passage are quite
remarkable in the context of ancient rabbinic literature, leading many scholars
to date it back to a time when Israel still enjoyed political independence. The
style emulates elements of biblical poetry, which is characterized by the literary
convention of "parallelism"; that is, expressing the same content in two different
wordings (a feature that does not always translate elegantly into English).

The prayer takes an unusually aggressive stance against heathenism, and
envisages a future redemption in which all of humanity—even the "wicked
of the earth"—will ultimately acknowledge the truth of Israel's God. This
triumphalist attitude is not often in evidence in standard Jewish prayer.

The Hebrew allows for a certain ambivalence as to whether the sentences
describing the future redemption should be understood as descriptions
(declarative sentences in the future tense) or as prayerful wishes.

As noted, the original liturgical setting for this prayer was restricted to Rosh Hashanah. During the Middle Ages, it was introduced into daily worship, so that it is now recited at the conclusion of each one of the three daily services.

Various liturgical blessings

In Jewish tradition, the recitation of a blessing in conjunction with an action or experience is the most basic way of imbuing it with religious significance. The simplest form of the liturgical blessing is "Blessed are you, Lord" followed by a descriptor that relates to God's relationship to the thing or event being blessed. When the blessing is recited upon partaking of a pleasure or benefit, it serves as a way of declaring one's appreciation for the God who is the source of the benefit—or, for that matter, of a misfortune, since Jewish law also requires that God be blessed as "the righteous judge" who is the ultimate source of losses and tragedies as well (see below). In some cases, the blessing does not seem to relate directly to the thing or event that occasions it, but rather it provides an opportunity to praise the Lord.

A common type of blessing is the one recited when one is performing a commandment. In essence, it is the act of recitation that transforms an otherwise neutral action into a religious observance. The standard formula for such blessings is "Blessed are you, Lord our God, king of the universe, who has sanctified us through his commandments, and commanded us to . . ."

Miscellaneous blessings

[Before eating bread:] Blessed are you, Lord our God, king of the universe, who produces bread from the earth.

[Before eating fruit (of a tree):] Blessed are you, Lord our God, king of the universe, who creates the fruit of the tree.

[Before eating vegetables:] Blessed are you, Lord our God, king of the universe, who creates the fruit of the earth.

[On seeing lightning or experiencing other manifestations of the power of nature:] Blessed are you, Lord our God, king of the universe, creator of the work of creation.

[On hearing thunder:] Blessed are you, Lord our God, king of the universe, whose power and might pervade the universe.

[On seeing a rainbow:] Blessed are you, Lord our God, king of the universe, who recalls the covenant and is faithful in his covenant and fulfills his word.

Comments

The allusion is to Genesis 9:12–17 where God established the rainbow as the sign of an everlasting covenant with humanity and promises that he will never again destroy them all with a flood as he did in the time of Noah.

Miscellaneous blessings (continued)

[On receiving bad news:] Blessed are you, Lord our God, king of the universe, the truthful judge.

[On receiving good news:] Blessed are you, Lord our God, king of the universe, who is good and does good.

[Blessing at a circumcision:] Blessed are you, Lord our God, king of the universe, who sanctified the beloved one from the womb, and placed the mark of his statute in his flesh, and sealed his offspring with the sign of the holy covenant.

Therefore as a reward for this, living God, our portion, our rock— decree that the beloved portion of our flesh be saved from destruction, for the sake of his covenant that he has placed in our flesh. Blessed are you, Lord, who establishes the covenant.

Comments

This is an example of a "poetic blessing" that incorporates several of the literary characteristics of liturgical poetry (see below), including extensive use of synonyms and scriptural allusions. **"The beloved one"** an allusion to Isaac (see Genesis 22:2). In Genesis 17 God informs Abraham that he will have a son and commands him to circumcise his sons as a sign of the covenant. The rabbis inferred from this that the command to circumcise Isaac was issued before his birth, as expressed poetically in this blessing.

From the "seven blessings" recited at a wedding ceremony

Blessed are you, Lord our God, king of the universe, who created everything for his glory.

Blessed are you, Lord our God, king of the universe, who fashions the human being.

Blessed are you, Lord our God, king of the universe, who fashioned man in his image, in the image of the likeness of his form, and who established for him and from him an eternal edifice.

Blessed are you, Lord, who fashions the human being.

Comments

The initial blessings in the sequence celebrate the physical and erotic dimensions of marriage, evoking the story of the creation of the first man and woman in the garden of Eden where, according to midrashic tradition, God acted as the "best man" to bring together Adam and Eve.

"established . . . an eternal edifice" This refers to the biblical account of God creating Eve out of Adam's body to be his constant companion.

*From the "seven blessings" recited at a wedding
ceremony (continued)*

Bring great gladness, and cause the barren woman to be merry because of the gathering of her children to her in gladness.

Blessed are you, Lord, who causes Zion to rejoice in her children.

Bring happiness, indeed, to the beloved companions, as when you brought happiness to your creation in the garden of Eden long ago. Blessed are you, Lord, who brings joy to the groom and the bride.

Blessed are you, Lord our God, king of the universe, who has created gladness and joy, the groom and the bride, cheer and song, delight and jubilation, love and fraternity, peace and fellowship.

Speedily, Lord our God, may there be heard in the towns of Judah and in the streets of Jerusalem the voice of joy and the voice of gladness, the voice of the bridegroom and the voice of the bride, the sound of the celebrations of grooms from their canopies and the music of young people at their feasts. Blessed are you, Lord, who makes the groom rejoice with the bride.

Comments

The joyous uniting of the bride and the groom is linked thematically with the future rebuilding of Jerusalem, both as a metaphor for the reunification of the city (portrayed as a forsaken mother) with her exiled children and as an ideal example of the happy occasions that will be celebrated in the redeemed future.

The phraseology and imagery of the blessing draw much of their inspiration from the imagery of Jeremiah 33:10–11: "Thus says the Lord: Again there shall be heard in this place—of which you say, It is desolate, without man and without beast—in the cities of Judah, in the streets of Jerusalem that are desolate . . . the voice of joy and the voice of gladness, the voice of the bridegroom and the voice of the bride . . . For I will cause the captives of the land to return as at the first, says the Lord."

The Passover Haggadah

The festival of Passover (Hebrew: *Pesaḥ*) commemorates the liberation of the ancient Israelites from centuries of slavery in Egypt, as described in the book of Exodus in the Torah. One of its pivotal observances is a ceremonial meal held on the first night of the festival (as well as on the second night in diaspora communities that add days to the biblical holidays). This meal has come to be known as the *seder*, "order," after the complex order of procedures, prayers and rituals that make up the traditional observance.

The seder as it has evolved in Judaism is a convergence of two main themes rooted in the Bible:

- First, there was a sacrificial meal built around the roasted lamb that was eaten by family groups along with various symbolic foods. With the cessation of sacrifices following the destruction of the Jerusalem Temple, the lamb itself was no longer offered, but other foods, especially the unleavened bread and bitter herbs (see below), continued to be eaten.
- Additionally, the Torah stresses the obligation to tell the story of the exodus to one's children. The annual seder meal was identified as the main occasion for the "telling"—in Hebrew: "*haggadah*"—and the name Haggadah was attached to the liturgy recited at the Passover table. The standard text of the Passover Haggadah has evolved over many centuries. Much of it is rooted in early rabbinic expositions that are contained in the Mishnah, Talmud and Midrash.

From the Passover Haggadah

This is the poor bread that our ancestors ate in the land of Egypt.

Comments

This passage is recited in Aramaic at the Passover meal as unleavened bread, *matzah*, is placed before the participants.

   "**Poor bread**" in the English reflects an Aramaic translation of the Hebrew expression that is usually rendered as "bread of affliction" in Deuteronomy 16:3: "seven days you shall eat matzot, the bread of affliction; for in haste did you come forth out of the land of Egypt; that you may remember the day when you came forth out of the land of Egypt all the days of your life." As related in Exodus 12:39, when the Israelites were freed from Egypt, they left in such haste that there was no time for their bread to rise, and therefore the eating of unleavened bread was designated a central ritual of Passover.

From the Passover Haggadah (continued)

Let anyone who is hungry come and eat, let anyone who is in need come and partake of the Passover offering.

Comments

"**come and partake of the Passover offering**" The Aramaic invitation is actually a verb derived from the same root as "passover." Ordinarily (as translated here), it has the meaning of "partake of the Passover offering" and would apply to the time when the Jerusalem Temple existed and sacrifices could still be offered. In a more general sense, however, it can mean just "celebrate the Passover." This would be more consistent with the context of the following lines where it is presupposed that the participants are in a state of exile from the homeland and are subjugated to foreign rulers.

From the Passover Haggadah (continued)

This year we are here. Next year in the land of Israel.
  This year we are slaves. Next year—free people.
  Why is this night different from all other nights?

Comments

One of the defining features of the Passover holiday is the injunction (Exodus 13:14) "when your son asks you in time to come, saying, 'What is this?' that you shall say to him, 'By the might of his arm the Lord brought us out of Egypt, out of the house of bondage.'" The Mishnah's description of the Passover ritual lists four questions that a child is expected to ask the father, all of which are provoked by unusual features of the feast. The Mishnah's version, reflecting the time when the Temple was in existence, includes a question about the lamb that was offered as a sacrifice. This was later replaced by a question about reclining.

From the Passover Haggadah (continued)

For on all other nights we eat either leavened or unleavened bread, but tonight only unleavened bread.
  For on all other nights we eat other kinds of vegetables, but tonight *maror* [bitter herbs].

Comments

The eating of bitter herbs, a symbolic recollection of the misery of slavery, is commanded in Exodus 12:8.

From the Passover Haggadah (continued)

For on all other nights we do not dip even once, but tonight twice.
  For on all other nights we eat either sitting upright or reclining, but tonight entirely reclining.

Comments

"reclining" The theme of freedom is expressed at the Passover meal by virtue of the fact that the meal is modeled after a formal banquet of the sort that was customary among the ancient Mediterranean aristocracy. At such banquets, it was customary for the main meal to be preceded by several appetizers that were eaten as dips. Then the main course was enjoyed while reclining on a couch, as each diner had a small individual table set out in front of them.

The next section begins the father's reply to the child's questions as he recounts the story of how the Israelites were enslaved in Egypt and then miraculously freed from there by God.

From the Passover Haggadah (continued)

> We were slaves to Pharaoh in Egypt, and the Lord our God took us out of there with a mighty hand and an outstretched arm. If the Holy One had not taken our ancestors out of Egypt, indeed we and our children and our children's children would still be enslaved to Pharaoh in Egypt.
>
> Even if we were all wise, if we were all understanding, if we were all elders, if we all had knowledge of the Torah—it is still incumbent upon us to relate the story of the exodus from Egypt. And the more one tells about the exodus from Egypt, the more praiseworthy it is.
>
> It once happened that Rabbi Eliezer and Rabbi Joshua and Rabbi Eleazar ben Azariah and Rabbi Akiva and Rabbi Tarfon were reclining at a feast in Bnai Brak as they were telling about the exodus from Egypt throughout that night; until their disciples came and said to them: our Masters, the hour has arrived to recite the morning *Shemaʿ*.
>
> Said Rabbi Eleazar ben Azariah: Behold, I am around seventy years old, but I have never been able to demonstrate that the exodus from Egypt must be mentioned at night, until Ben Zoma expounded it. For it says (Deuteronomy 16:3): "that you may remember the day when you came forth out of the land of Egypt all the days of your life"—
>
> "The days" refers to days.
> "All the days" refers to nights.
>
> But the sages say:
>
> "The days" refers to this world.
> "All the days" comes to include the days of the messiah.

Comments

The story about the five rabbis feasting in Bnai Brak (the Judean town that was home to Rabbi Akiva) is not actually connected to the subsequent statement by Rabbi Eleazar ben Azariah.

"to demonstrate that the exodus from Egypt must be mentioned at night" This statement deals with a technical liturgical question about whether the exodus must be mentioned in the blessing following the evening recitation of the *Shemaʿ*. Although this was the prevailing practice, Rabbi Eleazar had been unable to find a scriptural source for it. Ben Zoma adduced a proof that was based on the midrashic premise that every word of sacred scripture must be essential, and hence if the verse in Deuteronomy says "*all* the days" when "the days" would ostensibly have sufficed, then it must have been in order to expand the scope of the obligation to include night-time as well as daytime.

The "sages" (unidentified rabbis) employ the same form of reasoning to prove that even in the days of the great final redemption, the older redemption from Egypt will not be forgotten and will continue to be recalled.

Piyyuṭ—Hebrew liturgical poetry

Yannai

Yannai was one of the most brilliant and prolific authors of Hebrew liturgical poetry (*piyyuṭ*), though most of his oeuvre had to be rediscovered in the twentieth century with the help of newly discovered manuscripts from the Cairo Genizah. It is generally assumed that Yannai lived in the land of Israel under Byzantine rule (a situation that, as we shall see, is reflected in his poems), but we still do not know when he lived.

His *piyyuṭ*s were composed to serve as substitutes for the cantor's recitation of the Eighteen Blessings prayer on Sabbaths and festivals; on those days a shorter version of the prayer, consisting of only seven blessings, was recited. Each *piyyuṭ* relates to the opening verse or verses of the designated scriptural reading for the day according to the triennial cycle that was in use in the Palestinian rite, and is enriched by allusions to verses from other sections of the Bible (in the manner of midrashic expositions). After the development of the theme, the relevant biblical verses are recited, and then a brief transition is made to the theme of the respective blessing from the Eighteen Blessings.

An English translation cannot hope to convey the intricate formal and rhetorical features of classical *piyyuṭ*. For example, the opening stanzas contain acrostics of the twenty-two letters of the Hebrew alphabet, and then of the poet's name. The dense language alludes constantly to biblical expressions and to midrashic passages and expositions; and the style is governed by ingenious word-plays based on the multiple meanings of Hebrew lexicographic roots. A distinctive feature of the rhetoric is that the major figures are never identified explicitly by name, but rather by (often cryptic) epithets.

A full *piyyuṭ* of this type consists of eight elaborate sections. The present translation covers only the first two blessings.

Yannai: Piyyuṭ *for Exodus 7:8–9*[3]—*Part 1: Shield of Abraham*

Then you beheld the future.
To your chosen one you then showed it.

The secrets of the foe's heart you knew.
The word that he would say to them you made known to them.

COMMENTS

As befits a prayer, this *piyyuṭ* is addressing God. It focuses on four main themes suggested by Exodus 7:9 (cited below):

1   God knows in advance that Pharaoh will refuse Moses' and Aaron's demand to let the Israelites go.
2   The wonders that will be performed by means of Moses' staff.
3   The transformation of Aaron's rod into a serpent. The Hebrew word that is translated here as "serpent" has numerous associations in the Bible, and may be rendered as "dragon," "crocodile" and other terms.
4   Pharaoh's self-destructive stubbornness as he continues in his obstinate refusal.

"your chosen one" an epithet for Moses.
   "you then showed it" that is, God informs Moses that Pharaoh will refuse to comply.
   "the foe" Pharaoh.

Yannai: Piyyuṭ *for Exodus 7:8–9 (continued)*

The staff that was created to afflict him

COMMENTS

This alludes to a midrashic tradition that lists Moses' staff among other miraculous objects that were created specially at twilight on the first Friday of the creation.
   "him" Pharaoh.

Yannai: Piyyuṭ *for Exodus 7:8–9 (continued)*

and to answer the fool according to his folly,

COMMENTS

See Proverbs 26:5, cited below.

Yannai: Piyyuṭ *for Exodus 7:8–9 (continued)*

to show him the creeping of the serpent
to make him drink the venom of serpents.

COMMENTS

Compare Deuteronomy 32:24 "I will also send against them . . . the poison of serpents of the dust" and 32:33 "the cruel venom of cobras."

Yannai: Piyyuṭ *for Exodus 7:8–9 (continued)*

> The idiocy of his heart will prevail.
> He will rage with anger like a creeping thing.
> The power of the staff will overcome him
> when the wonder is performed when he speaks.

COMMENTS

Pharaoh will begin to bring about his own humiliating defeat when he angrily insists that Moses and Aaron show him a supernatural sign.

At this point, in keeping with the standard structure of such poems, we are given a list of the verses from all over the Bible that inspired the interpretation.

Yannai: Piyyuṭ *for Exodus 7:8–9 (continued)*

> As it is written: "When Pharaoh shall speak unto you, saying: Show a miracle for you; then thou shalt say unto Aaron: Take thy rod, and cast it before Pharaoh, and it shall become a serpent" (Exodus 7:9).
>
> And it says: "Who sent tokens and wonders into the midst of thee, O Egypt, upon Pharaoh, and upon all his servants" (Psalms 135:9).
>
> And it says: "A whip for the horse, a bridle for the ass, and a rod for the fool's back" (Proverbs 26:3).
>
> And it says: "Answer a fool according to his folly, lest he be wise in his own conceit" (verse 5).
>
> And it says: "A servant will not be corrected by words; for though he understand he will not answer" (Proverbs 29:19).
>
> Open up for us a response
> And loosen our reins
> By virtue of the righteousness of the one who sat at the opening (see Genesis 18:1–2).
>
> Blessed are you, God, shield of Abraham.

COMMENTS

The prayer leader turns from his scriptural homily back to actual prayer. The transition is from the theme of liberation (the story of the exodus from Egypt) to the personality of Abraham. The connection is made rather artificially by playing with the dual significance of the Hebrew word that can designate both the opening of restraining bonds and the opening of a tent door. In rabbinic legend, Abraham was distinguished for his moral qualities of hospitality and lovingkindness, as he would sit in front of the open door of his tent eagerly hoping to host travelers (see Genesis 18:1).

Yannai: Piyyuṭ *for Exodus 7:8–9 (continued)—Part 2: God's power*

> The staff that is called by the name of God
> is also called by the name of the two brothers.
> They inflicted signs and wonders
> upon the denizens of Noph, Moph and Naphtuhim.

COMMENTS

"called by the name of God" See Exodus 4:20: "And Moses took the rod of God in his hand."
   "by the name of the two brothers" Exodus 7:9: "Take thy rod . . ."
   "Noph, Moph and Naphtuhim" names of places in Egypt that are mentioned in various places in the Bible.

Yannai: Piyyuṭ *for Exodus 7:8–9 (continued)*

> The envoys did not delay to obey
> and to promptly deliver their monarch's missive.

COMMENTS

"envoys" Moses and Aaron. They are being praised here for immediately carrying out their orders.
   "their monarch"—God.

Yannai: Piyyuṭ *for Exodus 7:8–9 (continued)*

> The inner walls of their hearts hastily
> became enraged and they were bereft of intelligence.

COMMENTS

The subject has now shifted to Pharaoh and his servants who, in glaring contrast to Moses and Aaron, harden their hearts to angrily and stupidly resist God's command.

Yannai: Piyyuṭ *for Exodus 7:8–9 (continued)*

> The messengers, as soon as they appeared,
> they conveyed their message forthwith.

They prophesied mighty words from the king's lips.
Courageously they approached him with boldness.

As it is written: "And Moses and Aaron went in unto Pharaoh, and they
did so as the Lord had commanded; and Aaron cast down his rod before
Pharaoh, and before his servants, and it became a serpent" (Exodus 7:10).

And it says: "He sent Moses his servant; and Aaron whom he had
chosen" (Psalms 105:26).

And it says: "They showed his signs among them, and wonders in the
land of Ham" (verse 27).

COMMENTS

According to the biblical genealogy, the Egyptians were descended from
Noah's son Ham.

Yannai: Piyyuṭ *for Exodus 7:8–9 (continued)*

And it says: "Speak, and say: Thus says the Lord God: Behold, I am
against thee, Pharaoh king of Egypt, the great dragon that lies in the
midst of his rivers, who has said: My river is my own, and I have made
it for myself" (Ezekiel 29:3).

And it says: "A fool vents all his feelings, but a wise man holds them
back" (Proverbs 29:11).

And it says: "A fool has no delight in understanding, but in expressing
his own heart" (Proverbs 18:2).

As his heart considers,
By means of the divine understanding
May he bless us with life-restoring dew.

Blessed are you, God, who resurrects the dead.

COMMENTS

The last-quoted verse from Proverbs mentioned the theme of understanding
(and the fool's lack thereof). The poet uses this as the textual hinge for
turning now in prayer to address the God who understands all things.

"life-restoring dew" The seasonal petition for dew (during the summer
months when it does not rain) is incorporated into the blessing about God's
power, and it is intimately associated with the theme of resurrection of the dead.

Yannai: Piyyuṭ *for Exodus 7:8–9 (continued)*

Your rod guides me
and the crook of your staff

when you direct against Edom
your scourging whip.
Raise up a great miracle
for the dragon in the great sea,
as when you gave a great sign
to the great serpent.
Let loose the staff of your might
and the rod of your power,
the scepter of your pride,
the pole of your strength.
Lord, you released one wonder over Egypt.
Let loose many wonders against the oppressors.

COMMENTS

Until now, the poet has been expounding verses that described the freeing of the Israelites from the oppression of Egypt in the distant past. At this point he turns his attention to the present situation, when Israel is being oppressed by the wicked Roman-Byzantine empire (identified by the rabbis with the biblical nation of Edom). He implores God to once again manifest his supreme power by wreaking even mightier vengeance on the Roman "serpent/dragon" with a figurative staff of chastisement—an idea that is expressed rhetorically with the help of numerous synonyms and scriptural allusions.

Yannai: Piyyuṭ *for Exodus 7:8–9 (continued)*

As it is written: "And I will show wonders in the heavens and in the earth, blood, and fire, and pillars of smoke" (Joel 2:30).

And it says: "The Lord shall send the rod of thy strength out of Zion: rule in the midst of your enemies" (Psalms 110:2).

And it says: "But You are holy, enthroned in the praises of Israel" (Psalms 22:4).

Kinnot (Elegies)

The *kinnah* is a genre of *piyyuṭ* that is written to be recited on the Ninth of Ab, the annual commemoration of the destructions of the first and second Jerusalem Temples, as well as of various other national catastrophes that occurred on the same date. The Bible itself contains a prototypical example of that genre, the book of Lamentations, traditionally ascribed to the prophet Jeremiah who experienced the destruction of Jerusalem at the hands of the Babylonians.

The following *kinnah*, which is of unknown authorship, is closely bound to the closing (fifth) chapter of the book of Lamentations and usually serves

as a transitional bridge between the reading of the biblical text and the recitation of *Kinnot* poems. It follows Chapter 5 line by line: the first line of
each couplet is an actual quotation of the first half of the biblical verse,
while the second line is fashioned so as to rhyme with the first. (I have made
no attempt to reproduce the rhymes or poetic rhythms in this English translation.) Like many *kinnot*, this one was crafted to be recited as a litany, with
alternating congregational responses of "Alas" (Hebrew: *oy*) and "Alas,
what is come upon us!" The emotional impact of such litanies can be quite
powerful when recited by a congregation.

The majority of the verses in Lamentations Chapter 5 describe the sufferings and degradations faced by the Jews at the time of the destruction of the
Temple. In keeping with a frequent theme of biblical theology, the poet
regards each indignity as a punishment for a sin, and the second line of the
couplet shows how each particular punishment was a fair retribution for a
specific sin (some of these are based on the chastisements in the words of the
biblical prophets or rabbinic interpretations).

The closing verses of the Lamentations chapter shift to somewhat different
themes, addressing God directly, whether in pleas for forgiveness and
salvation, or in plaints at the protracted suffering of the people of Israel.
The *kinnah* merely quotes these verses verbatim without embellishments.
As is the standard practice in the liturgical reading of Lamentations in
the synagogue, the verse "Turn thou us unto thee . . . renew our days as
of old" is repeated at the end in order to conclude on a more upbeat and
optimistic note.

Alas, what is come upon us!

"Remember, O Lord what is come upon us." Alas!
Consider, and behold our reproach. Alas, what is come upon us!
"Our inheritance is turned to strangers." Alas!
"Our houses to aliens" Alas, what is come upon us!
"We are orphans and fatherless" Alas!
Our mothers lament in the month of Ab Alas, what is come upon us!
"We have drunken our water for money" Alas!
Because we scorned the water libation Alas, what is come upon us!
"Our necks are under persecution" Alas!
Because we pursued needless hatred Alas, what is come upon us!
"We have given the hand to the Egyptians" Alas!
And Assyria hunted us like game Alas, what is come upon us!
"Our fathers have sinned, and are not" Alas!
While we suffer for their wrongdoings Alas, what is come upon us!
"Servants have ruled over us" Alas!
Because we abrogated the emancipation Alas, what is come upon us!
    of slaves
"We got our bread with the peril of our lives" Alas!

Because we clenched our hands from giving to the poor	Alas, what is come upon us!
"Our skin was black like an oven"	Alas!
Because they exchanged their true glory [the Torah] for frivolity	Alas, what is come upon us!
"They ravished the women in Zion"	Alas!
Because they committed adultery and lewdness	Alas, what is come upon us!
"Princes are hanged up by their hand"	Alas!
Because they robbed and oppressed the poor	Alas, what is come upon us!
"They took the young men to grind"	Alas!
Because they were found in brothels	Alas, what is come upon us!
"The elders have ceased from the gate"	Alas!
Because they perverted the judgment of the orphan and the widow	Alas, what is come upon us!
"The joy of our heart is ceased"	Alas!
Because we ceased our pilgrimages	Alas, what is come upon us!
"The crown is fallen from our head"	Alas!
Because our holy Temple was burned down	Alas, what is come upon us!
"For this our heart is faint"	Alas!
For the splendor of our most coveted place has been removed	Alas, what is come upon us!
"Because of the mountain of Zion, which is desolate"	Alas!
For upon it was offered the "abomination that makes desolate" [an idol; see Daniel 11:12]	Alas, what is come upon us!

"Thou, O Lord, remainest for ever, thy throne from generation to generation.
"Wherefore dost thou forget us for ever, and forsake us for so long?
"Turn thou us unto thee, O Lord, and we shall be turned; renew our days as of old.
"But thou hast utterly rejected us; thou art very wroth against us"
"Turn thou us unto thee, O Lord, and we shall be turned; renew our days as of old."

T'khinnes

As was noted previously, the formal official liturgy that is recited in the synagogue deals largely with national and eschatological hopes and allows little flexibility for the spontaneous expression of individual feelings or for conducting a personal conversation with the Creator. To the extent that people did address God individually, such intimate activity usually left no written records. Nevertheless, we may obtain some idea of the everyday religious experiences of common Jews from collections of prayers that were printed, usually in the spoken language, for the use of those who did not know Hebrew, the language of the standard liturgy.

The texts cited here are from collections of *t'khinnes*, personal prayers and blessings composed in Yiddish, the German-Jewish vernacular of Ashkenazic Jewry, and intended to be recited by women. As such, they have no official status in the formal Jewish liturgy; but precisely for that reason, they come closer to expressing the intimate hopes and spiritual values of the women who recited them.

The texts are so honest and unassuming that they require little explanation. From them emerges a simple faith of people who identify emotionally with the pious women of the Bible, and who believe that God and the angels are constantly among them watching over all their deeds. Unlike the official prayers, which speak on behalf of the entire people, often in abstract terms, the entreaties of the *t'khinnes* are for immediate, tangible requests, like the economic sustenance and general welfare of their families.

From a Yiddish women's prayer (T'khinneh) recited before putting a loaf of bread in the oven

> Lord of the world, in your hand is all blessing. I come now to revere your holiness, and I pray that you bestow your blessing on these baked goods. Send an angel to guard the baking, so that all will be well-baked, will rise nicely, and will not burn, to honor the holy Sabbath which you have chosen so that Israel your children can rest thereon, and over which one recites the holy blessing, as you blessed the dough of Sarah and Rebecca our mothers. May the Lord God listen to my voice; you are the God who hears the voices of those who call to you with their whole heart. May you be praised to eternity.

From a T'khinneh recited upon the lighting of the Sabbath candles[4]

> Blessed are you, Lord God, king of the universe, who has sanctified us with his precepts and commanded us to kindle the Sabbath lamp.

Comments

"Blessed are you, etc." This is the normal blessing recited before kindling the ritual candles at the onset of the Sabbath, on Friday evening. Since ancient times (as noted in the Mishnah) it was recognized that this precept is usually performed by women.

From a T'khinneh recited upon the lighting of the Sabbath candles (continued)

> In honor of God, in honor of our precept, in honor of the beloved holy Sabbath, which our master God has given us, and he has commanded us to observe the beloved precept of candle-lighting, may I be capable of

fulfilling it and may it be considered as if I had fulfilled all of the six hundred and thirteen commandments together with all Israel. Amen, may this be your will.

Comments

"As if I had fulfilled, etc." This probably alludes to the fact that women are exempted from many of the Torah's commandments and other Jewish religious rituals. The prayer therefore expresses the hope that for purposes of obtaining merit and reward, her performance of the precepts that are specifically assigned to women should be given the same weighting as all those that can be observed by men.

From a T'khinneh *recited upon the lighting of the Sabbath candles (continued)*

May it be your will, Lord God and God of our ancestors, that the Temple be rebuilt speedily in our days, and grant us a portion in your Torah. And there we may serve you reverently as in the days of old and in ancient times. "Then shall the offering of Judah and Jerusalem be pleasant unto the Lord, as in the days of old, and as in former years" (Malachi 3:4).

Comments

This paragraph appears at the the conclusions of several sections of the standard Hebrew liturgy.

From a T'khinneh *recited upon the lighting of the Sabbath candles (continued)*

Master of the universe, let my commandment of kindling the lamps be accepted by you like the commandment of the High Priest when he would kindle the lamp in the beloved holy Temple.

"Thy word is a lamp unto my feet, and a light unto my path" (Psalms 119:105) which means: Thy word is a lamp unto my feet, and may my children walk in God's way and let the precept of kindling my lamp be acceptable, so that my children's eyes may shine in the beloved holy Torah. Furthermore, I beseech you by virtue of this light, O dear blessed God, that my precept of the light be acceptable to you like the eternal light that burned in the holy Temple and was never extinguished. May the merit of the light of this beloved Sabbath grant us protection as it did for the first man who was saved from immediate death. In the same way, may our merit from the lights grant us protection so that our children's eyes will shine with the light of the Torah, and their good fortunes will shine in the heavens and they will be able to provide a generous living for their wives and children; and all the precepts that we perform will be counted like the precepts of our patriarchs and matriarchs and of the holy tribes. May we be as pure as a newborn child with its mother. Amen.

Comments

This paragraph draws thematic associations between the light of the Sabbath candles and several biblical and other references to lamps and light. These include: the candelabrum and "eternal light" in the holy Temple (Exodus 25:31–40; Exodus 27:20–22; etc.) and the brightness of a child's eyes. In keeping with the dominant rabbinic interpretation, light was symbolically identified with Torah, and this theme permeates the words of this prayer.

The idea that Adam was rescued from immediate death by the onset of the Sabbath is found in the Midrash.

Note the numerous allusions to children, family and livelihood. These are typical female concerns and are far more pronounced in the *T'khinnes* than in conventional (male) prayer.

2 Aggadah and Midrash

Halakhic Midrash

The study of the Bible as it was carried on among the Jewish sages during the early centuries of the Common Era is known in Hebrew as "*Midrash*" from a Hebrew root whose primary meaning is "search, seek out." Midrashic interpretation was applied to the two chief areas of rabbinic study: Halakhah (law) and Aggadah (theology, morals and homiletics). The emergence of Midrash can be viewed as a logical outcome of the belief in the divine origin of the Hebrew scriptures: if the Bible was authored by God or through prophetic inspiration, then its text must have been composed with superhuman wisdom and precision, so that it deserves to be studied in the minutest detail. Indeed, the surviving literature from pre-rabbinic times, such as the Qumran ("Dead Sea") scrolls, attest to the intensive study of the Torah during the era of the Second Temple among diverse Jewish religious sects. The earliest traditions we have of a systematic formulation of exegetical rules are associated with the figure of Hillel the Elder who lived at the turn of the millennium (he died around 30 CE). Historical scholarship has pointed to the close relationship between Hillel's methods and the rules of interpretation that were applied by Hellenistic scholars and jurists to the works of Homer or to legal codes.

During the late first and early second centuries there was a flowering of midrashic scholarship that was reflected in the emergence of two distinct schools, associated with Rabbi Akiva and Rabbi Ishmael. Each of these schools produced a body of interpretations to sections of the Torah that can be recognized by characteristic hermeneutical logic, terminology and the rabbis who appear in their works. When applied to legal analysis, the midrashic approach of the school of Rabbi Ishmael is more likely to treat biblical Hebrew as a natural language that is subject to normal stylistic considerations. Rabbi Akiva, on the other hand, stresses the unique supernatural character of the revealed text, and derives new teachings from innocuous-looking features such as grammatical particles, superfluous words and letters, or unusual word choices. The hermeneutical differences are less pronounced in passages that are devoted to aggadic topics.

The following passages are translated from the *Mekhilta deRabbi Ishmael*, a Midrash on the book of Exodus from the school of Rabbi Ishmael.

Mekhilta deRabbi Ishmael Baḥodesh 6[1]

["Remember the Sabbath day to keep it holy" (Exodus 20:8).]

"Remember" and "observe" (Deuteronomy 5:12) were stated in a single utterance.

Comments

This passage is based on the apparent contradiction between the two versions of the revelation of the "ten commandments" as recorded in the Torah. The first version is part of the narrative in Exodus Chapter 20, and the second is found in Moses' review of his life in Deuteronomy Chapter 5. Although the descriptions are very similar, there are a number of differences in the wording, especially in the fourth commandment, the one ordaining the weekly sabbath. The Exodus version begins "*remember* the Sabbath day to keep it holy," whereas the Deuteronomy version has "*observe* the Sabbath day to keep it holy."

In general, the rabbis understood that "remember" refers to performing actions that express the holiness of the day, while "observe" refers to refraining from activities that would be done on normal weekdays. The Midrash here assumes that the inconsistency between Exodus and Deuteronomy cannot be ascribed to any inaccuracy in the story's transmission—since they believed that the text of the Torah contains a precise rendering of God's original words to Moses and the Israelites. Therefore it must be the case that both versions were uttered by God at Mount Sinai and each of them contains important teachings. Rather than being perceived as a challenge to the traditional Jewish belief in the Torah's divine origin, this duality is treated as a proof for that very claim: only God is capable of uttering two different messages simultaneously in the same act of speech.

The Midrash now proceeds to point out some other laws in the Torah that appear to contradict each other, and it notes how these instances provide additional evidence for the uniquely miraculous authorship of the Torah.

Mekhilta deRabbi Ishmael Baḥodesh 6 *(continued)*

"Everyone who profanes it shall surely be put to death" (Exodus 31:14) and "on the Sabbath day two lambs" (Numbers 28:9)—Both were spoken in a single utterance.

Comments

Performing acts of "work" on the Sabbath is a grave offense according to the Torah and may be punishable by death. And yet the verse from the book of Numbers commands the offering of sacrifices in the Temple on the Sabbath, though they require the performance of activities such as kindling a fire and cooking, which are normally prohibited on the Sabbath.

The rabbis understood that the Torah was designating the sacrificial worship as an explicit exception to the general Sabbath restrictions. As a general rule, they understood that the performance of positive commandments overrides prohibitions. At any rate, the fact that these two apparently antithetical laws can coexist in the Torah is also presented here as proof of its wondrous supernatural character.

It should be noted that during the era of the second Temple, this issue appears to have been a major matter of contention between the rival Jewish sects. Several of the Qumran documents indicate their authors' intense concern to avoid the possibility of conflicts between different laws of the Torah. This tendency is particularly evident in their calendar, which was structured in such a way that (unlike the Pharisaic and rabbinic calendars) no festival can occur on a Saturday. At any rate, the fact that the Sabbath additional offerings and the daily "continual" offering are offered on Sabbath is stated explicitly and clearly in the Torah.

Mekhilta deRabbi Ishmael Baḥodesh 6 *(continued)*

"You shall not uncover the nakedness of your brother's wife" (Leviticus 18:16) and "her husband's brother shall go in to her" (Deuteronomy 25:5) were both stated in a single utterance.

Comments

Marriage or sexual relations of a man with his sister-in-law, his brother's wife, is classified by the Torah as incestuous and the rabbis understood that the severe prohibition remains in force even after the death of the brother. And yet, if the brother should die childless, the Torah commands that the widow undergo the procedure of "levirate marriage" with her late husband's brother: "Her husband's brother shall go in to her, take her as his wife, and perform the duty of a husband's brother to her. And it shall be that the firstborn son which she bears will succeed to the name of his dead brother" (Deuteronomy 25:5–10). Thus, under the appropriate circumstances, an act that would otherwise have been punishable as a very grave sin has been transformed into an obligation. (The Torah also sets out a ceremony for releasing the parties from the obligation when they choose not to proceed with the levirate marriage.)

Mekhilta deRabbi Ishmael Baḥodesh 6 *(continued)*

"You shall not wear a garment of different sorts, such as wool and linen mixed together" (Deuteronomy 25:11) and "you shall make tassels" (Deuteronomy 25:12) were both stated in a single utterance.

Comments

The Torah (Numbers 15:38) prescribes that ritual "tassels" or "fringes" (*ṣiṣit*) be tied to the corners of one's garments. Mingled among them was a special thread that was to be colored blue or purple (Hebrew: *tekhelet*); according to the rabbinic tradition, this was a dye derived from a particular shellfish. Linen, derived from flax, was one of the most common fabrics used for clothing, though wool was one of the few materials that could be dyed effectively. Normally, the mixing of wool and linen is forbidden by the law of the Torah; however, the juxtaposition of the law forbidding "mingled stuff" and that requiring "twisted cords" in Deuteronomy 22:11–12— "Thou shalt not wear a mingled stuff, wool and linen together. Thou shalt make thee twisted cords upon the four corners of thy covering"—was understood as a statement of special permission to use woolen threads for the ritual tassels on linen garments.

Mekhilta deRabbi Ishmael Baḥodesh 6 (*continued*)

This is something that cannot be said about a human being, as it says: "God has spoken once, twice I have heard this" (Psalms 62:11); and it also says "Is not My word like a fire?" says the Lord, and "like a hammer that breaks the rock in pieces?" (Jeremiah 23:29).

Comments

The verses from Psalms and Jeremiah were expounded as allusions to the belief that divine speech can bear multiple messages or meanings. As regards Jeremiah, the image seems to be of a blacksmith's hammer creating many sparks when it strikes a rock. Look up the verses in their original contexts and consider whether these interpretations are warranted.

Mekhilta deRabbi Ishmael Baḥodesh 6 (*continued*)

"Remember" and "observe".
"Remember" before it and "observe" after it.
Based on this, they declared: One adds on from the profane to the sacred.
This may be illustrated by the parable of a wolf that is lurking in front of and behind a person.

Comments

This is a different way of accounting for the two different terms that are employed in the commandment to keep the Sabbath (perhaps taking into account that there are numerous other mentions of the Sabbath scattered through the Torah). According to this interpretation, these verses refer not to the Sabbath proper, which extends from sunset on Friday until Saturday night, but rather to a separate obligation to add on the sanctity of the Sabbath by extending it for an unspecified amount of time before and after—which is perceived as taking time out of the "profane" weekday and · sanctifying it as an extension of the holy Sabbath.

The text and meaning of the parable are unclear and it has been explained in diverse ways. Perhaps the wolf is meant to represent the hazards and spiritual challenges of workaday existence lurking around the sheltered refuge of the Sabbath day. Accordingly, it is recommended to establish a kind of "safety zone" around the sacred haven that is afforded by the Sabbath day.

Mekhilta deRabbi Ishmael Baḥodesh 6 (continued)

Eleazar ben Hananiah ben Hezekiah ben Garon says: "Remember the Sabbath day to keep it holy"—be conscious of it from Sunday. Thus, if you should happen upon a choice morsel, you should designate it for the Sabbath.

Rabbi Isaac says: "You should not count in the manner that others count; instead you should count in relation to the Sabbath."

"To keep it holy"—"to keep it holy" by means of a blessing.

Based on this, they declared: one sanctifies it over wine at its onset.

Comments

These interpretations all propose ways in which the Sabbath is made holy by means of "remembering" (the Hebrew term also suggests "mentioning"), as is implied by the wording of the biblical verse. Eleazar ben Hananiah speaks of being conscious of the Sabbath throughout the week so that everything that one does during the weekdays looks ahead to the Sabbath and is perceived as a preparation for it. His attitude is similar to that of Shammai the Elder, one of the prominent teachers at the turn of the millennium. A different approach was advocated by Shammai's colleague and rival, Hillel, who declared that one should live each day for its own sake.

What Rabbi Isaac seems to be saying is that the holiness with which Jews view the Sabbath is reflected in their practice of designating the days of the week. Unlike the "others" (non-Jews) who indicate the days of the week by names or other criteria, the convention in Hebrew is to refer to the days by number in relation to the Sabbath. Thus, Sunday is referred to in Hebrew as "the first day in the Sabbath cycle," Monday is "the second day," and so forth.

The third interpretation states that a person fulfills the obligation of remembering the Sabbath to keep it holy by reciting the "Sanctification" blessing [*Kiddush*] at the beginning of the Sabbath, on Friday evening. This is indeed the venerable and universal practice among Jews. It is customary to recite the Kiddush as a liturgical blessing over a cup of wine.

Mekhilta deRabbi Ishmael Neziqin Mishpaṭim *10*[2]

"And if an ox gore a man or a woman to death, the ox shall be surely stoned" (Exodus 21:28).

From this I only know of an ox. From where can I learn to treat all beasts like an ox?—I draw the following analogy: Here it says "ox" and it also says "ox" elsewhere. Just as with respect to the "ox" that is mentioned at Sinai it treated all animals like an ox, so too with the ox that is mentioned here, reason would dictate that we should treat all animals like the ox.

Comments

The passage in Exodus teaches that an ox that kills a human must be stoned to death. The Midrash wants to demonstrate that this law is not restricted to oxen, but applies to any animal that kills a human. It derives this by analogy from the wording of the Sabbath commandment given at Mount Sinai in the Ten Commandments. There it states that it is forbidden to make one's animals work on the seventh day (Deuteronomy 5:14): "nor your ox, nor your donkey, nor any of your cattle." Just as "ox" in that verse is explicitly listed alongside all other types of (domestic) animals, the Midrash assumes that the same applies here with regard to animals who kill humans, even though the other animals are not mentioned here.

This form of analogy between the occurrences of identical words in different contexts is known in Hebrew as "*gezerah shavah*."

Mekhilta deRabbi Ishmael Neziqin Mishpaṭim *10* (continued)

And from where do we learn to treat all ways of killing like goring?

I draw the following analogy: Since the dangerous ox is subject to stoning and the tame ox is subject to stoning, if you have learned with regard to the dangerous one that all ways of killing are treated as equivalent to goring, so too with respect to the tame one, let us treat all ways of killing as equivalent to goring.

Comments

In formulating its law about an ox that kills a human, the Torah speaks of causing death by goring. The Midrash wants to prove that the same law extends to other ways of killing people.

It is understood that this verse (28) is dealing with a "**tame**" ox; that is, one that has not previously been attacking people. The rule for a "**dangerous**" ox—one that has a previous record of goring—is dealt with in a separate section. In referring to manslaughter by a dangerous ox, the Torah says "it has killed a man or a woman." "Killed" is, of course, a more general term than "gored" and applies to any manner of killing. The Midrash initially assumes that it can transfer the rule from the one case to the other, to infer that in the case of the tame ox who kills, the law is applied equally whether the killing is done by goring or in other ways.

Mekhilta deRabbi Ishmael Neziqin Mishpaṭim *10 (continued)*

No. Granted that you can say this with respect to the dangerous ox, which is liable to pay the ransom—would you say it about a tame ox that is not subject to the ransom?

Comments

The Midrash rejects the initial attempt to prove its case, arguing that one cannot automatically equate the laws governing the dangerous ox with those of the tame ox, because we know that the former is treated more stringently when it kills a person. This stringency is evident in the law of "ransom" as set out in verses 29–30: "the ox shall be stoned and its owner also shall be put to death. If there is imposed on him a ransom, then he shall pay to redeem his life, whatever is imposed on him." This means that an owner who has been notified that his animal is dangerous, and yet does not take adequate precautions to keep it from killing a human being, is considered as though he were deserving of death and is required to pay the "ransom" payment to redeem himself from that responsibility. The Torah does not apply that law of "ransom" to the owner of an animal that has hitherto been tame and harmless.

The Midrash is arguing that just as the dangerous animal is treated more stringently than the tame one with regard to the ransom obligation, so too it might be treated more stringently with respect to punishing animals who kill in ways other than by goring.

Mekhilta deRabbi Ishmael Neziqin Mishpaṭim *10 (continued)*

For the expression "and it kills a man or woman" [in the same verse] can only have been included in order to draw a verbal analogy [*gezerah shavah*], as follows: It says here "a man or a woman" and it says elsewhere "a man or a woman." Just as elsewhere it treats all deaths like goring, so also here, it follows logically that all ways of killing are treated like goring.

Comments

The Midrash concludes that, though its desired conclusion cannot be derived by logical analogy, it can be proven by a *gezerah shavah*, a verbal resemblance (see above). The expression "a man or a woman" appears superfluously both in the passage dealing with the dangerous ox and in the one dealing with the tame one. This is perceived as an intentional signal by the Torah that we are supposed to apply details that are specified with respect to the one situation (where it refers to any form of killing) to the other situation as well. Because this kind of verbal analogy is not based on logical comparison, it is not open to the previous objection about the more stringent status of the dangerous ox.

Mekhilta deRabbi Ishmael Neziqin Mishpaṭim 10 *(continued)*

And from where do we derive the ruling that the killings of minors are treated the same as adults?

I reason as follows: Seeing as a tame ox is subject to stoning and a dangerous ox is subject to stoning—if you have learned regarding a dangerous ox that minor [victims] are considered like adults, so too with a tame ox we shall treat minors like adults.

No. If you have said this with respect to the dangerous ox, that is because [its owner] is subject to payment of the ransom, and hence with respect to it minors are treated like adults; but would you also say so with respect to a tame ox—for which ransom is not demanded—that minors should be treated like adults?!

For this reason it has to teach explicitly "Whether it has gored a son or gored a daughter, according to this judgment it shall be done to him" (verse 31).

Comments

The argumentation follows the same pattern as in the previous section. The Midrash wants to prove that when a hitherto tame ox kills a child, it is stoned just as when it kills an adult. Initially it seeks to demonstrate this by drawing a logical analogy from the case of a "dangerous" ox regarding which the Torah states explicitly "whether it has gored a son or gored a daughter." This analogy is rejected, however, because it is conceivable that the case of the dangerous ox would be treated more stringently, as indicated by its special requirement of "ransom" payment.

Aggadic Midrash: homiletic

Like most homiletical midrashic passages, the following one is closely tied to the schedule of liturgical readings from the Bible which took place in the synagogues, primarily during the Sabbath morning services. Normally, the five books of the Torah were read in sequence as part of the weekly services. In those communities that observed the ancient Palestinian liturgical rite, the Torah was divided up into relatively short sections so that it would be read in its entirety over a period of about three and a half years. (In the Babylonian custom, which was eventually adopted by all Jewish communities, the cycle is completed in a single year.)

There are, however, occasions when the Torah-reading sequence is interrupted for special occasions, such as the annual festivals. The collection known as *Pesiqta deRav Kahana*, from which this text is taken, consists of midrashic homilies and interpretations for those special readings.

In preparation for Passover, which begins in the middle of the springtime month of Nissan, a special reading was ordained to be read on the Sabbath immediately preceding the beginning of that month. The reading consists of Exodus Chapter 12 which relates how God informed the Israelites that they were about to be redeemed from centuries of slavery, and that they should prepare themselves for a sudden departure. The biblical portion includes a detailed description of the ritual observances associated with the Passover, and its public reading served as a reminder and prelude for the approaching holiday. The passage opens with the words "Now the Lord spoke to Moses and Aaron in the land of Egypt, saying, 'This month shall be your beginning of months; it shall be the first month of the year to you.'"

This text from the *Pesiqta deRav Kahana* exemplifies the most common rhetorical structure of rabbinic sermons, to which scholars have given the name "*petiḥa*" or "*petiḥta*"—an opening or interpretation. A standard *petiḥa* begins with a verse from a section of the Bible other than the one that is being read that day in the synagogue, and culminates with the opening words of the synagogue reading. It is probable that these sermons were delivered immediately before the reading of the Torah and served as a kind of preamble to it. A well-crafted *petiḥta* produced a degree of suspense in the audience as they tried to anticipate how the preacher would make the connection to the Torah reading (though in the present example, the general direction of the transition is relatively predictable and straightforward). Hundreds of *petiḥa* homilies are preserved in the ancient rabbinic compendia.

This passage assembles several alternative homilies to Song of Songs 2:8. The Song of Songs is a remarkable book of the Hebrew Bible, consisting entirely of sensuous love poetry. It was included among the Jewish sacred scriptures on the understanding that it was to be interpreted as an allegory, a symbolic representation of the relationship between God (the male figure) and Israel (the female figure). It is customary for Jews to read the Song of Songs on Passover. In the verse that is being expounded in this text, the woman speaks with excited anticipation of the imminent arrival of her beloved whose voice she hears approaching. This provides powerful imagery to represent Israel's mentality on the eve of the exodus from Egypt after they have been informed that their lengthy enslavement is about to reach its end.

Pesiqta deRav Kahana Ha-Ḥodesh Hazzeh 5:7[3]

"The voice of my beloved! Behold, he comes leaping on the mountains, skipping on the hills" (Song of Songs 2:8).
Rabbi Judah and Rabbi Nehemiah and the Rabbis.

Comments

This is to say, that the Midrash will now bring three different expositions of the verse, by Rabbis Judah and Nehemiah and by an unidentified group of rabbis.

Pesiqta deRav Kahana Ha-Ḥodesh Hazzeh 5:7 *(continued)*

Rabbi Judah says: "The voice of my beloved! Behold, he comes" refers to Moses. When Moses came and told Israel "In this month you shall be redeemed," they said to him: Our master Moses, how can we be redeemed? Did the Holy One not say to our ancestor Abraham "Know of a surety that your seed shall be a stranger in a land that is not theirs, and they shall serve them, and they shall afflict them four hundred years" (Genesis 15:13)? However only two hundred and ten of those years have elapsed!

He replied to them: Because he desires your redemption, he is over-looking your precise calculations. Instead, "he comes leaping on the mountains, skipping on the hills."

He comes leaping over the set times and over the calculations and over the intercalations. And in this month you shall be redeemed: "This month shall be to you the beginning of months: it shall be the first month of the year to you" (Exodus 12:2).

Comments

The prophet Moses is identified allegorically as "the voice of my beloved," the spokesman of God. At this point in the biblical narrative, Moses has notified the Israelites that God will shortly be taking them out of Egyptian bondage.

The people's response is perhaps surprising and has no obvious basis in the biblical story. Instead of experiencing feelings of relief and reassurance, they protest to Moses that he must be mistaken, because the conditions for redemption have not been fulfilled. The enslavement of the people had been foretold to their forefather Abraham in the covenant ceremony described in Genesis 15. In that passage the length of the slavery had been set at four hundred years—and yet barely half that time-span had elapsed at this point! Indeed, this is a discrepancy that has troubled biblical exegetes since ancient times, and many different solutions were proposed to account for it.

Rabbi Judah's solution is evidently inspired by the wording of the verse in Song of Songs: "he comes leaping on the mountains, skipping on the hills," which he understood as if it were saying that God was taking a sort of short-cut; in his impatience to redeem his beloved people, God was willing to contradict his own explicit declaration to Abraham and take them out of Egypt after only two hundred and ten years. This is a theologically powerful idea, as it boldly implies that God is ready to forego absolute truth out of his love and compassion for his creatures.

"**Intercalations**" refer to the addition of days to months or of months to years in the reckoning of the Hebrew calendar; this was a prerogative of the religious courts in ancient times (before the establishment of a permanent calculated calendar). It is not entirely clear how the concept fits into the present context, and it is possible that it may have been inserted here by mistake, since the subjects of the Hebrew religious calendar and the courts' authority over intercalation are a frequent theme in other midrashic interpretations of Exodus 12:2.

To fully appreciate the impact that this exposition had on its original audience, we should bear in mind that the Jews in the land of Israel at that time were suffering under the oppressive yoke of Roman imperialism, which they regarded as the embodiment of evil and idolatry. The story of the Egyptian exodus served them as a hope-inspiring paradigm for their future redemption and the overthrow of Rome. Rabbi Judah's homily effectively imbued them with the confidence that (notwithstanding their discouraging experiences of failed revolts against Rome), God could bring about their liberation at any moment, even if they had not necessarily satisfied all the conditions for the advent of the messianic redemption.

Pesiqta deRav Kahana Ha-Ḥodesh Hazzeh 5:7 *(continued)*

Rabbi Nehemiah says: "The voice of my beloved! Behold, he comes" refers to Moses. When Moses came and told Israel "In this month you shall be redeemed," they said to him: Our master Moses, how can we be redeemed as long as the land of Egypt is filled with the filth of our idol-worship?!

He replied to them: Because he desires your redemption, he is over-looking your idol-worship. Instead, "he comes leaping on the mountains, skipping on the hills." "Mountains" here is an allusion to idolatrous temples, even as you say "They sacrifice on the tops of the mountains, and burn incense on the hills" (Hosea 4:13).

Comments

Rabbi Nehemiah's exposition is almost identical to that of Rabbi Judah, except that it mentions a different reason why the Israelites thought they were not ready to be redeemed: because the centuries that they had spent as slaves in Egypt had succeeded in bringing them down to the disgraceful spiritual level of the Egyptian heathens.

As in Rabbi Judah's exposition, the people's objection is inferred from a close reading of the verse in Song of Songs, focusing on the superfluous detail "mountains." Basing himself on the comparison with the text in Hosea, Rabbi Nehemiah sees in this an allusion to idolatry.

Of course, this kind of interpretation is not very convincing, but it is a well-known trope of rabbinic interpretation known as the *"gezerah shavah"* ("comparison of equals"; see above). A similar method of comparing how a difficult word is used in other contexts can be quite useful in scholarly lexicography, but the rabbis like to use the *gezerah shavah* in more playful and creative ways, as we saw here—more in the sprit of a literary figure of speech than of serious exegesis.

Pesiqta deRav Kahana Ha-Ḥodesh Hazzeh 5:7 *(continued)*

And the Rabbis say: "The voice of my beloved! Behold, he comes" refers to Moses. When Moses came and told Israel "In this month you shall be redeemed," they said to him: Our master Moses, how can we be redeemed, when we possess no good deeds?!

He replied to them: Because he desires your redemption, he is overlooking your evil deeds. Whom does he look at? At the righteous among you, such as Amram and his court.

"Mountains" here is an allusion to courts, even as you say: "And she said to her father, Let this thing be done for me: let me alone two months, that I may go up and down on the mountains" (Judges 11:37).

Comments

This passage is structured very similarly to the previous expositions, except that here the flaw that is claimed to prevent the Israelites' redemption is identified as a general lack of merit through good deeds and righteousness. As in Rabbi Nehemiah's homily, the claim is inferred from the word "mountains" in the Song of Songs verse.

Here, however, the proof is even less persuasive. The instance of "mountains" in the story of Jephthah's daughter has no visible association with courts, righteousness or any of the topics in Rabbi Nehemiah's interpretation. (A variant reading equates the mountains with "elders," judges.) In its original context, Jephthah uttered a rash vow to offer up the first creature he saw after he returned successfully from battle, and it turned out to be his daughter. The girl asked for a reprieve of two months in which to lament her fate in the mountains. This Midrash, however, is probably alluding to a tradition according to which she appealed to a religious court in order to try to have the vow annulled. It is only after that obscure premise is conceded that the verse can be construed as having any connection to courts—and even then, it is not particularly obvious that courts are equivalent to good deeds or righteousness.

Pesiqta deRav Kahana Ha-Ḥodesh Hazzeh 5:7 *(continued)*

> Rabbi Judan in the name of Rabbi Liezer the son of Rabbi Yosé the Galilean; Rabbi Huna in the name of Rabbi Liezer son of Jacob: "The voice of my beloved! Behold, he comes"—this refers to the anointed [*mashiaḥ*] king. When he arrives and says to Israel "In this month you shall be redeemed," they say to him: Our master, anointed king—how can we be redeemed? Did not the Holy One declare that he would subject us to seventy nations?
>
> And then he responds to them with two answers, saying to them: If one of you has been exiled to Barbaria and one of you to Sarmatia, it is counted as if you were all exiled.
>
> And furthermore, this wicked empire conscripts soldiers from each and every nation. So if a single Cuthean comes and subjugates you, it is as if his entire nation has subjugated you. If a single Ethiopian comes and subjugates you, it is as if his entire nation has subjugated you.
>
> And in this month you shall be redeemed! "This month shall be your beginning of months."

Comments

This section expounds the same verse from Song of Songs in connection with the future redemption of Israel rather than the redemption from Egypt as in the previous sections.

In keeping with traditional Jewish eschatological concepts, the person who will lead the nation to freedom at that time will be the "anointed king"—in Hebrew, *melekh hammashiaḥ*, employing the word that has entered the English language as "messiah." This refers to a descendent of the royal house of King David who will one day restore Jewish political sovereignty. Anointing the head of a monarch or high priest with olive oil was part of the biblical ceremony for installing them as legitimate leaders. The advent of the messiah accordingly became synonymous with the future redemption of Israel from foreign subjugation (by imperial Rome) and exile.

The dialogue between Israel and the messiah follows the same pattern as that between Israel and Moses in the previous interpretations. The messiah informs the people that they are on the threshold of redemption. This appears to imply that the future redemption was expected to take place in the same month as the Egyptian exodus. This assumption is, in fact, consistent with a rabbinic tradition that depicts Nissan as the month designated for both the past and the future redemptions.

The people object to the messiah's announcement, arguing that the time is not yet ripe for the redemption because it cannot occur until all Israel has been scattered among all the seventy nations of the world. In fact, it is not quite obvious what the source was for such a belief, and the Midrash does not adduce a specific biblical verse in support of the idea. Although there are several scriptural passages that speak in a more general way of Israel being scattered around the world, our text takes this to a radical extreme by insisting at first that every individual Jew will be oppressed by every one of the seventy nations.

As in the previous homilies about Moses, the Israelites are reassured here that God will interpret his declaration leniently in order to facilitate their immediate redemption by means of a kind of legalistic loophole. It is not, as they had feared initially, that the redemption will have to wait until every Jew has been exiled to every land. God will consider the conditions to have been fulfilled if even one person has been in each land (and for this purpose the preacher refers proverbially to the farthest frontiers of the empire: the Barbary coast of Africa and Sarmatia in far-off eastern Europe).

Furthermore, it is not necessary that the Jews be subjugated by entire nations. Rather, because the Roman army included soldiers from so many diverse ethnic origins, it will be counted as if each soldier represented his entire nation. Now that God, moved by his love for his people, is interpreting the condition so loosely, there remains no impediment to the imminent coming of the messianic era.

This brief passage offered us a fine illustration of how the rhetorical structure of a homily integrated with the interpretation of biblical texts and with thematic development in order to create an effective literary unit that brought hope and reassurance to the congregation who heard it in the synagogue. (The complexity of the passage suggests that a later editor combined what were originally a number of shorter, separate homilies.) The exposition conforms to the accepted rules of a *petiḥta* as described above, beginning from Song of Songs 2:8, developing its interpretations in various ways, and then culminating with the beginning of Exodus Chapter 12, the Torah text designated for reading on that Sabbath.

Thematically, the passage draws a close parallel between the liberation of Israel in the distant past from their enslavement in Egypt, to the future redemption from the oppression of Roman imperialism. To Jews who might be losing hope because they believe that the necessary conditions for redemption are far from being fulfilled in their generation, the homilist retorts that the same doubts existed in the days of Moses, but the Almighty's love for his people is powerful enough to "skip over" any obstacles that might appear to stand in the way of the final redemption.

Aggadic Midrash: exegetical

The following section is taken from a midrashic commentary to the book of Esther that is incorporated into the tractate *Megillah* of the Babylonian Talmud. The selection covers the beginning of Chapter 6 of Esther. It is a pivotal chapter in the biblical narrative. Until that point, the Jews of the Persian empire have been imperiled by an edict of Prime Minister Haman ordering that they be massacred on an assigned date. Unknown to King Ahasuerus, his own queen is Esther, a Jewish woman who, along with her relative, the courtier Mordecai, is preparing a plan to expose Haman's plot at a banquet to which Esther will invite Ahasuerus and Haman.

When we read Esther without a commentary or from outside a religious perspective, it comes across as a very secular story. The name of God is not mentioned, and all the events are propelled by human actions or by apparent coincidences. One of the prominent functions of the midrashic versions is to point out (or inject) the divine hand that is guiding the outcome.

Babylonian Talmud Megillah 15b–16a[4]

> "*On that night the king's sleep wandered*" (Esther 6:1).
> Says Rabbi Tanḥum: The sleep of the king of the universe wandered.
> And the rabbis say: The upper ones wandered and the lower ones wandered.

Comments

The simple meaning of the verse is that King Ahasuerus was suffering a bout of insomnia on the fateful night in question. This turns out to be very fortuitous for Mordecai and the Jews, as Ahasuerus will ask to have the royal chronicles read before him. This will serve to remind him that Mordecai once saved his life but was never rewarded.

From a religious perspective, it is natural to understand that it was God who caused the king's sleeplessness. However, Rabbi Tanḥum takes this idea a step further, alluding to an approach mentioned elsewhere in rabbinic literature, which states that references in Esther to "the king"—as distinct from "King Ahasuerus"—refers to God rather than to the Persian monarch. When our current verse is read in this manner, we have a poignant and almost mythic portrayal of the almighty God being so upset by the danger hanging over the Jews that he is unable to remain at ease.

The statement by the (unidentified) "rabbis" appears to convey a similar idea. Perhaps they intend to assert that Rabbi Tanḥum's interpretation is not incompatible with the plain meaning of the verse, in that both God and Ahasuerus were unable to rest on that night.

Babylonian Talmud Megillah 15b–16a (continued)

> Rava says: The sleep of Ahasuerus, literally.
> A worry fell into his heart. He said: Why did Esther make a special point of inviting Haman? They are conspiring against "that man" to murder him.

He went on and thought: If it is so, there is not a single person who is friendly to me, who will come and tell me.

He went on and said: Is there a person who has done a favor for me and I have not rewarded him?

At once he ordered "the book of records of the chronicles; and they were read" (Esther 6:1).

Comments

Rava accepts the literal meaning of the scriptural passage. However, he tries to provide a credible psychological account of why Ahasuerus was overcome by sleeplessness on that particular occasion, and why his response was to order a reading of the "book of records and chronicles." Rava's solution is actually quite plausible. Esther had inexplicably invited him and Haman to a banquet. From the king's point of view, she might well be plotting with Haman to assassinate him (a common scenario in ancient political intrigues). Under the circumstances, this was a good time to make sure that he had allies to support him and that he had not alienated any potential friends by failing to reward favors that were due to them. This line of reasoning led naturally to a review of the royal chronicles.

Note the use of the circumlocution "**that man**" as a substitute for "me." This was a common way of referring to oneself in a negative context, based on the belief that the mention of an unwanted situation might actually help cause it to occur.

Babylonian Talmud Megillah 15b–16a (continued)

Says Rabbi Yoḥanan: Shimshai Haman's son was reading, and when he reached the account of Mordecai's exploit he rolled it [the scroll], but the columns would then roll themselves back.

And some say: The letters cried out saying "that Mordecai had told of Bigthan and Teresh," as it says: "and they *were read* before the king."

"And it was found written etc." (Esther 6:2).

"Wrote" it should have said!

—Says Rabbi Isaac Nappaḥa: This teaches that Shimshai is erasing and Gabriel is writing.

Says Rabbi Asi: Rabbi Shela of Kefar Tamarta expounded: And just as the lower writing which is in Israel's favor is not erased, the celestial writing all the more so!

Comments

The reader of the scroll of royal chronicles, whose identity the biblical narrator has concealed behind the anonymity of a passive verb, is identified by Rabbi Yoḥanan as Shimshai. The name Shimshai appears in the book of Ezra as the secretary of Rehum the governor of Samaria who "wrote a letter against Jerusalem to Ahasuerus the king" (Ezra 4:9) persuading him to halt the construction of the second Temple. That passage is the only other place in the Bible where Ahasuerus is mentioned, and according to the rabbis, Ahasuerus and Haman were complicit in the campaign to prevent the Temple's reconstruction after it had been commanded by the emperor Cyrus.

As a general rule, Midrash is uncomfortable with the appearances of minor or anonymous characters in Bible stories who appear only once, and it likes to identify such figures with more prominent personalities. In the present instance, not only do the rabbis identify Ahasuerus' anonymous scribe with the scribe Shimshai in Ezra, but Rabbi Yoḥanan also transforms Shimshai into Haman's son. In this way, the Midrash creates a vivid scene in which the hostile Shimshai, after reluctantly being commanded to read out the chronicle, tries to avoid reciting Mordecai's praiseworthy deed, hoping to fool the king by quickly turning the scroll or by erasing the section. However, God does not allow him to succeed. He rolls back the scroll, or (through the agency of the angel Gabriel) rewrites what was erased.

The homiletic point is evident. Contrary to the impression created by the unembellished biblical narrative, where the developments occur by fortunate happenstance and as a result of the actions of the human characters, the Midrash shows that God is personally manipulating the events, and the stratagems of Mordecai and Esther could not have succeeded without divine or angelic intervention.

Babylonian Talmud Megillah 15b–16a (continued)

> "And the king said, What honor and dignity hath been done to Mordecai for this? Then said the king's servants that ministered unto him: There is nothing done for him" (Esther 6:3).
>
> It was taught: Not because they love Mordecai, but rather because they despise Haman.

Comments

When Ahasuerus asked whether Mordecai had been rewarded for his service to the king, the servants replied honestly and without hesitation that he had not. Evidently the talmudic interpreter found it difficult to believe that heathen servants would have been so quick to divulge information that was to the advantage of the Jewish hero. For this reason it is proposed that the servants' readiness to help Mordecai did not arise out of any affection or sympathy that they felt toward him, but was motivated by their hostility to Haman. The Talmud does not explain the reason for that hostility.

Babylonian Talmud Megillah *15b–16a (continued)*

"And the king said: Who is in the court? Now Haman was come into the outward court of the king's house, to speak unto the king to hang Mordecai on the gallows that he had prepared for him" (Esther 6:4).

A baraita teaches: "For him" he had prepared it—for himself.

Comments

"For him . . . for himself" The midrashic commentator observes that the ambiguity that is created by the use of a pronoun ("him") allows for a wry and ironic double entendre. Although according to the plain sense of the passage, the verse is referring to the gallows that Haman prepared for *Mordecai*, it can also be understood to presage the reversal that will take place at the conclusion of the story, when it is the villain *Haman* who is hanged on that same gallows he intended to be the instrument of his villainy.

3 The literature of halakhic discourse

In the following section we will be studying a specific question in Jewish religious law ("halakhah") as it developed from its sources in the Torah through the interpretations and discussions of scholars in talmudic literature, commentaries and codifications of Jewish law over the generations. Hopefully, this will provide us with a suitable opportunity to appreciate the lively intellectual experience of halakhic debate that occupies a central place in Jewish spirituality.

Passages from the Torah

Deuteronomy 6:4–9

> Hear O Israel, the Lord is our God, the Lord alone. You must love the Lord your God with all your heart and with all your soul and with all your might. Take to heart these words with which I charge you this day. Impress them upon your children. Recite them when you stay at home and when you are away, when you lie down and when you get up.

Deuteronomy 11:18–20

> Therefore impress these My words upon your very heart: bind them as a sign on your hand and let them serve as a symbol on your forehead, and teach them to your children—reciting them when you stay at home and when you are away, when you lie down and when you get up, and inscribe them on the doorposts of your house and on your gates.

Comments

"**Recite them . . . when you lie down and when you get up**"—The precise meaning of this passage is not entirely clear. The main questions that concern us are:

1 What exactly is to be recited?
2 When is it to be recited?

As regards the first question, the meaning of the passage might be that the whole of God's teachings should be recited. Thus the medieval Spanish commentator Rabbi Abraham Ibn Ezra asserts: "The true meaning of 'these words' is: All the commandments." Other commentators claim that it refers to the Torah in general, to Moses' discourses in the Book of Deuteronomy, or to the covenant (involving a blessing or curse that are promised for obedience or disobedience to God's commands) at the end of the book of Deuteronomy.

As for the second question: the meaning of the passages seems to be that a person should continually be reciting and contemplating God's word at every minute of the day and through all one's activities.

Traditional Jewish legal interpretation, halakhah, interpreted the verses in question in a very different way. Most talmudic sources presume that the Bible is here commanding that these actual two passages in Deuteronomy are to be recited at designated times of the day. This recitation is known as the "*Shema'*," taking its name from the first word of the Hebrew text of Deuteronomy 6:4 ("Hear . . .").

As has been noted previously, the special ways the rabbis had of reading the verses of the Bible (or other sacred texts) are called "Midrash." The function of the Midrash in our case may have been to turn an infinite (and therefore ultimately impossible-to-fulfill) command—to recite a limitless body of teaching (the divine Torah) at all times and throughout one's life—into a more manageable and finite obligation.

Admittedly, if we choose to understand the the rabbis' motives in that way, then their midrashic exegesis might appear to be a trivialization of a lofty religious ideal. However, such apparent literalism can at times be a pretext for deeper theological or spiritual ideas. In our case too, the fact that Jewish law orders the reading of the *Shema'* passages is not merely the result of a contrived way of reading the Bible, but reflects an emphasis on certain values and ideas which the rabbis considered central to Jewish belief.

Mishnah

The next passage is from the Mishnah, the most important collection of Jewish teachings after the Bible. The Mishnah consists for the most part of concise statements of law, frequently presented in the form of disputes between various rabbis (called "*Tannaim*") who lived between the second half of the first century and the beginning of the third century CE. The following excerpt is from the beginning of the first Tractate of the Mishnah, entitled *Berakhot* ("Blessings"), which deals with the prayers and blessings of the daily liturgy.

Mishnah, Berakhot 1:1

From when is the *Shema'* recited in the evenings?—From the time when the priests enter to eat from their heave-offering [*terumah*] until the end of the first watch. These are the words of Rabbi Eliezer.

And the Sages say: until midnight.

Rabban Gamaliel says: until the dawn comes up.

Comments

"**the Shemaʿ recited**" The Mishnah presumes that there exists an obligation to recite the passages: Deuteronomy 6:4–9, Deuteronomy 11:13–21 and Numbers 15:37–41 in the evening and in the morning.

"**heave-offering**" A segment of all produce must be set aside for support of the **priests** (Kohanim), the descendants of the biblical Aaron (Moses' brother) who are charged with the performance of the worship in the Jerusalem Temple.

Though the required proportion for heave-offering is not defined in the Torah, the rabbis declared that one-fiftieth is a proper amount for an average person. The priest may eat of the *terumah* only when he is in a state of ritual purity. If he was in a state of ritual impurity, he can usually purify himself in the following manner, as set out in Leviticus 22:5–8:

> "Whoever touches a creeping thing by which he may be made impure or a man from whom he may derive impurity, whatever his impurity may be, the soul that touches anything of that kind shall be impure until the evening, and shall not eat of the holy things, unless he bathe his flesh in water. And when the sun is down, he shall be pure, and afterwards he may eat of the holy things.

"**first watch**" The first third or quarter of the night (the definition is subject to a dispute in the Talmud). It is important to bear in mind that the ancients did not use mechanical clocks, but measured day and night in terms of the actual light and darkness.

The Babylonian Talmud

One of the most impressive intellectual and spiritual creations of the Jewish tradition was the Babylonian Talmud. Composed between the beginning of the third century and the seventh century CE, it consists of a very detailed commentary on the Mishnah, in which the rabbis of the later era (called "*Amoraʾim*") meticulously examined every word of the Mishnah, trying to trace its sources, compare it with other traditions, and draw practical and theoretical implications from its teachings.

Babylonian Talmud, Berakhot 2a–2b

When do the priests eat heave-offering ?

It was stated in a *baraita*: The indication for this is when the stars come out.

Comments

The Mishnah linked the earliest time for reciting the evening *Shema'* to the time when priests eat their heave-offering, though the latter definition appears to be scarcely less obscure than the former. The Talmud clarifies the matter somewhat by citing a *baraita*—a teaching that is contemporary with the Mishnah though not included in it—to the effect that both criteria can be equated with a more standardized and objective measurement: the appearance of the stars in the night sky.

The Talmud will now proceed to quote a number of alternative definitions of the time from which one may recite the evening *Shema'*, and will try to establish whether those varied definitions reflect contradictory views—all without yet explaining exactly what times these definitions in fact refer to.

Babylonian Talmud, Berakhot 2b

The master said: "from the time when the priests enter to eat from their heave-offering."

They pointed to a contradiction [from the following source]:

From what time may one recite the *Shema'* in the evenings?—From the time when the poor man enters to eat his bread with salt until the time when he stands up from his meal.

Comments

"**The master said**" This is a standard formula for quoting from a source that was previously cited in full. It probably reflects the respectful form of address of a student speaking to his teacher (In some cultures and languages it is considered overly familiar to speak to one's teacher or superior directly in the second-person ("you") form.)

"**They pointed out a contradiction**" The Aramaic expression for pointing out a contradiction literally means "they threw them together." The unstated subjects are the scholars of the academy.

Thus far the quotation from the *baraita*. Now the Talmud proceeds to discuss it and uses it to prove a point.

Babylonian Talmud, Berakhot 2b, *continued*

The last clause certainly contradicts the Mishnah. Must one say that the first clause also contradict the Mishnah?

—No. The "poor man" and the "priest" are the same measurement.

Comments

"**The last clause . . .**" Clearly the *baraita*, which speaks of the comparatively early time when one stands up from the evening meal, does not agree with any of the opinions expressed in the Mishnah about the *latest* time for the recitation of the *Shema'* (midnight or dawn).

However, it is possible to ask regarding the *earliest* times: is the time of the "poor man" (in the *baraita*) necessarily different from that of a priest (in the Mishnah), as would seem to be implied by the need to mention two different categories of people?

To this question the Talmud replies that it is possible that the two criteria may actually refer to the same time.

Note that the Talmud has not come to prove that the Mishnah and *baraita* agree. Rather (as is common in talmudic dialectic), it merely wishes to say that the contrary hypothesis (i.e. that the sources necessarily disagree with each other) has not been proven.

Babylonian Talmud, Berakhot 2b, *continued*

They pointed out a contradiction: From what time may one begin to recite the *Shema'* in the evening?

From the time when people go in to eat their bread on Sabbath evenings. These are the words of Rabbi Meir.

But the Sages say: From the time when the priests are entitled to eat their heave-offering.

The indicator for this is the appearance of the stars.

And even though there is no real proof of it, there is an allusion to it. For it states: "So we labored in the work, and half of the men held the spears from daybreak until the stars appeared" (Nehemiah 4:21).

And it says (verse 22): "that they may be our guard by night and a working party by day."

What is "and it says"?

Comments

"They pointed out a contradiction" The contradiction here is occasioned by the *baraita* that offers different ways of determining the time for reciting the evening *Shema'*. In the course of its presentation of the Sages' position, the *baraita* quotes a passage from the biblical book of Nehemiah that relates how the Judeans who returned to Jerusalem after the Babylonian captivity faced dangers from various groups who were opposed to the rebuilding of Jerusalem's walls. Therefore the builders had to labor while bearing arms, and the men were divided into day and night shifts. Verse 21 seems to equate the end of day and the start of night-time with the appearance of the stars.

"What is 'and it says'?" The Talmud now, before building its case, clarifies a problem in the *baraita*: Why is it necessary to quote a second proof-text? This is a standard question that is asked whenever a *baraita* quotes more than one verse to prove a single point. This type of objection is based on the premise that every word of a religious text is precious and therefore the authors would not "waste" words by bringing two proofs where one would have sufficed.

Babylonian Talmud, Berakhot 2b, continued

—If you should argue that the night begins when the sun sets, but that they went out late and came back early—then: Come and hear: "that they may be our guard by night and a working party by day."

Comments

That is to say: from the first verse alone we cannot conclude that "the appearance of the stars" is meant to be synonymous with the beginning of the night. Taken by itself, it might only indicate the hours in which the people worked and stood guard, but without intending to provide actual definitions of daytime and night-time. That the stars are always the boundary between day and night is proven only after we have compared the two verses:

"So we wrought in the work . . . *till the appearance of the stars.*"
"And may labour in the *day.*"

In this way we prove conclusively that the day, according to biblical Hebrew usage, lasts until the appearance of the stars, at which point night begins.

After this digression, the Talmud is ready to try to prove from this *baraita* that the mealtime of the poor man is not the same as that of the purified priest.

But first of all we must introduce an additional assumption:

Babylonian Talmud, Berakhot 2b, continued

You assume that the "poor man" and "people" are the same measure.
    And if you should say that the poor man and the priest are the same measure, then the Sages would be [saying] the same as Rabbi Meir!

Comments

This cannot be so, since the wording of our *baraita* makes it clear that they disagree.

Babylonian Talmud, Berakhot 2b, continued

Rather, learn from this that the "poor man" has one time and the priest has one time!

Comments

Or, to give the argumentation a quasi-mathematical formulation:

$$\text{"Poor man"} = \text{"people"}$$
$$\text{"People"} \neq \text{"priest"}$$
$$\text{Hence: "Poor man"} \neq \text{"priest"}.$$

Babylonian Talmud, Berakhot 2b, *continued*

No. [Perhaps] the poor man and the priest have the same time, but the poor man and the people do not have the same time.

Comments

To this the Talmud now retorts: no, your argument is founded on an unproven assumption: there is no necessary basis for supposing that the times of the "poor man" and the "people" are identical. If we want, we can arrange the facts in a different way.

The Talmud will now continue to test the hypothesis that the times of the "poor man" (in the *baraita*) and "priests" (in the Mishnah) are identical (as shown below).

Babylonian Talmud, Berakhot 2b, *continued*

But do the poor man and the priest really have the same time?
    But they pointed out a contradiction:
    From what time may one begin to recite the *Shema'* in the evenings?—
From the time that the Sabbath day becomes sanctified on Sabbath evenings. These are the words of Rabbi Eliezer.

Comments

In terms of Jewish religious law, the holiness of the Sabbath is expressed by means of the prohibitions of many kinds of activities ("work") during the period extending from Friday evening until Saturday night. The commencement of the Sabbath normally occurs during the twilight period on Friday, before it has become completely dark, and well before the stars come out.

As Rashi explains in his commentary to this Talmud passage, the Sabbath restrictions are accepted so early because of uncertainty, as a way of creating a margin of safety. In the gradual transition from day to night, people cannot be absolutely certain at which precise point in time the Sabbath begins, and therefore they accept it (and refrain from forbidden activities) from the earliest possible moment, at the beginning of twilight, in order to preclude the possibility of violating the severe Sabbath restrictions.

Babylonian Talmud, Berakhot *2b, continued*

Rabbi Joshua says: from the time when the priests are purified in order to eat their heave-offering.

Rabbi Meir says: from the time when the priests immerse themselves in order to eat from their heave-offering.

Rabbi Judah said to him: but do not the priests immerse themselves while it is still day-time?

Rabbi Ḥanina says: from the time that the poor man enters to eat his bread with salt.

Rabbi Aḥai [and some say: Rabbi Aḥa] says: from the time that most people enter to take their seats [to dine].

Comments

The details of the dispute between Rabbi Meir and Rabbi Judah are discussed in a short, but difficult, passage in the Talmud, which we have omitted.

Here concludes the quotation from our *baraita*. The style of the *baraita* presumes that all the rabbis are in disagreement with one another.

Babylonian Talmud, Berakhot *2b, continued*

Now, if you say that the poor man and the priest have the same time, then Rabbi Ḥanina and Rabbi Joshua would be saying the same thing!

From this must you not conclude that the poor man has one time and the priest has another time?

Draw that conclusion!

Comments

The Talmud, despite its attempts to avoid reaching a conclusion, must admit in the end that the "poor man" criterion is not the same as our Mishnah's "priest" criterion—as indeed all the opinions expressed refer to different times (though we have not defined them all). The Talmud does not help us very much here. It concludes (for reasons which the commentators have difficulty in accepting, and which we will not explore in detail) that the "poor man" time is later than the "priest" time.

As regards the question of "twilight", this in fact is one of the more complex problems of talmudic law. It refers to the period between sundown and night, a time when either we are uncertain whether it is day or night, or perhaps a mixture of both. The talmudic rabbis offer a range of opinions on the matter. Some say it is an indefinable split-second point in time, while others define it in terms of the deepening darkness, the reddening of the western horizon, or other criteria. All the opinions refer to this period that extends from sundown until starlight.

Babylonian Talmud, Berakhot 2b, *continued*

Which one of them is later?
—It stands to reason that the "poor man" is later. For if you were to say that the "poor man" is earlier, then Rabbi Ḥanina would be the same as Rabbi Eliezer!
Rather, should you not learn from this that the poor man is later? Learn from this.

Comments

The reasoning is not entirely clear, but the proof seems to run as follows: we presume that Rabbi Eliezer's measure of the time when the Sabbath becomes sanctified constitutes the earliest of the possibilities (based on the convention of ushering in the Sabbath as early as possible on Friday evening, as described previously). If we accept that the "poor man" criterion is also an early one, then it would be identical to Rabbi Eliezer's, and yet the *baraita* presents their opinions as conflicting! Hence, we are left with no other logical possibility but to conclude that the "poor man" time is a later one.

Babylonian Talmud, Berakhot 3a

There is a contradiction between Rabbi Meir [of one *baraita*] and Rabbi Meir [of the last *baraita*]!
—There are different *Tannaim* according to Rabbi Meir.

Comments

The Talmud is unable to explain away the blatant differences between the views of Rabbis Meir as reported in the two *baraita*s. In such cases, the Talmud sometimes falls back on a dubious solution that does not so much resolve the difficulty as explain how it came to be. Because these traditions about what the early rabbis had said were classified as belonging to the "oral Torah," they were known to the later scholars by virtue of the fact that they were transmitted by human agents who memorized and recited them. These memorizers were known as *tanna*s (as a secondary development, that term came to be applied to the sages whose words they were transmitting). In the course of the transmission, it is assumed that there developed differing versions of those traditions, whether because of inaccurate recollection or (as appears more likely) because of the interpretations that were given to them by later scholars.

This explanation, which raises implied questions about the general reliability of the rabbinic tradition, is only invoked as a last resort, but in our passage it is evidently considered acceptable.

In the following exchange, the same approach is used initially to deal with the discrepancy between the views ascribed to Rabbi Eliezer in the last *baraita* and in the Mishnah.

Babylonian Talmud, Berakhot 3a

There is a contradiction between Rabbi Eliezer and Rabbi Eliezer!

—There are two *Tannaim* according to Rabbi Eliezer's opinion.

Or if you wish, I can say: The first clause of the Mishnah is not R. Eliezer's.

Comments

The last explanation resolves the contradiction by proposing a different manner of reading the Mishnah. When the author of this Mishnah passage said "From the time when the priests enter to eat from their heave-offering until the end of the first watch. These are the words of Rabbi Eliezer," he may have meant that the attribution to Rabbi Eliezer refers only to the issue of "until when," but not to the question of "from when." This is not as forced as it might seem at first, seeing how the subsequent dispute in the Mishnah relates only to the second issue and not at all to the first.

We will see later on that the question of how we are to view the authorship of the opening clause of the Mishnah is of considerable importance for the determining of its legal weight. A central principle of talmudic legal decisions declares that, in disputed cases, the law generally follows the anonymous view in the Mishnah, since presumably it expresses the view of the majority of the rabbis. If, on the other hand, the ruling is presented in the name of an individual sage, then its authority is weaker. In our particular case, this would not seem to be terribly significant, since the Mishnah does not record any dispute as regards the beginning-time for the *Shema'*. Nevertheless, in view of the various opinions reported in *baraita*s, this distinction can prove to be significant.

You likely feel confused by all the different criteria mentioned in the various *baraita*s quoted in the passage. Most of these different opinions are not really explained by the Talmud, which only seems to be interested in the specific issues that it raises.

One of the leading modern scholars of the Talmud, Professor Louis Ginzberg, tried to put some order into the labyrinth of different opinions by applying to the texts a bit of historical methodology. His basic hypothesis is that all the sources really can be reduced to two different positions, which in turn are interpretations of a single ancient source. According to Ginzberg, the earliest tradition on the matter is the one preserved in our Mishnah, which defines the time for the *Shema'* as the time when the priests "enter to eat of their heave-offering." Ginzberg argues that the Hebrew phrase translated here as "enter to" often has the meaning of "prepare to," and that in early times a disagreement developed surrounding the correct interpretation of the phrase. According to one view, it referred to the time when the priests went in to immerse themselves in the ritual bath, in order to purify themselves; while another interpretation said that it was the time when, having already bathed, they were ready to go in and partake of their evening meal. The first view indicated a time around sunset, and the latter, closer to the appearance of the stars.

These times were relevant to people who lived when the laws of ritual purity were actually observed, especially while the second Jerusalem Temple was standing. Ginzberg, like a number of other scholars, argues that the priests did not bathe in the ritual bath only when they knew that they had become impure; but rather, in order to avoid all doubts, they made immersion a daily routine at evening time. Hence, especially in Jerusalem, the stream of priests to and from the baths would constitute a visible indication of the time. After the destruction of the Temple in the year 70 CE, the observance of the laws of purity eventually became impossible to observe, and new criteria had to be set down.

One tradition translated the references to a more universally observed ritual, the Sabbath. Therefore we find sources that define the time for the reading of the *Shema'* in terms of "when the Sabbath becomes hallowed," around when the stars come out; or an earlier time—when they sit down for the Friday-night meal.

A Babylonian *baraita* (Rabbis Ḥanina and Aḥa have associations with Babylonia, and the *baraita* in which they are quoted does not appear to have been known outside the Babylonian Talmud) records a third pair of reference points, relating to weekday activities, also divorced from any specifically Temple-related observances: the later time is defined as when a poor man eats his food (he is likely to stay longer in the market to search for scraps that others have left behind); the earlier is the time when people sit down to eat (probably referring to weekday meals).

As we said above, this is a hypothetical reconstruction of the evolution of the views expressed in the various *baraita*s. The Babylonian Talmud does not normally approach sources from such a perspective, and hence the conclusions that they drew were much different.

The Babylonian *Geonim*

In the following pages, we will begin to explore some of the conclusions that were drawn by scholars of the halakhah (Jewish religious law) who lived after the era of the Talmud and claimed to base their legal decisions upon the talmudic texts that we studied.

The earliest codifications of Jewish liturgical practice follow the view of our Mishnah, interpreting it according to the talmudic explanations that are found in our passage in *Berakhot* and elsewhere.

The next two citations are both taken from the works of *Geonim*, the successors of the Babylonian talmudic academies after the completion of the Babylonian Talmud. Amram served as head of the academy during the ninth century CE, and the renowned Saadiah during the tenth century. We have already had occasion to refer to Saadiah's prayer book in connection with the text of the liturgy, and we will encounter him later on as a theologian and philosopher.

Amram Gaon, Seder Rav Amram[1]

He who recites the evening *Shema'* before the appearance of the stars has not fulfilled his obligation, since it was taught in a *baraita*: "From what time may one begin to recite the *Shema'* in the evening? From the time when the priests are entitled to eat their heave-offering. An indicator for this is the appearance of the stars."

And it was taught in another *baraita*: "He who recites it earlier has not fulfilled his obligation."

And how many stars must have appeared for it to be considered night?—It was taught (*Shabbat* 35b): "Rabbi Nathan says: One star is still day, two are twilight, three are night."

Saadiah Gaon, Siddur[2]

The time for this prayer, that is, the evening service, is from the appearance of the stars.

Comments

The next source, which also originated in the geonic academies, introduces us to the main problem that will concern us for the duration of this section: in contrast to the talmudic sources that we have been studying, which seem to make it quite clear that the evening *Shema'* may not be recited before the appearance of the stars, it seems that the universal practice in Jewish communities during the Middle Ages was to recite the evening prayer service much earlier than that, while it was still light outside.

In order to understand the following source, it will be necessary to supply some background information about the structure of the daily Jewish liturgy.

In its liturgical usage, the *Shema'* which must be recited every evening and morning includes not only the designated passages from the Torah, but also a surrounding framework of blessings on various themes. The blessing that follows the scriptural texts is on the theme of redemption: "Blessed are you, Lord, the redeemer of Israel."

In addition to the *Shema'*, the halakhah also prescribes that another prayer, which it calls "*Tefillah*" ("Prayer"), must be recited three times daily—in the morning, afternoon and evening.

Morning Tefillah = *Shaḥarit*, or: *Tefillat ha-Shaḥar*
Afternoon Tefillah = *Minḥah*
Evening Tefillah = *'Arvit* or: *Ma'ariv*

Now, in the Talmud there is found a discussion about the best way to arrange the various prayers:

Said Rabbi Yoḥanan: Who is deserving of the world to come?
—It is the one who juxtaposes "Redemption" to "Prayer" in the evening.
Rabbi Joshua ben Levi says: The *Tefillot* were ordained in the middle.

The meaning of this dispute is as follows: according to Rabbi Yoḥanan the recitation of the *Shema'* must always precede that of the Tefillah. In this way, the blessing about redemption will be followed immediately by the Tefillah, thereby linking the two central ideas of Redemption and Prayer. Rabbi Joshua ben Levi, on the other hand, believed that the *Shema'* should be the first prayer recited in the morning, but the last in the evening; accordingly, the evening *Shema'* should come after the Tefillah. Evidently he insists on a literal understanding of the phrase "when you lie down and when you wake up," which implies, in his view, that the *Shema'* should be the first thing one should say upon waking and the last before going to bed. The law was decided unanimously in favor of Rabbi Yoḥanan's position.

	Rabbi Yoḥanan	**Rabbi Joshua ben Levi**
Evening service	*Shema'*; Tefillah	Tefillah; *Shema'*
Morning service	*Shema'*; Tefillah	*Shema'*; Tefillah

A second principle that we must understand is that Jewish tradition assigns great importance to the institution of communal prayer—that is to say, when possible, one should attempt to recite one's prayers within a congregation of at least ten Jews.

"A responsum of our Rabbi Hai of blessed memory"[3]

Regarding your enquiry about a congregation who pray the evening service and recite the *Shema'* before the appearance of the stars, and no-one is able to stop them.

Since, owing to our sins, several communities have been acting leniently in this matter and pray prior to the appearance of the stars—which option is to be preferred? Should a person pray the "Eighteen Benedictions" with the community, because "the king's glory is in the multitude of people" (Proverbs 14:28), and then wait until the appearance of the stars before reciting the *Shema'* with its accompanying blessings? Or, alternatively: Should one wait altogether until the stars have appeared and only then "join Redemption to Prayer," in keeping with the dictum of Rabbi Yoḥanan (*Berakhot* 4b)?

The Rabbis of the Land of Israel act as follows: They recite the evening prayer, and afterwards recite the *Shema'* at its proper time, without worrying about joining Redemption to Prayer.

Our own opinion is that it is preferable to recite *Shema'* at its proper time, the indicator for which is the appearance of the stars. This is a commandment of the Torah, and therefore has precedence over the joining of Redemption to Prayer, in cases where it is impossible to fulfill both rulings. If one is able to recite the service with the congregation as a voluntary devotion, and repeat it later in fulfillment of one's obligation, then it is preferable to do so.

Comments

The formulators of this question to Hai Gaon were faced with a need to decide between a number of alternative possibilities, and to establish a set of priorities for dealing with the various halakhic principles outlined above. At the root of the question stood the basic problem: granted that the halakhah is that the *Shema'* may not be recited before nightfall—what does one do when the congregations do not act according to the talmudic rulings? Ought a Jew who wishes to observe the law in its proper form simply recite his prayers privately, ignoring the erroneous practice of the rest of the community; or should the ideal of communal prayer stand paramount in the scale of values, impelling the individual to refrain from withdrawing from the community even if it involves compromising the details of correct liturgical practice?

A compromise solution is also suggested: That the evening Tefillah be recited earlier ("the Eighteen Benedictions" is a common synonym for the Tefillah, based on its original format), and only afterwards, after the stars have come out, is the *Shema'* recited. (Apparently the strictures regarding the time of the evening Tefillah were not viewed as seriously, perhaps owing to its non-obligatory status.) This would involve a violation of the ruling of Rabbi Yoḥanan in the Talmud about joining Redemption to Prayer.

Hai's basic position is that the highest priority should be given to reciting *Shema'* at its proper time, since this is a command of the Torah, the highest authority in Jewish law. If this can be accomplished only at the expense of the rule about joining Redemption to Prayer, then the Torah statute must take precedence over a less authoritative rabbinic law. However, an effort ought to be made to satisfy all the demands—by praying twice: once to fulfill the duty of praying with the community, though not actually fulfilling the obligation of reciting the *Shema'* at its ordained time; and a second time, in order to perform the recitation properly, though in private.

Note the reference to the custom of "the rabbis of the land of Israel," which is similar to Hai's own ruling: they recite the evening prayer (Tefillah) while it is still light, and then wait until the stars appear before reciting the *Shema'*. In doing so, they do not fulfill the dictum about joining Redemption to Prayer (i.e. having the Tefillah follow immediately upon the *Shema'*). Hai would allow this, though he would prefer reciting the *Shema'* an extra time "as a voluntary devotion," in order to fulfill all the requirements.

Who exactly are these rabbis of the land of Israel? The reference might be to contemporaries of the Gaon, unknown other than from this reference. It is, however, quite likely that the reference is to the passage given below from the Palestinian Talmud, from the beginning of the tractate *Berakhot*.

Palestinian Talmud Berakhot

[A *baraita*] taught: He who recites the *Shema'* earlier than this [the appearance of the stars] has not fulfilled his obligation. If so, then why do they recite it in the synagogue? Said Rabbi Yosé: They do not recite it in the synagogue in order to fulfill their obligation, but rather in order to stand in prayer (*tefillah*) out of words of Torah.

Comments

It is not entirely clear how we are to reconstruct the practice being described by the Palestinian Talmud. However, it appears most reasonable to suppose that it is identical with Hai's own recommendation: The *Shema'* was recited together with the Tefillah before its proper time, and then again, privately, after the appearance of the stars. Perhaps we should interpret Hai Gaon's description of the custom of the rabbis of the Land of Israel accordingly.

We shall see that this passage from the Palestinian Talmud will become central to the subsequent discussions of the medieval rabbis in their attempts to harmonize and explain the discrepancy between the rulings of the Mishnah and the prevailing customs of their communities.

The Sephardic codes of Jewish law

At this point in our presentation we attempt to trace the development of our issue among the talmudic authorities of Spain and Provence (the southern part of France which served as a cultural buffer in the Middle Ages between the Islamic and Christian worlds). We shall begin our study with a passage from the talmudic code of Rabbi Isaac Alfasi, who lived and taught in Spain (1013–1103). In order to appreciate his comments, some background should be supplied about the nature of Alfasi's Code.

The important point to keep in mind is that the Code is, for the most part, not a separate literary creation, but rather a condensation of the Talmud. Alfasi copied out the text of the Talmud, omitting passages that were not required for the derivation of practical law. He left out aggadic (non-legal) sections, as well as legal sections involving matters that were not in practice in his time (laws relating to the Temple, sacrifices, ritual purity and agricultural laws that were only observed in the land of Israel), as well as much of the purely theoretical discussions that did not affect the actual practice of the law. Sometimes he would add traditions from the *Geonim* or his predecessors; but his own contribution was usually limited to indications of which of two or more conflicting views was to be accepted, or brief explanations of unclear passages.

Rabbi Isaac Alfasi, code (beginning of Berakhot)

> We learn that both the Mishnah and the *baraita* accept that the permissible time for reciting the *Shema'* according to the Sages is from the hour when the priests enter to eat their heave-offering; that is, the time when the stars appear. This is the halakhah according to the accepted principle that the law follows the majority opinion.

As regards the Talmud's finding a contradiction between two statements of Rabbi Eliezer—since a *baraita* teaches "From what time may one begin to recite the *Shema'* in the evening?—From the time that the Sabbath day becomes sanctified on the Sabbath eve; these are the words of Rabbi Eliezer"; and yet we learn in our Mishnah: "From the time that the priests enter in order to eat their heave-offering until the end of the first watch; these are the words of Rabbi Eliezer."—This is not to imply that the Mishnah's statement "from the hour when the priests enter to eat of their heave-offering" is only the individual opinion of Rabbi Eliezer. On the contrary, both Rabbi Eliezer and the Sages accept this view, since the Sages disagree with Rabbi Eliezer only with regard to the end time, Rabbi Eliezer saying "until the end of the first watch," while the Sages say "until midnight." But the statement "from the hour when the priests enter to eat their heave-offering" is not disputed, because if the Sages do not accept "from the hour when the priests enter in order to eat their heave-offering" and it is only the view of Rabbi Eliezer, then the Sages ought to have disagreed with him about the beginning time as they disagreed about the end time. Since they disagree only about the end time, we may deduce that both Rabbi Eliezer and the Sages are of the opinion that the beginning time is from the hour when the priests enter to eat their heave-offering. Since Rabbi Eliezer agrees with the Sages that it is from the hour when the priests enter to eat their heave-offering, and we find in a *baraita* that he says "from the hour when the Sabbath becomes hallowed on the Sabbath eve," the Talmud points out the contradiction between his two statements and resolves it by saying that we have two different tannaitic traditions according to Rabbi Eliezer. According to the second solution, in which we say "Or if you wish you might say: The end clause is Rabbi Eliezer but the first is not Rabbi Eliezer," the matter is clear that "from the hour when the priests enter to eat their heave-offering" is stated according to the Sages and not Rabbi Eliezer.

Therefore according to both the first and second solutions, the statement of the Mishnah "from the hour when the priests enter to eat their heave-offering" is the view of the Sages, and hence we follow that view.

Comments

According to the first solution, which agrees that the opening clause of the Mishnah is also Rabbi Eliezer's view, Alfasi seems to be arguing that the position actually represents a consensus for which Rabbi Eliezer is grouped with the rest of the Sages. This is not really the simple meaning of the Talmud, where it is quite clear that they regard this clause as the view of Rabbi Eliezer alone. In any case, since the Mishnah presents no other opinion about the beginning time for the reciting of the *Shema'*, Alfasi could have argued that we are meant to rule according to that view, even though other views can be found in the *baraita* (the authority of a Mishnah is superior to that of a *baraita*).

In the light of the foregoing description of the nature of Alfasi's code, it is remarkable that this lengthy discussion of the issue should be found at all in it.

What does this fact teach us?

It most probably is to be viewed as an indication that Alfasi regarded the question as problematic or controversial, as something that could not be dealt with in a simple legal ruling without adding some justification and argument. In fact, Alfasi is likely to have encountered a conflict between the accepted practice of his community and the dicta of the Talmud.

From Alfasi's statements, one does get the impression that he is responding to arguments that had been proposed, to the effect that the Mishnah's statement "These are the words of Rabbi Eliezer" applies not only to the immediately preceding clause ("until the end of the first watch"), but to the entire Mishnah up to that point, including the rule "From the time that the priests enter in order to eat their heave-offering." In that case, there would be some justification for regarding the Mishnah as an individual's view, and not the accepted opinion of the majority of the Sages.

Alfasi's most distinguished successor was Moses Maimonides, who composed his great works on Talmud, Jewish Law, philosophy and medicine in twelfth-century Egypt. Maimonides' monumental code of law, the Mishneh Torah, summarizes the law according to rigorous principles of classification, without discussing the sources or reasons for the decisions.

Maimonides, Mishneh Torah, Laws for the Recital of the Shema' 1:9

What is the time for reciting the *Shema'* at night? The proper time is from the appearance of the stars, until midnight.

Maimonides, Mishneh Torah, laws of prayer (Tefillah) 3:7

> One should recite the Sabbath night service on Friday before sunset. Similarly, one may recite the evening service for the outgoing of the Sabbath during the Sabbath [day]; since the Evening Service is not mandatory we are not so strict about its time, as long as he recites the *Shema'* at its proper time, after the appearance of the stars.

Comments

As regards the times for reciting the *Shema'*, Maimonides simply rules according to the Mishnah, following Alfasi, without any reference to alternative possibilities or practices.

His ruling concerning the time for the evening Tefillah is of considerable interest. Maimonides accepts the precedents that speak of talmudic rabbis reciting the Friday night and Saturday night Tefillah on the preceding afternoon. However, he does not expand this precedent to other days of the week (though it is possible that he would accept the argument that the rule would apply all the more so when Sabbath-violation is not at issue). It is clear that Maimonides is speaking only about the Tefillah, and not the *Shema'* as well.

Maimonides recommends advancing the recitation of the Friday night prayers in accordance with the rabbis' urging to "add on to the Sabbath" as an expression of our fondness for it. As to the early recitation of the Saturday night service, Maimonides' sees this as a result of the Talmud's ruling that the evening Tefillah is not mandatory at all. Because this is so, we really should not be that concerned about its proper time. This shows that he does not accept an earlier time for the evening Tefillah, nor, of course, for the *Shema'*.

Rashi and the medieval French and German commentators

The great eleventh-century talmudic commentator Rashi (Rabbi Solomon ben Isaac of Troyes, France) was troubled by the contradiction between the apparently unambiguous ruling of the Mishnah in *Berakhot* and the prevalent practice in his own community. In explaining the Mishnah he also cites the above-mentioned passage from the Palestinian Talmud, which he ties in with another custom, mentioned in the Babylonian Talmud.

Before examining Rashi's own words, something should be said about the custom of the recital of the "bedtime *Shema'*." The talmudic source for this is the following passage, which portrays the recitation as a kind of protective charm against demons and other dangers that might otherwise beset a person while sleeping through the night.

Babylonian Talmud Berakhot 4b–5a

> Rabbi Joshua ben Levi says: Though a person has recited the *Shema'* in the synagogue, it is proper conduct [*miṣvah*] to recite it again upon his bed.

Rav Asi says: What is the scriptural source? "Tremble and sin not; commune with your own heart upon your bed, and be still, Selah" (Psalm 4:5).

Rav Naḥman says: If he is a rabbinic scholar, then it is not necessary.

Abayé says: Even a rabbinic scholar should recite one verse of supplication, such as: "Into thy hand I commit my spirit. Thou hast redeemed me, O Lord, thou God of truth" (Psalm 31:6).

Rabbi Isaac says: If one recites the *Shema'* upon going to bed, it is as though he held a two-edged sword in his hand. [Rashi: to slaughter the demons]. For it is said (Psalm 149:6): "Let the high praises of God be in their mouth, and a two-edged sword in their hand."

How does it indicate this?

—Mar Zuṭra [or if you prefer: Rav Ashi] says: from the beginning of the passage. For it is written (ibid. verse 5): "Let the saints exult in glory, let them sing for joy upon their beds," and it is written afterwards: "Let the high praises of God be in their mouth, and a two-edged sword in their hand."

And Rabbi Isaac says: If one recites the *Shema'* upon his bed, the demons keep away from him.

Babylonian Talmud Berakhot 60a

One who goes in to sleep upon his bed recites from "Hear O Israel" until "And it shall come to pass if you hearken."

Commentary of Rashi (Rabbi Solomon ben Isaac) to Berakhot 2a

"Before this time [i.e. the time specified in the Mishnah] it is not considered the time for lying down. Therefore "he who recites it earlier has not fulfilled his obligation. If so, why do they recite it in the synagogue?—In order to stand for prayer out of words of Torah."

Thus is it brought down in the Jerusalem Talmud. Therefore we ought to read it after dark. And one can fulfill his obligation by means of the first paragraph, which is recited upon going to bed.

Comments

Rashi's solution is similar to that of Rav Hai Gaon, which was also based on the ruling of the Jerusalem Talmud; except that for Rashi the main recital of the *Shema'* is the one that is recited upon going to bed.

If you compare Rashi's observations with the texts we have just presented describing the recitation of the *Shema'* at bedtime, it appears that the prophylactic function of the bedtime recitation is not entirely consistent with Rashi's claim that one fulfills thereby one's obligation of reciting the

Shema' in the evening. At any rate, certain contradictions and difficulties were felt by Rashi's strongest critics—his students and descendants whose debates and comments are recorded in the notes entitled "Tosafot" (additions) in the margins of the Talmud editions. The rabbis whose teachings comprise the Tosafot included the leading talmudic scholars in Germany and France in the centuries following Rashi. The first to be quoted in the following passage is the famous Rabbi Jacob ben Meir Tam—known as "Rabbenu Tam," one of the most independent and intellectually versatile students of the Talmud in any age. He was Rashi's grandson.

Tosafot Berakhot 2a

Rashi commented: "And how is it that we recite [the *Shema'*] while it is still daytime and do not wait until the appearance of the stars, as stipulated in the Talmud?

For this reason Rashi explained that the *Shema'* recited upon going to bed is the main one, which is recited after the appearance of the stars. And thus do we find in the Jerusalem Talmud: "If he recited it before this time he has not fulfilled his obligation. If so, then why do we recite the *Shema'* in the synagogue?—In order to stand for prayer out of words of Torah" (Thus far a quotation from Rashi).

However his explanation is incomprehensible. The prevailing custom in reciting the bedtime *Shema'* is to recite only the first paragraph (*Berakhot* 60b), whereas according to Rashi's explanation they should recite all three paragraphs.

A further difficulty: in the recitation of the evening *Shema'*, they should also include two blessings before and afterwards (Mishnah *Berakhot* 1:4).

Moreover: the *Shema'* is recited at bedtime only to protect against demons, as explained below (*Berakhot* 5a), and a scholar is exempted from it.

And an additional difficulty: if Rashi is correct, then that implies that we rule in accordance with the view of Rabbi Joshua ben Levi who stated: the Tefillah services were ordained in the middle; that is, midway between the two recitals of the *Shema'* in the evening and in the morning. Whereas we really accept the view of Rabbi Yohanan who says below (4b): "Who is deserving of the world to come? It is he who joins redemption to prayer in the evening."

Comments

As you may recall, the dispute between Rabbi Joshua ben Levi and Rabbi Yohanan concerns the question of whether the evening *Shema'* should be recited after the Tefillah (in which case the two daily Tefillahs would be sandwiched in between two *Shema'*s) or before it (in which case the prayer for redemption, the last blessing after the *Shema‘*, would immediately precede and adjoin the "Prayer," the Tefillah). No one has ever seriously doubted that the ruling of Rabbi Yoḥanan is the accepted one according to normative Jewish law.

Before we return to the solutions to the Tosafot's objections, it is necessary to remind ourselves of the relationship between the *Shema‘* and the evening Tefillah. Given that the two sections of the evening service are supposed to be recited consecutively, it would be reasonable to presume that the times stipulated for them should be the same. Thus far we have examined most of the talmudic sources that deal with the fixing of the earliest time for reciting the evening *Shema‘*. However, an examination of sources that define the correct times for the evening Tefillah might supply us with additional possibilities for resolving our difficulties. Moreover, since the evening service follows the afternoon service, it is also worth looking at the rabbis' views concerning the latest time at which the afternoon Tefillah may be said. Such a discussion is to be found in the following passage.

Mishnah Berakhot *4:1*

> The afternoon Tefillah [is recited] until evening.
> Rabbi Judah says: until the *pelag ha-minḥah*.
> The evening Tefillah is not fixed.

Comments

According to a talmudic tradition, the prayer services were instituted by the ancient Jewish authorities so as to parallel the daily sacrifices that were offered up in the Jerusalem Temple (see Numbers 28:4: "The one lamb shall you offer in the morning, and the other lamb shall you offer at dusk"). The evening Tefillah was supposed to correspond to the burning of the remaining limbs which was to continue through the night (Leviticus 6:2). Rabbinic tradition states that the afternoon sacrifice was offered usually at 9.5 hours of the day (talmudic chronology divided the daylight into twelve equal hours; thus 9.5 hours would turn out at approximately 3:30 p.m. according to a modern clock). Rabbi Judah disagrees and extends the time to the middle of the period between 9.5 hours and sunset (which is at the twelfth hour)—i.e. at 10.75 hours (about 4:45 p.m.). This point, an hour and a quarter before sunset, is termed *pelag ha-minḥah*; literally, the half of the afternoon service.

It would be reasonable to suppose that according to Rabbi Judah, the end of the permissible period for the recitation of the afternoon prayer would also mark the beginning of the permissible time for reciting the evening *Shema‘* and Tefillah.

With this background in mind, we may now resume our study of the Tosafot.

Tosafot Berakhot 2a (continued)

For these reasons [the objections that were raised against Rashi's explanation], Rabbenu Tam explained that, on the contrary, the *Shema'* recited in the synagogue is the principal one.

And if you should ask: How can we recite it while it is still light?—It may be answered: because we follow the view of Rabbi Judah, who stated that the time for the afternoon Tefillah is until the *pelag ha-minḥah*; i.e. until eleven hours less one-quarter [4:45 p.m.]. And the time for the evening service begins immediately upon the conclusion of the time for the afternoon service.

Comments

As we read through Rabbenu Tam's skillful argumentation, we should not overlook some fundamental difficulties in his approach. First of all, we should take note of the fact that, in trying to fix a time for the recitation of the evening *Shema'*, he disregarded all the sources that deal explicitly with that question—all of which point toward a time near the appearance of the stars—and, instead, based his ruling on indirect inferences from sources that deal with a very different question: the recitation of the afternoon Tefillah. Note as well that even if we concede that the latest time for reciting the afternoon Tefillah would also be the earliest time for the evening Tefillah—a premise that is far from obvious—it would still not follow naturally that the times stipulated for the recitation of the evening Tefillah are the same as those for the recitation of the *Shema'* [for example, the *Shema'* and Tefillah of the morning service have different time stipulations].

Moreover, by deciding the dispute in the Mishnah *Berakhot* 4:1 in favor of Rabbi Judah, Rabbenu Tam has put himself at variance with one of the basic rules of talmudic legal decision-making, which declares that whenever there is a disagreement in the Mishnah between an anonymously presented view and one whose author is identified, the law is to be decided according to the anonymous view, because it is assumed to be the majority position. Here Rabbenu Tam has decided according to Rabbi Judah against the anonymous view that permits the reciting of the afternoon Tefillah until sunset.

Note also that, after having extended the permissible time-period for the evening service, Rabbenu Tam seems to have also shortened the time for the afternoon prayer. Had he accepted the decision of the anonymous view in the Mishnah, it would have been permissible to recite the Minḥah service until sunset—but now he may only do so until an hour and a quarter before sunset, contrary to the prevalent practice. Thus, in resolving a contradiction between the common custom and the theoretical law concerning the evening *Shema'*, he has created a similar contradiction with regard to the afternoon Tefillah.

This problem was pointed out in the continuation of the Tosafot.

Tosafot Berakhot 2a, *continued*

> Should you object: how do we recite the afternoon service just before dark, after the *pelag ha-minḥah?*
>
> —It may be answered: We follow the view of the Sages who state that the afternoon service is recited until evening.
>
> Moreover we say below (*Berakhot* 27a): "Now that the law was not decided according to either of the two masters [Rabbi Judah or the anonymous Sages], one who acts according to either view has acted properly."
>
> In any case, it remains difficult: this is like accepting two contradictory lenient rulings, since the only reason we recite the evening prayer right after the *pelag ha-minḥah* is because we say that the *minḥah* time has expired, according to Rabbi Judah, and thereby it immediately becomes the time for the evening prayer. And yet with regard to the afternoon service itself we do not follow Rabbi Judah's position, but that of the Sages!

Comments

The objection should be clear. Though the Talmud does in fact allow us to choose between the positions of the Sages (the anonymous opinion in the Mishnah *Berakhot* 4:1) and Rabbi Judah, it nevertheless seems irresponsible to select only those parts of both positions that would lead to lenient decisions, when the decisions derived thereby would prove to be mutually contradictory.

The Tosafot appear to accept the above objections to Rabbenu Tam's interpretation, and offer as an alternative a somewhat different explanation, cited in the name of Rabbi Isaac of Dampierre, one of the major French talmudic authorities of his time.

Tosafot Berakhot 2a, *continued*

> For this reason Rabbi Isaac says that the *Shema'* recited in the synagogue is nevertheless the main one. And we who recite the evening service while it is still daylight are following the view of the Tannaim cited in the Talmud who define the time as "the hour when the day becomes hallowed [on Friday evening]", or "from the hour when people come home to sit down to their meals"; referring to the Friday meal which was eaten by daylight, which marks the time for the [evening] prayers.
>
> Evidence may also be cited from the fact (*Berakhot* 27b) that Rav would recite the Sabbath evening prayers on Friday afternoon, and he presumably also recited the *Shema'*.

Comments

The Talmud in *Berakhot* 27b gives a number of examples of rabbis who would recite the Sabbath evening prayers while it was still light on Friday afternoon; and even of rabbis who recited the evening prayer for the conclusion of the Sabbath, which should normally be recited on Saturday night after the appearance of the stars, on Saturday afternoon. This indicates that those sages accepted the ruling of Rabbi Judah in the Mishnah, not only where it involved adding to the length of the Sabbath (which needs no other justification, as there is a halakhic principle that favors extending the length of the Sabbath), but even—as in the case of ending the Sabbath on Saturday afternoon—where it resulted in shortening the Sabbath.

Tosafot Berakhot 2a, *continued*

> On the basis of all these proofs it may be concluded that the *Shema'* recited in the synagogue is the main one.
>
> And as to the statement of the Jerusalem Talmud: "Why did they recite it in the synagogue . . ."—Rabbenu Tam says that they used to recite the *Shema'* before their prayers just as we recite "*Ashrei*" (Psalm 145) beforehand, and that the *Shema'* functions in this case merely as a way to stand for prayer out of words of Torah.
>
> From this it would appear that one who recites the *Shema'* at bedtime should not say blessings, nor should one recite more than the first paragraph.

Comments

Rabbenu Tam is trying to explain the passage from the Jerusalem Talmud upon which Rashi based his interpretation that the recitation of the bedtime *Shema'* was in fact the mandatory one, through which one fulfills the obligation of the evening recitation; whereas the *Shema'* that is included in the evening synagogue service is merely a custom intended to introduce some Torah-study (or at least, a biblical text) into the service.

Rabbenu Tam argues that the Jerusalem Talmud is in fact speaking of the afternoon service, not the evening service. The mandatory afternoon service consists merely of the Tefillah, without a recital of the *Shema'*. The accepted custom is to precede the Tefillah with Psalm 145, according to a dictum found in the Talmud that this Psalm should be read every day. Rabbenu Tam claims that the custom described in the Jerusalem Talmud was a similar one, of reading the *Shema'* before the afternoon Tefillah without any intention of fulfilling thereby any specific obligation. The authors of the Jerusalem Talmud were not denying that the obligatory recitation of the evening *Shema'* was, as commonly understood, in the evening synagogue service before the Tefillah. From the Tosafot's last comment it would appear that there were those who, accepting Rashi's ruling that the bedtime *Shema'* was really the principal one, augmented it to include all the trappings of the "official" recitation: the inclusion of all three chapters, along with the full framework of blessings before and after. The Tosafot conclude, however, that in view of their claim that the synagogue recitation is really the main one, there is no need to do so.

Rabbenu Tam's position here is typical of his attitude to Jewish law. He held that the accepted practice of the community has a sanctity of its own, and even if it should appear to contradict the rulings of the Talmud, some means should be sought to re-interpret the talmudic passages in order to uphold the ancestral custom. As we shall see, not all talmudic authorities agreed with this approach.

As we have seen, the French and German rabbis found a way to legitimize an early recitation of the evening *Shema'* by means of Rabbenu Tam's audacious assertion that Rabbi Judah's definition of the latest time for reciting the afternoon service—the *pelag ha-minhah*—is also the earliest time for reciting the evening *Shema'*. With all its difficulties, this solution gained widespread acceptance in subsequent generations.

However, people soon began to realize that even Rabbenu Tam's explanation was not really adequate to justify the popular custom. Rabbenu Tam had, as it were, given permission for reciting the *Shema'* from the *pelag ha-minhah*, an hour and a quarter before nightfall. Unfortunately, the people were saying the *Shema'* much earlier than this.

In the following sources, we will read from various authorities who attempted to cope with this difficulty.

First, we will look at a brief comment by Rabbi Meir Ha-Kohen of Rothenburg, author of *Hagahot Maimoniot*, a work whose purpose was to supplement the decisions of Maimonides' code with material from the Franco-German schools, especially from the teachings of the author's famous teacher, the great thirteenth-century scholar Rabbi Meir (ben Baruch) of Rothenburg.

Rabbi Meir Ha-Kohen of Rothenburg, Hagahot Maimoniot *to* Hilkhot Tefillah *ch.3*

> (Maimonides: "As long as he recites the *Shema'* at its proper time, after the appearance of the stars.")
>
> Thus ruled the Alfasi, and so wrote Rabbenu Hananel in the name of our masters the *Geonim*, and this seems to be the sense that emerges from Rashi's remarks at the beginning of the tractate, that a person does not fulfill the obligation of reciting the evening *Shema'* until the appearance of the stars. This is also implied in the opening mishnah of the first chapter, which accords with the view of the Sages in the *baraita*. So too has it been taught explicitly in a *baraita* in the Jerusalem Talmud: "He who recites it before the appearance of the stars has not fulfilled his

obligation." So too wrote the Master Rabbi Eleazar the son of Judah ben Rabbi Kalonymos who reported concerning Rabbi Isaac ben Abraham who used to recite the *Shema'* with the congregation when they would say their prayers by day; since "a person's prayers are heard only when recited with the congregation." Then, after the appearance of the stars, he would again recite the *Shema'* with its blessings upon retiring to bed. However, Rabbi Eleazar himself wrote as follows: "Nevertheless the principal obligation is to recite the *Shema'* with its blessings and to join 'Redemption to Prayer' after the appearance of the stars."

It is of course true that Rabbenu Tam has written that from the *pelag ha-minḥah* onward is considered night-time for both the Tefillah and the *Shema'*, since we accept the ruling of Rabbi Judah who stated in *Berakhot* Chapter 4 that from the *pelag ha-minḥah* onward is considered night; and as we find in the Talmud that Rav and several Tannaim and Amora'im used to recite the Sabbath service on Friday afternoon, as well as reciting the Kiddush [sanctification of the Sabbath] over a cup of wine. So too would they recite the Havdalah [the ceremony for the conclusion of the Sabbath] on Saturday afternoon, as we find there [in the Talmud]. The same applies to the recitation of the *Shema'*, seeing that we accept the view of Rabbi Yoḥanan who ruled that the *Shema'* is recited before the Tefillah, and a *baraita* supports him; as against the position of Rabbi Joshua ben Levi who claims that the Tefillahs should precede the *Shema'*. The Mishnah at the beginning of our tractate (*Berakhot*) accords with Rabbi Eliezer . . .

However, the accepted halakhah is not according to that view, nor according to the Jerusalem Talmud which I quoted above, but rather it accords with Rabbi Judah here, since Rabbi Meir in Chapter 1 agrees with him, claiming that the proper time is from the hour when the priests immerse themselves. Nor does Rabbi Judah disagree with him, except for the fact that according to his definition twilight consists of three quarters of a *mil* etc.

Thus have the Tosafot, the Raviah [Rabbi Eliezer ben Rabbi Joel Ha-Levi] and Rabbenu Simḥah written.

However, on this all agree: that one who recites the *Shema'* or the evening service before the *pelag ha-minḥah*, in the middle of the afternoon, more than an hour and a quarter before nightfall has not fulfilled his obligation as regards either the *Shema'* or the evening Tefillah. And whoever chooses to conduct himself according to the view of Rabbenu Tam should recite the afternoon service before the *pelag ha-minḥah*, whereas he may recite the evening service and the *Shema'* after the *pelag ha-minḥah* directly. Thus wrote the Raviah, that one should make every effort to be precise about the times. And he who desires to act according to the rulings of the Geonim can recite the afternoon service up until nightfall; i.e. until sunset, which is the appearance of the stars. However, he should not recite the evening service or the *Shema'* until after the appearance of the stars. Certainly it would be inconceivable to recite both the afternoon and evening services between the *pelag ha-minhah* and the appearance of the stars, since this would entail the acceptance of two contradictory lenient rulings. Since for purposes of the afternoon service he is defining it as daytime, in keeping with the Geonim who rule according to the Sages in Chapter 4 (against Rabbi Judah), whereas in the case of the evening service they are accepting the view of Rabbenu Tam who ruled according to Rabbi Judah.

Comments

By now you should have been able to understand all the arguments and references in the lengthy and complex discussion of the *Hagahot Maimoniot*, and it could serve as a thorough review of the main lines of halakhic discourse encountered up till now.

What is new in this excerpt is primarily the author's emphasis on the limitations of Rabbenu Tam's solution. Rabbenu Tam was able to justify the advancing of the time for the evening *Shema'* as far as the *pelag ha-minh ah*—but not before. Rabbi Meir Ha-Kohen does not refer explicitly to actual practice, but comparison with other sources shows us that European Jewish communities were definitely reciting the *Shema'* earlier than 1.25 hours before nightfall.

Later halakhic authorities

Rabbi Moses Isserles (c. 1530–1572) was one of the leading Polish halakhic authorities of his day. He composed two principal works. The first, from which we will be reading now, is entitled the *Darkei Moshe*, and consists of selections from the Ashkenazic [French-German-Eastern European] works, presented as a supplement and commentary to Rabbi Jacob ben Asher's Ṭur. This selection is mostly a quotation from Rabbi Israel Isserlein's *Terumat Ha-Deshen*. Note the reference to scholars who are accustomed to separating themselves from their communities. This sociological phenomenon indicates a certain weakening in the unity and solidarity of the communal authority, which will become a significant factor in coming generations.

Rabbi Moses Isserles, Darkei Moshe, Oraḥ Ḥayyim #235

And Rabbi Israel Isserlein wrote in the same responsum that there are places where they recite their prayers as early as three or four hours before nightfall, and the custom has become widespread as a result of widespread frailty. People are hungry and thirsty and crave food while it is still mid-afternoon. Thus they begin to pray early and then eat immediately afterwards. Even a scholar ought not to separate himself from the community if he cannot protest against their praying so early, unless he is accustomed to separating from the community in other matters as well. If so, then he may also pray after nightfall.

Comments

The most widely accepted halakhic code is the *Shulḥan ʿArukh* of Rabbi Joseph Caro. Caro, a victim of the expulsion of the Jews from Spain in 1492, wandered through Turkey and the Land of Israel, especially in the center at Safed. He composed two important works. The first, the *Beit Yoseph*, consisted of a lengthy commentary on the *Ṭur*, in which he would trace the sources of each of Rabbi Jacob ben Asher's rulings, and compare the different opinions and interpretations that had been proposed by halakhic authorities until his time. The conclusions were presented in his own code, the *Shulḥan ʿArukh*, arranged according to the order of the *Ṭur*. In general, Caro based his rulings on three "pillars": Rabbi Isaac Alfasi, Maimonides and the *Ṭur*.

The ruling here is quite unambiguous, that the proper time for reciting the *Shemaʿ* is only after the stars have come out (and they must be small stars, which are visible only somewhat later). Post facto, however, he recognizes that if one has recited it earlier with its blessings, he may not recite the blessings a second time, since after-the-fact the recitation is recognized as valid.

Rabbi Joseph Caro, Shulḥan ʿArukh Oraḥ Ḥayyim #235

The proper time for reciting the *Shemaʿ* at night is from the appearance of the small stars. And if it is a cloudy day one should wait until he is no longer in any doubt. If he read it earlier, he must again recite it without the blessings. And if the congregation recites the *Shemaʿ* earlier, while it is still light, he should recite the *Shemaʿ* and its blessings with them, and recite the evening service with them; and when the proper time arrives for the *Shemaʿ* he should recite the *Shemaʿ* without any blessing.

Comments

As we mentioned above, the sources for the decisions of the *Shulḥan ʿArukh* were all Spanish authorities (only the *Ṭur*, via his German-born father, introduces some Ashkenazic traditions into the work). As a result, the code, in its original form, could not readily be used by Jews who followed the traditions that had evolved in the talmudic academies of France, Germany and eastern Europe. In order to remedy this limitation, Rabbi Moses Isserles composed a set of glosses on the *Shulḥan ʿArukh* in which he incorporated the teachings of the European authorities. This work succeeded so well in rendering Caro's code usable by Ashkenazic Jews that it came to be considered an inseparable part of the *Shulḥan ʿArukh*, and is invariably printed with it.

His comments here are also based on Rabbi Israel Isserlein's *Terumat Ha-Deshen*, quoted above.

The idea that, by being too conspicuous in one's piety and religious observance, one might be guilty of arrogance or haughtiness, is found in the Talmud.

Rabbi Moses Isserles, *glosses to* Shulḥan ʿArukh Oraḥ Ḥayyim #235

> However he should not recite the evening prayer again even if the congregation recited it long before nightfall, unless he is accustomed to separate himself and act with special piety in other respects as well, since in that case it does not have the appearance of haughtiness when he repeats his prayers.

Comments

The following passage is excerpted from the Mishnah commentary *Tifʾeret Yisrael* [Glory of Israel] by Rabbi Israel Lipschutz (1782–1860), a German scholar who served much of his rabbinical career in Danzig [Gdansk]. As is evident from his discussion here, Rabbi Lipschutz was fascinated with the scientific discoveries of modern times. His discussion here revolves around the disparity between the assumptions of the classic rabbinic texts and the realities of northern Europe when it comes to defining day and night. In some localities, including his native Danzig, darkness comes so late in the summer months and so early in the winter that it makes the standard halakhic definitions of day and night awkward and inconvenient; and if one travels far enough to the north, to the "land of the midnight sun" or to the North Pole itself, then one encounters extended days without any sunset (or alternatively, without sunrise), situations in which the halakhkic categories appear to break down entirely.

Rabbi Israel Lipschutz, Tifʾeret Yisrael, *commentary to the Mishnah,* Berakhot *chapter 1*

> I am in doubt regarding the northern lands such as our city of Danzig, or Copenhagen, Stockholm and similar localities, where throughout June and July the night is as bright as day—or at least, it is possible there even in the middle of the night to distinguish clearly between *tekhelet* and white—in such places, what would be the correct time for donning ritual tassels [ṣiṣit]?
>
>   It is not possible to suggest that we ought to calculate according to the times in Nissan and Tishri [May and September], for we can see quite clearly that on the festival of Shavuot, when it is customary for people to stay awake all night, that they recite the [morning] prayers at

the break of dawn. This shows that they do not calculate the times according to Nissan and Tishri.

And furthermore, God forbid that we should also follow the Nissan and Tishri times with regard to the Sabbath times in those localities—for even though this would result in a greater stringency when it comes to the onset of the Sabbath, at any rate it would lead to a leniency with respect to the conclusion of the Sabbath.

Similarly, there are doubts that arise in connection with the recitation of the evening *Shema*ʿ and the Tefillah, and on fast days.

Comments

The Talmud defines the earliest hour when it is permissible to wear the ritual tassels or recite the *Shema*ʿ as when it is light enough "to distinguish between *tekhelet* [a shade of blue] and white"—as long as it is too dark to see the distinction, it is still night, and those precepts must be observed by day. In the northern latitudes, however, there are times in the summer when it is always light enough to see the distinction.

Rabbi Lipschutz briefly considers the possibility of calculating the halakhic times not according to the actual current state of the sun, but with reference to more "manageable" seasons in the spring and fall when night and day are of equal length. He quickly dismisses that possibility by noting that prevailing practice has never measured time in that way. His proof is from the widespread custom (of kabbalistic origin) of observing an all-night vigil of Torah study ["*tiqqun*"] on the Shavuot holiday [Feast of Weeks] which commemorates the giving of the Torah. Those who have been participating in the vigil make a point of holding a morning prayer service at the earliest permissible time, which is measured according to the astronomical dawn on that date, and not averaged out to the equivalent time in fall or spring.

He also notes that if one were to follow the fall or spring times for measuring the extent of the Sabbath day, it would result in ending the Sabbath at around 6 or 7 p.m. in mid-summer, even though it will not get dark until many hours later. While there is no halakhic objection to extending the Sabbath, and making people observe its restrictions earlier than they would according to the traditional mode of reckoning, this would create an extreme leniency in allowing people to commence weekday activities earlier than they could if they were measuring the day according to the current state of the sun. Jewish religious law normally eschews such leniency.

Rabbi Israel Lipschutz, Tif'eret Yisrael, *commentary to the* Mishnah, Berakhot *chapter 1 (continued)*

> To be sure, I have no problems regarding the variations between differing localities—that in one place night falls earlier while in another

place it falls later. For it is perfectly reasonable that every person must act in accordance with the place and time in which he is found.

However, our main uncertainty relates only to northern lands during the summer, where there is no actual night in June and July—what would be the times for recitation of the *Shema'*, the Tefillah, donning ritual tassels [*ṣiṣit*] and for the Sabbath?

Comments

It is very unusual for a rabbinic text to refer to months by their non-Jewish names, as Rabbi Lipschutz does here when he speaks of "June and July."

Rabbi Israel Lipschutz, Tif'eret Yisrael, *commentary to the* Mishnah, Berakhot *chapter 1 (continued)*

Initially, there would also appear to be a question regarding someone who happened to be traveling near the North Pole during the summer, since there are consecutive months of actual daylight there during the summer, and it is possible to observe the sun making the full circuit of the horizon—east, south, west and north. So how should a Jew conduct himself if he finds himself there among the sailors who journey there to hunt whales? When should he recite his Tefillah and *Shema'* in the mornings and evenings, and when should he refrain from work on the Sabbath?

Comments

The picture of Jews participating in whaling expeditions to the North Pole is a very intriguing one, and it would be remarkable to infer from this text that religiously observant Jews in the nineteenth century were involved in such exotic activities. (It should be noted that whale oils and fats, the main reasons for which they were hunted, are not kosher.) However, it would appear that Rabbi Lipschutz is merely inventing a hypothetical example of why a person might be traveling to the Arctic regions.

Rabbi Israel Lipschutz, Tif'eret Yisrael, *commentary to the* Mishnah, Berakhot *chapter 1 (continued)*

We can answer that people there have a different indicator, since the sun there makes the circuit of all the directions in the course of a twenty-four hour period. Therefore a person will know that each full circuit of the sun is equal to one day. Consequently, if he arrived there on a Sunday according to his calculation, he will know that the seventh circuit of the sun is the Sabbath—although he still will not know the precise times for the morning and evening prayers, nor will this system enable him to know the times for the beginning and end of the Sabbath.

So how should he conduct himself—should it be in accordance with the inhabitants of Europe or the inhabitants of America? Indeed it is known regarding those two localities, that one is located on one side of the globe while the other one lies opposite it. Hence, at the time that the Sabbath is sanctified in Europe, in America it is only the beginning of Friday, and when the Sabbath is concluded with the Havdalah blessing in Europe, it is still Saturday morning in America. So if our traveler is in the vicinity of the North Pole and observes the sun shining brightly at both the European and the American times, when should he begin and end his Sabbath there?

Even if we were to rule that "we should apply to him the stringencies and the leniencies of his place of origin," there remains the question of how he can be expected to know the starting times of the evening and morning in his place of origin.

Comments

In a talmudic discussion about how to deal with cases of people who are traveling between towns that observe differing local customs, one of the halakhic positions that is mentioned is that such people should continue to observe the customs of the place from which they have come.

Rabbi Israel Lipschutz, Tif'eret Yisrael, *commentary to the* Mishnah, Berakhot *chapter 1 (continued)*

It is possible to resolve that doubt as well by means of a calculation, by counting backward from the exact hour indicated on one's clock. For example, if he arrives there at six o'clock according to his clock, and according to his calculations it is now 6 p.m. on Sunday, he can then count five more periods of twenty-four hours or five full circuits of the sun, and then he can begin to count and observe his Sabbath for twenty-four hours.

At any rate, it seems to me that if he were to perform an act of forbidden labor then, he would not be liable to a death penalty or a sin-offering, since his status would not differ significantly from that of a person who was wandering in the desert and lost track of the Sabbath.

It follows from this that if there were two people there, one from America and one from Europe, each of them would observe the Sabbath according to his own place of origin, and neither of them would incur the penalties of death by stoning or the obligation of a sin-offering, seeing as their obligation is merely of rabbinic origin.

Comments

This is a very radical conclusion. In effect, Rabbi Lipschutz is stating here that the Arctic conditions are so different from the circumstances envisaged by the Torah that the biblical Sabbath cannot really be observed at the North Pole, since the criteria for measuring days have broken down there entirely. Therefore Jews who observe the Sabbath in the far north are doing so only by rabbinic injunction, and are not subject to the biblical penalties for violations of the Sabbath prohibitions (death by stoning for intentional transgressions or the sacrificing of sin-offerings for unintentional ones).

Rabbi Israel Lipschutz, Tif'eret Yisrael, *commentary to the* Mishnah, Berakhot *chapter 1 (continued)*

> It also seems to me that they are permitted to recite the morning and evening prayers, and to recite the blessings "who brings on the evening" and "who creates light" even though for them the night is as bright as the day. Nevertheless, they should say those things according to the practices in their places [of origin].
>
> However, in the northern provinces such as our own city [Danzig] and similar localities, we still do not know what is the correct time for donning ritual tassels and reciting the *Shema'*.
>
> May the Holy One enlighten our eyes with the light of his Torah to observe and to perform and to uphold his precepts and his statutes and his instructions.

Comments

One of the most popular halakhic codes of our times is the *Mishnah Berurah* composed by Rabbi Israel Meir Kagan (1839–1933), a noted Lithuanian scholar widely known for his influential moralistic tract, the *Ḥafetz Ḥayyim* (about the evils of slander and gossip). The *Mishnah Berurah* consists of a commentary on the section of the *Shulḥan 'Arukh* that deals with daily conduct, liturgy and the cycle of the year (it is indicative that by this point in modern Jewish history these were the only areas of Jewish law that were of general relevance).

Note that for Rabbi Kagan, the idea that people would recite their evening prayers before the appearance of the stars is a rare anachronism, while most people wait until dark. The opinion of Rabbenu Tam, which we have seen as the dominant view among the medievals, is described here as a minority position opposed by most authorities.

Rabbi Israel Meir Kagan, Mishnah Berurah Oraḥ Ḥayyim #235

> The congregations used to [pray early] because of difficulty, since at times they would have to wait for the evening service until the appearance of the stars. So each person would go home and they would not participate in communal prayer, since it is inconvenient for them to assemble again. Also, there are many unlearned types who, if they did

not pray with the congregation, would not pray at all. For these reasons they rely on the view of Rabbi Judah who states that from the *pelag ha-minḥah* onwards it is considered the proper time for the evening service ... and since for the purpose of Tefillah it is considered night-time, their custom was to recite the *Shemaʿ* as well, even though most authorities do not consider this proper ...

Behold, in our times most people are accustomed to reciting the *Shemaʿ* and the evening service after the appearance of the stars, as prescribed by the law. However in some places the old custom is still prevalent in the synagogues, to pray immediately after the afternoon service, even though it is still somewhat light. It would seem that one who prays in such a place should go back and repeat the *Shemaʿ* when its proper time comes. At the least, it appears that he should read all the paragraphs at bedtime properly, and should have the intention of fulfilling thereby the positive precept of reciting the *Shemaʿ*. In some localities there exists a custom that the specially pious (*vatiqim*) do not recite the *Shemaʿ* along with the congregation, but remain silent until the Eighteen Benedictions, and afterwards join the congregation in prayer, and wait after the service until the appearance of the stars, and then they recite the *Shemaʿ* with its blessings. They do not worry about "joining Redemption to Prayer." This custom is also mentioned in the writings of the early authorities.

Comments

We have come to the end of our readings about the development of the halakhah related to the time for the evening *Shemaʿ*. The situation has come a full circle: the earliest sources, the Mishnah and *baraita*s, seem to prescribe the appearance of the stars as the earliest permissible time. Immediately following the Talmudic period, it seems that the prevalent practice in many communities was to recite it earlier. The Spanish and Provençal rabbis insisted on adherence to the rulings of the Talmud, at least for those know-ledgeable enough to know the correct procedure, while making certain allowances for the preservation of community solidarity. The Ashkenazic authorities worked from the assumption that their customs were correct, and they found ways to harmonize the Talmud to their own practice. As we get closer to our own era, the tendency has shifted back to scrupulous adherence to the times laid out in the Mishnah and Talmud.

In a brilliant study of the question at hand (upon which much of this presentation has been based), the distinguished Israeli historian Professor Jacob Katz suggested that the development of the halakhah here ought to be seen as a gauge of some important sociological processes in the evolution of Jewish communal life. Until the Emancipation of European Jews, which was marked largely by their being allowed to enter the general society at the expense of their own independent communal institutions, the Jews maintained a large degree of communal solidarity, and the rabbis who led them felt obligated to speak on behalf of their entire communities, not just particular segments. In recent centuries, under the influence of modern ideas and social forces, the communities became divided into subgroupings who did not necessarily acknowledge each other's legitimacy. Even among traditionally observant Jews, who often found themselves a minority within the larger community, sects developed with separate institutions. As a result, according to Professor Katz, we find that the local rabbis and halakhic scholars could no longer appear as spokesmen for all the Jews of their towns, but only for those who had voluntarily elected to accept their authority. The rabbi could therefore make more stringent demands on his followers, without paying attention to the fact that the majority of his coreligionists were acting according to different standards. Whether or not we are persuaded by the particular arguments of Katz's thesis, they do serve to add a new dimension to the study of halakhah as a whole. It reflects not only its own religious and legal content, but can also serve as an instrument for the study of the broader currents of Jewish history.

The finest minds of scholars and spiritual leaders devoted themselves for centuries to this and countless other ongoing conversations on diverse questions of Jewish religious law, generating a fascinating and engaging literature of codes, explanatory and critical commentaries and responsa. Hopefully, this chapter has provided enough of a taste of this literature to whet an appetite for further study.

4 Jewish Bible commentaries

Interpreting Balak

In the following texts we will be examining a representative sampling of classic Jewish biblical exegetes. The scriptural passages that they are interpreting come from Numbers Chapter 22. The story takes place as the Israelites, coming to the end of their forty-year sojourn in the Sinai desert, are about to finally enter and conquer the promised land. The Israelites' initial successes against neighboring nations impel Balak King of Moab to invoke supernatural assistance against them by hiring the Midianite prophet Balaam to curse the Israelites. Toward that end, Balak sends a delegation of Moabite and Midianite elders to Balaam in order to persuade him to accept the task.

Numbers 22

7] So the elders of Moab and the elders of Midian departed with divinations in their hand, and they came to Balaam and spoke to him the words of Balak.

8] And he said to them: Lodge here tonight, and I will bring back word to you, as the Lord speaks to me. So the princes of Moab stayed with Balaam.

9] Then God came to Balaam and said: Who are these men with you?

10] So Balaam said to God: Balak the son of Zippor, king of Moab, has sent to me, saying:

11] Look, a people has come out of Egypt, and they cover the face of the earth. Come now, curse them for me; perhaps I shall be able to overpower them and drive them out.

12] And God said to Balaam: You shall not go with them; you shall not curse the people, for they are blessed.

13] So Balaam rose in the morning and said to the princes of Balak: Go back to your land, for the Lord has refused to give me permission to go with you.

14] And the princes of Moab rose and went to Balak, and said: Balaam refuses to come with us.

15] Then Balak again sent princes, more numerous and more honorable than they.

16] And they came to Balaam and said to him: Thus says Balak the son of Zippor: Please let nothing hinder you from coming to me;

17] for I will certainly honor you greatly, and I will do whatever you say to me. Therefore please come, curse this people for me.

18] Then Balaam answered and said to the servants of Balak: Though Balak were to give me his house full of silver and gold, I could not go beyond the word of the Lord my God, to do less or more.

19] Now therefore, please, you also stay here tonight, that I may know what more the Lord will say to me.

20] And God came to Balaam at night and said to him: If the men come to call you, rise and go with them; but only the word which I speak to you—that you shall do.

21] So Balaam rose in the morning, saddled his donkey, and went with the princes of Moab.

22] Then God's anger was aroused because he went, and the angel of the Lord took his stand in the way as an adversary against him.

Comments

As we shall be seeing, there are several glaring problems and inconsistencies in this passage that had to be confronted by the commentators. Note for example the shifting between elders and princes, between Moabites and Midianites, and the like. A more substantial problem here arises from God's inconsistent treatment of Balaam. In verse 12 he forbids Balaam to accept the invitation of the delegation from King Balak, but then in verse 20, he tells him that he may accept it (under specified conditions)—and yet in verse 22 God is angry at Balaam for accompanying the delegation!

In the broader context (which would take us beyond the specific verses copied here), Balaam's personality and moral stature are riddled with inconsistencies. He is variously described as an authentic prophet of God and as a mere soothsayer or sorcerer. When Balak hires him to curse Israel, he insists throughout that he will only speak what God tells him to speak; and true to his promise, in the end what he utters consists of admiring blessings rather than curses—and yet in the end, Balaam is put to death for his complicity in seducing the Israelites to perform acts of sexual immorality that provoke a severe divine retribution. These and other difficulties inspired the Jewish exegetes to grapple with the text and to come up with coherent readings that would account for all the details.

The Babylonian Talmud Sanhedrin 105a

"So the elders of Moab and the elders of Midian departed"
It was taught in a *baraita*: Midian and Moab were never at peace.

This is analogous to two dogs in a pack who were enraged at each other. When a wolf attacked one of them, the other one thought: if I do not come to his assistance, then today he will kill him and tomorrow he will come after me. So the two of them joined forces and killed the wolf.

Comments

"Baraita"—(literally: external) refers to a rabbinic oral tradition from the era of the Mishnah, that is not included in the Mishnah.

It is hard to find a textual source for the Talmud's assumption that Moab and Midian were normally hostile to one another (Rashi refers us to Genesis 36:35, which hardly seems relevant). More likely, the interpretation is a rhetorical one and is colored by the later experiences and expectations of Jews living in a hostile heathen world. The remark should probably be read in the sense that even pagan nations that would otherwise be in conflict with each other will forget their differences and join forces to fight against Israel.

The Babylonian Talmud Sanhedrin 105a (continued)

Said Rav Pappa: This is in accord with the popular adage: The rat and the cat held a feast from the fat of the unfortunate one.

Comments

Rav Pappa (a fourth-century Babylonian scholar) often illustrates teachings by quoting popular sayings and adages. In the present instance it is rather odd that the Israelites are depicted as the wolf, the aggressor, especially when they were ultimately victorious over their enemies.

The Babylonian Talmud Sanhedrin 105a (continued)

"So the princes of Moab stayed with Balaam"
And where did the princes of Midian go to?—When he said to them, "lodge here tonight, and I will bring back word to you," they said: Is there a father who despises his children?

Comments

A glaring difficulty in the text, which many commentators tried to solve in diverse ways, is that verse 7 speaks of "the elders of Moab and the elders of Midian" coming to Balaam, but in verse 8 it is only the elders of Moab that stayed with him. What happened to the elders of Midian, and why?

The Talmud's answer here underscores the unique paternal relationship between God and Israel, which led the Midianite elders to conclude that their objective of cursing Israel (that is, directing divine disfavor against them) was futile, so they left.

The Babylonian Talmud Sanhedrin 105a (continued)

> Said Rabbi Naḥman: Insolence is effective even toward Heaven. At first it is written "you shall not go with them"; but later it is written "rise and go with them."

Comments

As we shall see later on, God's apparent inconsistency in first forbidding and then allowing Balaam to accompany Balak's envoys was regarded as a serious theological problem that had to be resolved. Rav Naḥman's approach seems naïvely and unabashedly anthropomorphic: it appears as if Balaam is being depicted as a stubbornly insolent child who keeps nagging his father until he finally relents and consents to the child's demand.

Rabbi Solomon ben Isaac (Rashi)

Rabbi Solomon ben Isaac of Troyes, France (1041–1105) was the most popular Jewish interpreter of the Bible, and his commentaries are included with most Jewish printed editions of the Hebrew Bible. His commentary to the Torah combines extensive quotations from the talmudic and midrashic sources with his own original observations.

Rashi to Numbers 22:6

> **"With divinations in their hand"**
> All sorts of divinations, so that he could not claim "I do not have the instruments of my craft with me." The elders of Midian brought this divination with them.

COMMENTS

Rashi is responding here to a twofold difficulty in the biblical text. First of all, the Hebrew word (*qesamim*) translated here as "divinations" is an unusual one that lends itself to diverse interpretations, as is evident from the various commentaries and translations. Furthermore, if we give it the most likely interpretation, as "paraphernalia for performing divination," then it is odd that the elders should bring them to Balaam; why could they not simply assume that Balaam, who was a professional diviner, had his own supply of equipment?

Rashi to Numbers 22:6 (continued)

> They said: If he will accompany us this time, that means that there is
> substance to him; but if he refuses us, then there is no advantage to be
> gained from him. For this reason when he told them "lodge here
> tonight," they said: we can expect nothing from him; so they left him
> and made their departure, as it says "So the princes of Moab stayed
> with Balaam" which indicates that the princes of Midian made their
> departure.

COMMENTS

Rashi is relating to the same problem that we saw above in the Talmud
passage, of the apparent disappearance of the Midianite princes. In what
ways (if at all) does his solution differ from the Talmud's?

Rashi to Numbers 22:20

> **"If the men come to call you"**
> If the call is yours and you are the one who expects to reap a reward
> for it, then "rise and go with them"; "but" in spite of yourself, "only the
> word which I speak to you—that you shall do."
> But nevertheless, "Balaam went." He said: perhaps I will succeed in
> persuading him.

Rashi to Numbers 22:22

> **"Because he went"**
> He saw that the thing was evil in the sight of the Omnipresent, and
> yet he still desired to go.

COMMENTS

Rashi (following in the footsteps of several midrashic and talmudic interpretations) explains the specific contradiction between verses 20 and 22 by
paraphrasing the texts so that God is not commanding, requesting or recom-
mending that Balaam consent to accept Balak's mission. Quite the contrary—
God is saying that he would prefer that Balaam turn down Balak's offer,
however, he will not compel him to refuse. He recognizes that Balaam is
driven by an overwhelming desire to go to Balak, whether because of his
greed for the immense wealth that the king has promised to bestow upon
him or out of his personal loathing for the Israelites and the values they
represent. God therefore concedes with reluctance that if Balaam insists on
going, he will not prevent him, provided that Balaam agrees to say what
God tells him—and not what Balak is hiring him to say.

For this reason, according to Rashi, God will still be justified in being angry at Balaam for making the wrong moral choice.

Rabbi Abraham Ibn Ezra

Rabbi Abraham ben Meir Ibn Ezra (c. 1089–c. 1164) was born and educated in the "Golden Age" of Muslim Spain. He excelled as a poet, philosopher, and grammarian, as well as biblical exegete. The latter part of his life was spent wandering in poverty through western Europe and the Middle East.

Ibn Ezra's works of biblical interpretation focus on grammar, lexicography, a sensitivity to the stylistic conventions of the Hebrew language, and a general concern for plausible and rational judgments. In adopting this approach, he frequently found himself in disagreement with the talmudic understanding that assumed that the word of God could not be subjected to human aesthetic standards. Ibn Ezra's critical sense led him to raise questions concerning the traditional claims about the authorship of biblical books, anticipating some of the conclusions of modern scholarship. In spite of his commitment to the plain meaning of the biblical text (*peshat*), Ibn Ezra used his commentaries to defend the rabbinic oral tradition against its detractors from the Karaite movement (the Jewish ideology that insisted on exclusive reliance on the Bible without the rabbinic "oral tradition"). He often cited Saadiah Gaon who had composed his own Arabic Bible translations and commentaries and had fought a fierce polemical campaign against Karaism.

Rabbi Abraham Ibn Ezra to Numbers 22:19[1]

> The Gaon (of blessed memory) said as follows:
>
> If someone should object that, once God had said (verse 12) "You shall not go with them," how can he then say (verse 20) "rise and go with them'?
>
> —It is possible to reply: The Lord did not want him to accompany the first delegation, until they were accompanied by distinguished princes.

COMMENTS

This passage again focuses on the discrepancy between God's responses to Balaam's two requests to agree to Balak's invitation. The first time he forbids it absolutely, whereas the second time he permits it.

Before presenting his own solution, Ibn Ezra quotes one in the name of an unnamed "Gaon" (head of the Babylonian talmudic academy). It is not clear who this Gaon is; Saadiah and Samuel ben Hofni composed important commentaries to the Torah, though this section of the book of Numbers is not included in the surviving remains of either commentary.

The Gaon's solution is based on an otherwise incidental difference between the two delegations that Balak sent to recruit Balaam. The first consisted of "the elders of Moab and the *elders* of Midian" (verse 7), whereas the second (verses 14–15) included "the *princes* of Moab." Evidently the Gaon is saying that the reason why God did not consent to Balaam's going with the first group was because they were beneath his dignity—or at least, beneath the dignity of God in whose name Balaam would be going and whose people he would be addressing. This interpretation is hinted at by the fact that God responds to Balaam's first request by asking him "Who are these men with you?" (verse 9).

Rabbi Abraham Ibn Ezra to Numbers 22:19 (continued)

However in my own view, this interpretation is unnecessary. Rather, the meaning is as in (Numbers 13:2) where it states "Send ye men [to spy out the land of Canaan]." For the Lord had said (Deuteronomy 1:21) "go up and possess it"; however, they did not place their faith in him, but instead they said (verse 22) "Let us send men before us," and it was at this point that Moses consulted with the Lord who told him "Send ye men."

In a similar vein, after the Lord had told Balaam "you shall not curse the people," why did he need to say "that I may know what more the Lord will say to me"? It was just that he was thinking evil thoughts in his heart. Therefore the Lord directed him to go with the men, but to take heed that he only speak that "which I speak to you."

And the confirmation my interpretation is correct is when it says "Then God's anger was aroused because he went."

COMMENTS

Ibn Ezra's own explanation, though it focuses on a different textual discrepancy, is similar in its main assumptions to that of Rashi outlined above. Like Rashi, he argues that—contrary to the assumption underlying the objection—verse 20 should not be understood as a divine injunction to Balaam to accept Balak's invitation, but merely as a reluctant concession to Balaam's unshakable determination to do so.

Ibn Ezra strengthens his case by reading verse 20 within the broader narrative and psychological contexts of the chapter. Once God made it clear that he was opposed to the mission, there was no purpose served by again consulting God on the same question. Clearly, Ibn Ezra concludes, the fact that Balaam still hoped nonetheless that God would give his consent reveals his true malevolent desires. Viewed in this way, God's answer was not a command to go, but a recognition that—since Balaam was determined, come what may, to go to Balak—he should be careful about what he would say.

In support of his interpretation, Ibn Ezra compares this passage to another episode in the Torah in which God becomes fiercely angry at people who appear to be obeying his instructions. The reference is to the account of the spies who were sent by Moses to scout out the land of Israel, as described in Numbers 13 and Deuteronomy 1. Those two passages are in fact inconsistent about who took the initiative in that ill-fated decision. Deuteronomy presents it as an idea that originated with the Israelites and was supported by Moses; while in Numbers it is God who appears to be commanding it. At any rate, the tragic story concludes with God punishing the people for accepting the discouraging report that was brought back by the spies, and sentencing them to remain in the desert for forty years until a new generation will be ready to enter the promised land.

Ibn Ezra is arguing that the only way of reconciling all the apparent contradictions there is by assuming that what appears at first sight to be a divine command to "Send ye men to spy out the land of Canaan" was not a command at all, but a reluctant acceptance of the faithless people's demand to send the spies. This is indeed the same approach that he is applying to the Balaam story.

Note how verse 22, which for Rashi was part of the problem (in that it posed a challenge vis-à-vis verse 20), figures in Ibn Ezra's commentary as validation for his solution to the discrepancy between verses 12 and 20.

Rabbi Samuel ben Meir (Rashbam)

Rabbi Samuel ben Meir (c. 1085–c. 1174) is generally known by the Hebrew acronym "Rashbam." He was a grandson of Rashi and the brother of Rabbi Jacob Tam. In addition to his works of biblical exegesis (his commentaries to other books of the Bible besides the Torah have mostly been lost), Rashbam was a prominent participant in the "Tosafot" school of critical commentaries to the Talmud, and he composed explanatory commentaries to some of the Talmud sections that Rashi had left uncompleted.

Rashbam's commentary to the Torah is distinguished by its commitment to scholarly objectivity, restricting itself to the plain, contextual meaning of the text without imposing the traditional rabbinic interpretations. He was sensitive to issues of grammar (he had some familiarity with the pioneering works of the Sephardic grammarians), and to the literary and rhetorical qualities of biblical Hebrew. He was outspoken and undiplomatic in dismissing the interpretations of previous authors when he felt that they were not justified by the facts of the text.

Rabbi Samuel ben Meir (Rashbam) to Numbers 22:7²

"With divinations [Hebrew: *kesamim*] in their hand"
They brought various magical instruments to Balaam, so that he could not plead "I do not have the necessary magical instruments."
This is as it is written: "In his right hand is the divination for Jerusalem" (Ezekiel 21:22).

COMMENTS

The Hebrew word describing what the elders were bringing to Balaam is an unusual one that lends itself to diverse translations (for example, the standard English "King James" version renders it as "rewards of divination," the fee that they intended to offer Balaam for his services). Rashbam interprets that the elders were bringing to Balaam the equipment that he would require in order to ply his trade. At first sight, this seems like an unlikely explanation. Could it not be assumed that Balaam owned his own instruments? Therefore Rashbam suggests that they wanted to avoid a situation in which he might plead that he could not perform the divination for them because for some reason he did not have the necessary equipment on hand.

Rabbi Samuel ben Meir (Rashbam) to Numbers 22:14

"With us"
He did not consider us important.
"Numerous and honorable"
More important and dignified than the first ones.

COMMENTS

These comments remind us of the explanation of the Gaon in Ibn Ezra's commentary, that Balaam's refusal to go with the first delegation was because they were not sufficiently important or dignified. For Rashbam this seems to describe the perspective of the envoys, and not necessarily that of Balaam himself (or of God).

Rabbi Samuel ben Meir (Rashbam) to Numbers 22:22

"Because he went"
Willingly, in his desire to curse them even though he was fully aware that the Holy One did not want this.

COMMENTS

Rashbam's view seems similar to that of Ibn Ezra and others, that what provoked the divine anger was Balaam's eagerness to curse Israel even after God had indicated his displeasure with the prospect.

Rabbi Hezekiah ben Manoah

Little is known about the life of this thirteenth-century exegete, apparently from France. His commentary, which has been included in the standard rabbinic Bibles since the sixteenth century, is quite eclectic, making use of traditional midrashic interpretations, Rashi (his main source), as well as many other commentators of diverse literal and homiletical orientations. Some of his explanations appear to be quite novel.

Rabbi Hezekiah ben Manoah, Hizzequni *to Numbers 22:6*

"With divinations in their hand"

Books of divinations, as Rashi explained it. And similarly in the "Jerusalem Targum": "with sealed letters in their hands," meaning: letters bearing the king's signature.

We find the following analogous usage: "In his right hand is the divination"; "he shakes the arrows, he consults the images, he looks at the liver" (Ezekiel 21:21).

COMMENTS

Without the reference to the Jerusalem Targum (an Aramaic translation of the Torah composed in the land of Israel), we would understand that the "books of divination" were manuals or books of spells and incantations. The reference to "letters bearing the king's signature" seems to be to something else, probably the official orders to Balaam to practice divination on behalf of the king. It is not clear whether these should be read as a single interpretation or as two separate ones.

The second quote from Ezekiel provides additional evidence about the nature of the practices that the Bible categorizes as "divination."

Rabbi Hezekiah ben Manoah, Hizzequni *to Numbers 22:6 (continued)*

An alternative explanation: They brought with them the wages to be paid to the diviners; as in "they will not collect '*qisma*' in Jerusalem" (Targum to Habakuk 3:17).

COMMENTS

Look up the verse in Habakuk. The Hebrew there contains no reference at all to divination or magic.

Rabbi Hezekiah ben Manoah, Hizzequni *to Numbers 22:8*

"So the princes of Moab stayed with Balaam"
Because they had no acquaintances in Midian, they lodged with Balaam. However, the elders of Midian lodged with their own friends.

Rabbi Hezekiah ben Manoah, Hizzequni *to Numbers 22:12*

"You shall not curse the people"
The plague that will take place in connection with Baal Peor is perfectly well known before the Holy One; so if Balaam were to curse them, the world would say that the plague had come upon them on account of his curse.

COMMENTS

The problem that seems to be bothering Rabbi Hezekiah (as it bothered many other commentators) is: why should God care if Balaam curses Israel if such curses have no independent power unless God wills them to take effect?

His response is that it could lead to a dangerous misunderstanding. God will in fact inflict a terrible plague upon Israel when they succumb to harlotry and idolatry in the cult of Baal Peor, as described in Numbers chapter 25. If Balaam were allowed to curse the people prior to that episode, then the plague would be perceived as the result of that curse, in defiance of God's will, rather than as the divine punishment that it was.

Rabbi Hezekiah ben Manoah, Hizzequni *to Numbers 22:19*

"That I may know what more the Lord will say to me"
Even though the Holy One had already said to him "You shall not go with them," he kept pushing himself to go and curse, since he thought that his curse would be effective. He thought in his heart: unless it was going to be effective, why is he preventing me from going?

Rabbi Hezekiah ben Manoah, Hizzequni *to Numbers 22:20*

"If the men come to call you"—to invite you to dine with them over a peace-offering, then you may **"go with them."**
And if you should argue: why is this episode different in that now he tells him "go with them" whereas previously he told him "you shall not

go with them"—rather, we must understand that from the beginning all that God was saying was that he should not go with them *in order to curse Israel*.

An alternative explanation: this does not constitute a discrepancy, seeing as [Balak] had now gone on to send more numerous and more honorable princes than previously.

An alternative explanation: **"If the men come to call you"**—If they are such idiots that they have come back yet again to invite you, after I already said to you **"you shall not go with them,"** then **"go with them"** and they will see that it will not do them any good.

Rabbi Hezekiah ben Manoah, Hizzequni *to Numbers 22:22*

"Then God's anger was aroused because he went"

For he had not given the permission willingly [literally: with a radiant countenance], as it states "If the men come to call you, etc." So Balaam should have grasped from that first time that the Holy One did not wish him to go.

We find a parallel instance in the affair of the spies where it says (Numbers 13:2) "send ye men" though it was unmistakably evident before him that the Holy One was not comfortable with their being sent.

An alternative explanation: **"Then God's anger was aroused because he went"**—Seeing that he had said previously "only the word which I speak to you—that you shall do" and hence Balaam was not to go until he knew what that word was; but impelled by his hatred he acted hastily and did not wait for his instruction.

The episode about Balaam was written in Scripture in order to make it known why the Holy One subsequently removed the holy spirit from the nations of the world. For this one arose from them and sought to curse them though they had done nothing to warrant it.

Rabbi Moses Naḥmanides

Rabbi Moses ben Naḥman (1194–1270), known in Hebrew by his acronym, "Ramban," was born in Gerona and spent most of his career in Barcelona in Christian Spain. He made important contributions to the principal disciplines of Jewish religious learning and was able to synthesize several distinctive scholarly approaches to religious thought and Talmud study that were current in Sephardic, French, Ashkenazic and Provençal cultural spheres. He was one of the first mainstream Jewish scholars to adopt the Kabbalah (which he designates "the way of truth") in his scriptural exegesis.

Naḥmanides' commentary to the Torah was completed late in his life after he had moved to the land of Israel in the wake of his participation in the religious disputation of Barcelona in 1263. It is very clearly the work of a mature scholar and religious personality who has given extensive consideration to the text and the issues that arise from it. He methodically weighs the interpretations proposed by previous commentators, including the talmudic and midrashic rabbis, Rashi and Ibn Ezra, as well as Moses Maimonides. Where appropriate, he tries to defend traditional readings, and he frequently proposes profound new explanations.

Rabbi Moses Naḥmanides to Numbers 22[3]

"Then God's anger was aroused because he went"

"He saw that the thing was evil in the sight of the Omnipresent, but he still desired to go"—this is cited from the Master [Rashi].

And Rabbi Abraham [Ibn Ezra] wrote . . . [Naḥmanides cites the interpretation in its entirety, as brought above.]

But all this avails me not.

As for what the Gaon said, it is not correct. For the Lord said to Balaam explicitly "You shall not go with them; you shall not curse the people, for they are blessed." Thus, the reason why God forbade him to go was to keep him from cursing the people, so how could it be permissible for him to accompany the other princes? He did not forbid him to go on account of the delegation's lowly status.

As to what Rabbi Abraham proposed—it is incorrect to suggest that God would change his mind and revoke his declaration on account of the questioner's intransigence. The matter of "send ye men" is not as he presents it; I have explained its meaning [elsewhere]. And God would never punish anyone for doing something that they were given permission to do, God forbid! The rabbis stated in the Midrash: from here you may learn that they allow a person to proceed in the direction in which he wants to go.

COMMENTS

Whereas Ibn Ezra (as well as Rashi) believe that God could be angry at Balaam for choosing the wrong course of action even if it was not explicitly forbidden, Naḥmanides rejects that position. He seems to be suggesting that God would not actually punish anybody under those circumstances; however, it is not obvious that Balaam was in fact punished for choosing to accompany Balak's messengers. Perhaps Naḥmanides has in mind Balaam's humiliating altercation with the talking ass in verses 23–35; though it is far from evident that this incident should be categorized as a punishment.

Rabbi Moses Naḥmanides to Numbers 22 (continued)

What strikes me as the correct explanation of the matter is that from the beginning God forbade him to curse the people "because they are blessed"; therefore, why should he accompany them, seeing as he was not going to curse Israel, and the envoys did not want him for any other purpose? For this reason God said "you shall not go with them; you shall not curse the people, for they are blessed." It is clear that Balaam made known to them what God had said.

Then Balak communicated to him a second time, since he did not believe him. This time he increased the honors he bestowed on him in the form of more numerous and more distinguished princes than the first ones. He also promised to increase his reward and his tributes. Now Balaam replied that the matter was not dependent on money or on his will; but rather it was entirely in the Lord's power, so he would consult with him again as to what he must do. In this he was behaving properly, for what did he know of the mind of the supreme being, and divine counsel is always a good thing, as he instructs sinners in the proper course and informs us what the messengers of the people should utter; or he might advise him what will befall them in the future. Now the Lord said to him: I have already told you that this people are blessed and you will not be able to curse them, so turn back now.

And the meaning of "if the men come to call you, etc." is that they should be persuaded to let you accompany them on the understanding that you will not curse the people, as I instructed you from the beginning. Then "rise and go with them; but only the word which I speak to you—that you shall do." This means that if I order you to bless them, then you should bless them and not be afraid of Balak. This is the meaning of "if the men come to call."

For this was the intention of the exalted Lord from the start: that Balaam should accompany them after he had made known to Balak that he must not curse them and that he must conduct himself, as regards their request, in accordance with God's command. For God's desire (may he be blessed) was to bless Israel from the mouth of the prophet to the nations. And behold, Balaam was expected to make all this known to Balak's princes and to say to them: the Lord has authorized me to accept your invitation on the sole condition that I must not curse the people, and on the understanding that if he commands me to bless them I shall bless them. But if they do not consent to these conditions, then they must leave me be.

For on this second occasion Balak said: "Come now, curse them for me." He did not wish Balaam to reveal future events or anything else, only to put a curse on the people. However Balaam, out of his intense desire to go, did not inform them of this, nor did he tell them anything.

COMMENTS

It would appear that according to Naḥmanides' interpretation, the cause of God's anger against Balaam was not that he agreed to go to Balak, and not that he consulted God after being told not to go (neither of those things was wrong in itself), but because he failed to convey to the king the specific conditions that God had attached to his mission.

Don Isaac Abrabanel

Isaac ben Judah Abrabanel (1437–1508) spent much of his life in Portugal and, later, Castile until the expulsion of the Jews from the Iberian peninsula in 1492 impelled him to emigrate to Italy. In all those lands he occupied important governmental posts involving state finances. It was in Italy that he composed most of his works, which consisted principally of biblical exegesis and treatises about topics of Jewish belief and theology.

In Abrabanel's commentary to the Torah, he commences each unit with a lengthy series of numbered questions aimed at difficulties in the text. In the course of his explanation, he notes how he has provided answers to each question in order. His explanations engage with previous interpreters, including Naḥmanides, but Abrabanel prefers to take novel approaches to elucidating the text. He makes very selective and critical use of midrashic traditions, and is committed to arriving at the plain meaning with particular attention to literary and theological topics.

Don Isaac Abrabanel to Deuteronomy 20

> The seventh question: If Balaam accurately conveyed to Balak's messengers the divine reply "the Lord has refused to give me permission to go with you" (verse 13), then why did Balak's princes emend the words to say "Balaam refuses to come with us" (verse 14)? When they ought to have said: "The Lord has refused to give Balaam permission to go with us."
>
> The eighth question: If God (may he be blessed) gave Balaam permission to go by saying "if the men come to call you, rise and go with them," then why does it say after he went that "then God's anger was aroused because he went, and the angel of the Lord took his stand in the way as an adversary against him"? After all, he went with God's express permission and by his word!

COMMENTS

With regard to the story of Balak and Balaam, Abrabanel felt it necessary to insert an introductory discourse in which he provides an original and profound perspective on a glaring discrepancy in the narrative, namely the fact that Balaam is occasionally depicted as a mere soothsayer or sorcerer, though in most respects he functions as an authentic prophet who conveys God's word to humanity. In keeping with a tradition that is found in the Talmud, several medieval commentators equated "soothsaying" with astrology, the ability to make predictions based on the mapping of the stars. Many medieval rationalists were convinced that this brand of "astral magic," which extended to the channeling of celestial energy through the timely use of talismans, was a perfectly legitimate science.

Don Isaac Abrabanel to Deuteronomy 20 (continued)

Note that sometimes Scripture refers to Balaam as a soothsayer, as it states (Joshua 13:22): "The children of Israel also killed with the sword Balaam the son of Beor, the soothsayer"; while at other times Scripture attests that the holy spirit spoke through him. Nor should you heed the words of those who claim that someone who predicts the future by means of astrology is designated a prophet. For indeed, Balaam undoubtedly attained to the rank of a true prophet, and this is the view of the talmudic sages that he attained to the highest level of prophetic ability.

However, the truth of the matter is that he was originally a soothsayer and was exceedingly knowledgeable in the workings of the stars, and he knew how to prepare talismans according to the designated times, by means of which he could draw down heavenly forces from the upper realms to the lower world, whether for good or for evil. This is what the ancient sages meant when they stated that he knew how to designate and select the time when Mars was in its ascendant and the malevolent stars were looking upon it, and at that moment he would fashion talismans to destroy, kill, and annihilate. Now, however, when the Holy One wished to facilitate Israel's conquest and inheritance of the holy land, he saw fit to pour out the spirit of his prophecy upon Balaam so that he would prophecy the future exploits of Israel's triumphs. This was done in order that all the nations who were hostile to Israel would hear Balaam's words and learn from Balaam's mouth that "this decision is by the decree of the watchers, and the sentence by the word of the holy ones" (Daniel 4:17) that Israel will inherit the land and that "as the Lord has purposed, so it shall stand" (see Isaiah 14:24), and with this they would tremble and quiver before them.

Thus, at first Balaam was a soothsayer in that he was an eminent astrologer, expert in the science of the stars which is a branch of soothsaying. And since he possessed much knowledge of that discipline, he continued to be referred to as a soothsayer until his dying day. A person who masters that subject also knows the future, and for that reason he knew how to bless those who were blessed and to curse those who are destined to be cursed. For astrology does not actually produce blessings or curses—it merely foretells them before they occur according to what the stars reveal in their trajectories. However, Balak thought that Balaam had the ability to make reality conform to his will by means of talismans, even in supernatural ways. For this reason he sent his messengers to him bearing charms; that is to say, the instruments that are required for soothsaying. For these types of talismans consist of bronze vessels and other items like breastplates and images. However, when

Balaam was transformed by the prophetic spirit which was governed by divine providence and not by the order of the stars, he insisted on ascribing it to prophecy and to the blessed Creator who was speaking through him. Balak, however, ascribed it to his astrological know-how. In this matter there was a difference of opinion: Balaam was making a persistent effort to declare that he was a prophet of the Lord, while Balak was claiming that this was untrue and that all his wisdom was limited to soothsaying and nothing else.

This is a major principle, that you should bear in mind when interpreting this episode.

. . . And Balaam replied to them (verse 7) **"lodge here tonight, and I will bring back word to you, as the Lord speaks to me."**

What he means is that the matter is no longer dependent upon charms or astrology as it was previously. For my role has undergone an immense and powerful transformation, in that I am now a prophet of the Lord. And because my prophecy comes in nocturnal dreams, you should therefore lodge here tonight so that I can give you my reply in the morning after the Lord speaks to me in my prophecy.

Now it states after this (verse 8) **"so the princes of Moab stayed with Balaam."** It would have sufficed for Scripture to say simply "and thus did they do" in order to convey the idea that Balak's emissaries did not know who was the Lord who was speaking to him, and for that reason they said to themselves "we shall not budge from here until the Lord comes to speak with him so that we might see who this angel is who speaks to him." But the reason that it says "so the princes of Moab stayed with Balaam" was because they actually stuck close to him and congregated around him there in order to behold this.

And Scripture goes on to say **"then God came to Balaam."** This comes to inform us that even though the emissaries were there with him, the prophecy that issued from God was apparent only to Balaam and not to the princes of Moab. This is analogous to "the men who were with me did not see the vision" (Daniel 10:7).

Now the Lord said to Balaam **"Who are these men with you?"** He was not really asking who they were or why they had come, for this was known. Rather, he was castigating Balaam, since after he had been elevated from the status of a soothsayer to the status of prophecy, what business did he have now with people who were coming for the purpose of soothsaying? This, then is the meaning of "Who are these men with you?": Surely I know that these men are not wandering about in order to seek out the word of the Lord, given that they are from the nations who listen to soothsayers and diviners (see Deuteronomy 18:14), so what business do they have with you? Have they come for the purpose of soothsaying as before?

This is comparable to the situation of a man who marries a promiscuous harlot, and he admonishes her: keep away from other men now that I have taken you to wife. Now if it should happen that he comes home to find men speaking with his wife, he will assume that they are approaching her for purposes of harlotry, and hence he will ask her "Who are these men with you?" In the same way, the Blessed One asked Balaam about the matter of the soothsaying, to which he replied truthfully, as it states (verse 10) "Balak the son of Zippor etc." It was in response to this that God said "You shall not go with them; you shall not curse the people, for they are blessed." That is to say: you shall not go with them because I am telling you not to curse them, and that you will not be able to curse them because they are blessed. For if in my providence I have blessed them, then how can the celestial systems curse them, since divine providence overrides the celestial systems and cannot be undermined.

However, Balaam in his wickedness did not tell Balak's emissaries all that the Lord had spoken. For if he had told them "you shall not curse the people, for they are blessed," then perhaps Balak would not have continued imploring him to go. Rather, all that he told them was that "the Lord has refused to give me permission to go with you." Therefore he thought that it might still be possible that he would give him permission to go with different princes. And because Balak's emissaries did not believe in his prophetic ability and they thought that his skill was confined to soothsaying as it had been in previous days, and that it was for purposes of self-aggrandizement that he was claiming to be a prophet and that the Lord was speaking with him—for this reason, when they returned to Balak they did not say to him "the Lord refuses to allow Balaam to come with us" as Balaam had said to them. Instead, they said "Balaam refuses to come with us," implying that he refused of his own volition to accompany them. Therefore Balak sent to him a different contingent of princes, numerous and more honorable than the first ones, and he sent him the message "please let nothing hinder you from coming to me"; that is to say: do not ascribe your refusal to come to the Lord, since you are the one who is refusing. Since I am now sending different, more honorable princes, "please let nothing hinder you from coming to me" . . .

. . . Indeed he replied to them that they should stay there tonight so that he may know what more the Lord will say to him regarding the matter of his going. Then he came to him in a prophetic dream and said, "if the men come to call you, rise and go with them; but only the word which I speak to you—that you shall do." The meaning of this statement is that he (may he be blessed) said to him at first "you shall not go with them; you shall not curse the people"—referring to two things: the going and the cursing, both of which he forbade him. But this time Balak had replied to him "please let nothing hinder you from coming to me"; that is to say, at least do not refrain from coming to me, so that we can meet and discuss it together, and if you choose not to curse, then do not curse. But at any rate, do not refrain from coming.

Behold, the standard convention regarding physicians is that if a physician is called to leave his land in order to cure a patient in a different locality, then he is compensated separately for the travel, following which they come to an agreement regarding the actual medical care, which amounts to a single wage. It was in this sense that God said when Balak asked Balaam to go there, that in any case "if the men come to call you"—that is to say: if the only thing they are asking of you is that you go there, then "rise and go with them" and claim compensation from Balak for your travel. However, when it comes to the cursing, you are not to utter a word, for I am notifying you that that matter is not subject to your authority or will. "But only the word which I speak to you—that you shall do." This applies equally with respect to blessing them, cursing them or refraining from either.

From all this it emerges that there has been no discrepancy or contradiction vis-à-vis what he told him previously, and that the Lord (may he be blessed) never allowed Balaam to go to curse them, but only to go. And Balaam ought to have figured out from this that the Holy One did not want him to curse Israel, so to what could be accomplished by his going? Accordingly, he should have stated explicitly to the envoys "indeed I shall accompany you, since it will be of no advantage to you and you will gain no profit whatsoever through either your actions or your imploring." However, he did not do this. Instead, he said to Balak's envoys that God had given him permission to accompany them. It was for this reason that "God's anger was aroused because he went." God's anger was aroused against Balaam because he chose willingly to go, knowing that it would not succeed.

And indeed, the Lord prevented Balaam from cursing the people, and at any rate he wanted him to bless them, not because Balaam was capable of obliterating the righteousness of their forefathers or the merit from their standing at Mount Sinai, or because "a foolish man could squander it" (see Proverbs 21:20)—rather, it was because Balaam's abilities with regard to blessings and curses were very famous among the nations when it came to making requests of God; as Balak said: "for I know that he whom you bless is blessed, and he whom you curse is cursed" (verse 6). So if Balaam were to curse Israel, then the nations of the land would place their trust in his curse and make a more concerted effort to fight against Israel on the strength of his curse.

However, when they heard from him that the Holy One was preventing him from cursing on their behalf and he made known that they are blessed, then all the inhabitants of the world and the denizens of the land would know and acknowledge that they are called by the name of the Lord, and they will realize that Israel's successes came from the Lord from heaven, and that "this decision is by the decree of the watchers, and the sentence by the word of the holy ones," "and who may say to him: What are you doing?" (Ecclesiastes 8:4)—and there will no longer rise up among them any spirit to wage war against Israel.

COMMENTS

As regards the discrepancy between verses 12 and 20—where God first forbids and then permits Balaam to go with Balak's envoys—Abrabanel resolves the difficulty by noting that what was forbidden was the cursing of Israel and what was permitted was merely to go to Balak without cursing them. This in fact is very close to Naḥmanides' interpretation; as is Abrabanel's castigation of Balaam for his failure to disclose the full content of God's prohibition of cursing. However, unlike Naḥmanides, Abrabanel finds the main reason for God's anger in Balaam's excessive willingness to travel to Balak (a theme that is stressed in the midrashic tradition), a failing that seems to take on greater importance in light of Balaam's ambivalent status as a soothsayer who was only recently "promoted" to the position of prophet.

In his closing observations, Abrabanel attaches much importance to the way that Balaam's actions might influence public opinion and morale in times of war, even if his blessings and curses have no independent reality. It is probable that these perceptive insights into the dynamics of Realpolitik were shaped by Abrabanel's extensive personal experiences in the upper echelons of the Spanish and Portuguese governments.

Rabbi Jacob Zevi Meklenburg

Rabbi Meklenburg (1785–1865) was a leader of the traditionalist faction in Germany in the nineteenth century, an opponent of the movements that were calling for religious reform in Judaism. He spent most of his career in Koenigsberg. His commentary on the Torah, *Ha-Ketav ve-ha-Kabbalah* (=the scripture and the tradition) was intended principally to demonstrate that the teachings of the talmudic "oral Torah" were neither a separate tradition independent of the written Bible nor an invention of the rabbis, but in fact had their basis in a profoundly close reading of the language of the Torah text. Toward that end, Meklenburg developed a penetrating sensitivity to the usages of biblical grammar and vocabulary that resulted in some very original explanations, albeit ones that were designed to uphold the tradition.

Rabbi Jacob Zevi Meklenburg, Ha-Ketav ve-ha-Kabbalah *to* Numbers 22:12

> **"You shall not go with them"**
> The first time God did not allow him to go, but the second time he gave him permission to go when he said to him "rise and go with them." This has given rise to great perplexity among the commentators.

It seems to me that there is no indication here that the divine will has changed, because there is an important distinction between the term "go" when it is attached to the word *'immahem* ["with them"; as in verse 12] and when it is attached to the word *ittam* ["with them"; as in verse 20] . . .

Thus, when God addressed him saying "you shall not go *'immahem*," this designated active going, that he should not take part in the going with them in order to fulfill their requests and to serve them by cursing the people. However, this term does not include a total prohibition against any kind of going.

However, on the second occasion God used the form "go *ittam*" and this term designates mere going without any specific purpose, such as for a stroll or to honor somebody.

Accordingly he explicitly forbade him to exert any kind of effort, as when he said "but only the word which I speak to you—that you shall do"; and as Rabbi Obadiah Sforno explained:

"If the men come to *call* you"—if all they want is to consult with you [as we find in such expressions as "called from the congregation" (Numbers 1:16) or "I have called you, that you may reveal to me what I should do" (1 Samuel 28:15)], then "rise and go with them" in order to admonish them that they should not sin.

Thus, the Torah revealed to us here Balaam's nefarious motives, in that what he really wanted was the opposite of what he had been commanded. For when it says "and he went with the princes of Moab" the verb "went" is linked to the term "*'im*" which indicates purposeful going in order to fulfill their desires and to serve them by cursing.

5 Philosophy and rational theology

The Arabic-speaking world was deeply affected by the discovery and translation of ancient Greek philosophical works that took place in the course of the Muslim expansion, especially in Syria. Traditional Jewish authors in that cultural sphere participated in this exciting rediscovery of the classical legacies of Plato, Aristotle and other great philosophers. Although the Jewish acquaintance with the philosophical tradition was mediated by syntheses that were first formulated by Islamic thinkers, the rationalist interpretation of religion was a more lasting trend in the Jewish community.

The favorable attitude toward philosophical study was based largely on the impression that it could be used to uphold the fundamental beliefs of Judaism, such as monotheism and the ethical values of the Torah. As people became more seriously committed to the philosophical method, they came to reinterpret the Jewish religion itself from a philosophical perspective. Most notably, the core value of the Torah was transformed from the performance of commandments as the expression of the covenantal commitment of the Jewish people to its God, to the perfect intellectual knowledge of an impersonal and incorporeal deity.

Saadiah ben Joseph al-Fayyumi (882–942) was raised in Egypt and spent some time in the holy land. In 928 he was invited to be *Gaon*, Head of the Babylonian talmudic academy of Sura in Baghdad. He excelled in virtually every known area of Jewish scholarship, including talmudic law, Hebrew linguistics, biblical studies and liturgical poetry, and had been involved in polemical disputes with the Jewish authorities in the holy land, and notably against the Karaite movement. His Arabic work on rationalist theology, *The Book of Doctrines and Opinions*, was not the first book of medieval Jewish philosophy, but it was the first such work by a major authority.

Saadiah's theological approach was close to that of the Muslim "Kalam" movement, which tended to subordinate the rationalist method to the authority of the revealed scripture. A central concern was a new philosophical understanding of the "oneness" of God, a conception that was not limited to the denial of other deities, but also insisted that God was incorporeal and removed from any attributes that imply space, emotions, change or any other form of multiplicity. Toward that end, Saadiah carefully interpreted the Bible in order to demonstrate that when it employed human-like terms to describe God, these should not be understood literally. Saadiah also offered systematic presentations of basic theological concepts from the Bible and rabbinic literature.

From: Saadiah Gaon's *The Book of Doctrines and Opinions*[1]

It is essential to append to this matter a section that is not to be skipped over, namely to pose the following question: If all matters of religion can be grasped through investigation and through proper reason, as the Lord has informed us, then what is the reason why the All-Wise one has given them to us by means of prophecy, and corroborated them by means of miraculous and visible signs, rather than through rational proofs?

To this we may respond, with the help of God (may he be exalted) with a satisfactory answer. We reply as follows: Because it is known before the All-Wise one that lessons that are derived through rational investigation only reach fruition after a lengthy period, if he were to direct us only to them for our knowledge of religion, then we would remain without religion for a long time, until we had completed the labor and concluded the task. If so, then it is possible that many of us would never complete the task owing to their imperfection, while others would not finish the matter on account of their impatience, or they would be overwhelmed with doubts, which would bring them to a state of confusion and block their progress.

It is for this reason that he (may he be praised and honored) freed us from all these burdens, and sent to us his messengers, and conveyed his teachings to us verbally, and allowed us to view with our eyes signs and miracles regarding them, so that no doubt can ever arise with respect to them, and you will never find any grounds for denying them; as he says (Exodus 20:22): "Ye have seen that I have talked with you from heaven." Furthermore, he spoke with his messenger in our presence, and in doing this thing he made it necessary for us to believe in him for all time, as he says (Exodus 19:9): "that the people may hear when I speak with thee, and believe thee for ever."

For this reason we were immediately obligated to accept the principles of the faith along with everything that they imply, because it had already been made evident by means of tangible proofs, and we were obliged to accept it as it had been given to us with the evidence of the faithful tradition, as will be explained. Furthermore, we were commanded to examine it methodically until the matter is grasped rationally. We did not budge from that state until the proof for it had been established within us. And we were obligated to believe in his religion through what our eyes beheld and our ears heard. And even though it might take a long time for us to ponder it until we reach the conclusion of our study, there is no harm in that. A person who lags behind because of some obstacle will not be left without any religious belief. Even for women and children, and those who are not intellectually equipped for rational speculation, their faith will nevertheless be perfect and cogent, since all people are equal when it comes to sensory knowledge. Praise the All-Wise, the Leader! For this reason you will find in the Torah that women and children are often mentioned with the fathers, when it speaks of signs and wonders.

Comments

The medieval philosophers were convinced that philosophy and scripture arrive at the same theological conclusion: a belief in the one incorporeal God who created the universe. What the prophets of old had taught on the basis of supernatural revelation, the philosopher could deduce by means of scientific and logical reasoning. Saadiah shared the widespread belief that the Greek philosophers had come to the belief in God purely through the exercise of their minds, unaided by revelation.

The question that Saadiah poses here follows naturally from that premise. If human beings are created with the intellectual equipment necessary to reach the correct conclusions about religious belief, what need was there for God to achieve the same objective by means of revelation. This is an issue that continued to be discussed through the history of religious philosophy, and is referred to as "the two sources of truth."

The solution proposed here by Saadiah was accepted, in roughly the same form, by most subsequent Jewish philosophers. He argues that the intellectual quest for theological truth is a very drawn-out process. It involves extensive training in the natural sciences and in logic. The ability to conceptualize a deity that is entirely unified, without matter or physical form, requires a major departure from our normal modes of thought and is a stage that people arrive at after years of disciplined study and speculation. History has produced only one Aristotle capable of understanding God without the benefit of revelation. Many people will never reach that level of sophistication at all due to their inherent shortcomings (Saadiah shares the medieval assumption that women are inherently unfitted for intellectual pursuits), or because of external impediments.

For this reason, God has given humanity (or, at least, the Jews who received the Torah) a kind of head start, supernaturally revealing to them the main doctrines of true religious faith. Provisionally, until they are able to arrive at that truth through philosophical deduction, they will be kept on the correct course by virtue of the doctrines that they have been taught as part of their conventional religious training. Society cannot afford the luxury of waiting for people to arrive unaided at their own spiritual perfection.

As the eighteenth-century German Jewish philosopher Moses Mendelssohn would later observe, rational truth is not susceptible to miraculous corroboration, nor can it be commanded. For Saadiah, miracles and commands are performed in support of religious doctrines only in the preliminary stage of religious development, when the truths of religion are accepted on authority, and not yet out of intellectual conviction.

Baḥya Ibn Paquda

Rabbi Baḥya ben Joseph Ibn Paquda was an eleventh-century Spanish theologian and moralist whose mystical philosophy was in the spirit of the Neoplatonic movement, stressing the struggle between spiritual values and the enticements of the material body. His Arabic masterpiece, the "Guide to the Duties of the Heart," was strongly influenced by Islamic Sufi ideas. Arguing against the prevailing Jewish approach that equated religious perfection with talmudic study and performance of the commandments of the Torah, Baḥya declared that that kind of religion was only a lesser degree of external acts of piety, "the duties of the limbs," whereas the true saint should strive to fulfill the "duties of the heart," the deeper intellectual virtues and values.

Baḥya Ibn Paquda, The Duties of the Heart[2]

The soul is a delicate light that was created out of the throne of Glory, and there is nothing comparable to it among human treasures. It is contained in the least of vessels, namely an earthenware vessel, the human body which was fashioned out of clay and mud. And it would have been impossible for one element to combine with the other were it not for the spirit of life that dwells within the sinews, which is the intermediary between the body and the soul. For a body is something that cannot be fruitful or multiply or increase. However, the spirit of life is drawn to the body, since the two of them when combined are able to be fruitful and multiply. And the soul is what hovers over the spirit of life. Even when the body is asleep and the spirit of life is in repose, and it descends to the deepest chambers of the body to digest the food—at that time, the soul longs to pursue its thoughts. In this manner dreams arise. As soon as the spirit of life becomes feeble, its strength diminishes, and then the soul returns to the place from which it was created. In the same way, the juice of the grape in the cask tends to run out—implying that the soul is external to the body. This is clearly proven by the words of Elijah, of blessed memory; as it states (1 Kings 17:21): "O Lord my God, I pray thee, let this child's soul come into him again"; and it continues (verse 22): "and the soul of the child came into him again, and he revived."

Comments

The nature of the human soul has always been one of the favorite topics of philosophical speculation. It was widely held that there were three different souls: the "vegetative," providing the most fundamental life forces; the "animate," enabling motion and activity; and the uniquely human "soul" that is necessary for achieving abstract thought, as expressed through the power of speech. For Baḥya, the soul is not a function of the form of the body, but a separate (though invisible) substance.

Baḥya's depiction of the divine origin of the soul ("created out of the Throne of Glory") is consistent with the biblical statements that humans are created "in the image of God" (Genesis 1:26, 27) and that God breathed his spirit into the first man, who was fashioned out of earth. This imagery dovetails nicely with the Neoplatonic doctrine that the soul is a divine element that has been imprisoned inside an earthly dungeon, and longs to be freed so that it can finally return to its true home. This kind of yearning for death is very alien to traditional Jewish values, but is encountered frequently in Neoplatonic writings.

Moses Maimonides

Rabbi Moses ben Maimon (1138–1204, known also as Maimonides or by the Hebrew acronym "Rambam") was a towering figure in the disciplines of Jewish religious law and philosophy. He was born in Cordoba, Spain, but fled with his family at a young age to Fustat (Cairo), Egypt, where he spent most of his life. He earned a living as a physician at the court of the sultan and published extensively on medical topics.

His law code, the *Mishneh Torah*, was the most ambitious project of its sort ever produced and is discussed elsewhere in this volume. In addition to its restatement of the full range of biblical and rabbinic law, the *Mishneh Torah* was distinguished by the fact that Maimonides opened it with a section on rationalist theological doctrines which he insisted were the ultimate purpose of the Torah. Given that Maimonides' theological system was based largely on Aristotle, his incorporation of it into a work on Jewish law provoked heated controversy.

Maimonides' *Guide of the Perplexed*, composed in Arabic, was the last of his publications. As he states in the book's introduction, he composed it in order to resolve the dilemmas faced by traditional Jews who were perplexed by the apparent contradictions between traditional Jewish religious teachings and the scientific and philosophical ideas of the day.

Moses Maimonides, Mishneh Torah, *The Laws of the Foundation of the Torah*[3]

The foundation of foundations and the pillar of wisdom is to know that there exists a first being who brought into existence all that exists; and all that exists in the heavens and on the earth, and whatever is between them, exists only by virtue of his existence.

And if it should enter your mind to suppose that he does not exist, then not a single thing would be able to exist.

And if it should enter your mind to suppose that nothing exists other than he—then he alone would exist, and would not cease to exist because their existence had ceased; because all things that exist are dependent on him, but he (may he be blessed) is not dependent on them, and he is not one of them. Therefore his truth is unlike the truth of any of them.

This is what the prophet said (Jeremiah 10:10): "But the Lord is the true God"—He alone is true, and no other being has a truth like his truth. This is what the Torah says (Deuteronomy 4:35): "There is none else beside him"—That is to say, there exists no true being like him other than himself.

This being is the God of the universe, the master of the whole earth, and he guides the sphere with a power that has no limit or end, with a power that never ceases. For the sphere turns continually, and it cannot turn without someone to turn it. And he (may he be blessed) is the one who rotates it without a hand or a body.

Comments

In very concise language, Maimonides presents a profound conceptual depiction of a God who is unlike anything that the human mind is able to imagine. He begins with a summary of the proof of God's existence as the original source of being. Since everything that now exists owes its existence to something ontologically prior to it, there must be a being that exists without having been caused by something else—and that is God. God is entirely self-sufficient, and does not rely on any other being for his existence. However, every other being in the universe relies on God for its existence. While it is possible to imagine God existing without the universe, it is impossible to conceive of the universe existing without God.

The "sphere" that is referred to here is the outermost of the concentric spheres that make up our universe according to Aristotelian cosmology. It is the sphere that houses the "fixed stars." Maimonides accepts as a proven fact that the motion of the sphere is infinite and eternal, an assumption that is not quite provable. Based on that premise, he deduces that the being that directs it and keeps it continually in rotation must be infinite.

Note Maimonides' ingenious use of scriptural quotations. The verses from Jeremiah and Deuteronomy contrast the God of Israel, creator of heavens and earth, with the illusory powers of idols. Maimonides interprets the texts as if they were making a philosophical declaration that God's uncaused being is metaphysically incomparable with any other beings.

Moses Maimonides, Guide of the Perplexed 1:54[4]

Be aware that the master of the wise, our teacher Moses (peace be upon him), submitted two requests, and received replies to both requests. The first request that he made was that God (may he be exalted) should make known to him his essence and the truth of his being. The second request, and it was the one that he submitted first, was that God should allow him to know his attributes.

And God (may he be exalted) answered him by promising that he would let him know all his attributes, and that these consist of his actions. And thus did he inform him that it is impossible to perceive his essence as it really is. Nevertheless he pointed out a theoretical perspective from which Moses could obtain the greatest amount of knowledge of God that it is possible for a human to attain. That which Moses (peace be upon him) obtained has not been attained by any human being either previous to him or since.

His requesting to know God's attributes was when he said: "Show me now thy ways, that I may know thee, that I may find grace in thy sight" (Exodus 33:13). Consider how many wondrous things are contained in this quote! The fact that he says "Show me thy way, that I may know thee" is proof that God (may he be exalted) is known through his attributes. For once a person knows his ways, he will know him. Moses' words "that I may find grace in thy sight" are evidence that the person who has knowledge of God is the one who finds favor in his eyes, rather than the one who merely fasts and prays. Furthermore, anyone who knows him is acceptable to him and near unto him, whereas one who has no knowledge of God is despised and distanced by him. The degree of satisfaction or hatred, of nearness or distancing, is in accordance with the degree of knowledge or ignorance.

We have already digressed from the subject of this chapter. I shall now return to the main point: When Moses asked to attain knowledge of God's attributes (may he be exalted), and he also asked for forgiveness for the people; he was then answered with respect to their forgiveness. Subsequently, he requested knowledge of his essence, as it says, "Show me thy glory" (verse 18). He was then answered with respect to his first request—that is to say: "Show me thy ways"—in that it says, "I will make all my goodness to pass before thee" (verse 19). However, in answer to his second request he was told, "Thou canst not see my face" (verse 20).

These words "all my goodness" allude to the fact that God presented before him the totality of existence, regarding which it says, "And God saw everything that he had made, and, behold, it was very *good*" (Genesis 1:31). In saying "presented before him the totality of existence," what I mean is that Moses attained an understanding of their nature and of their interconnections, so that he understood how God controls them all, and how it is in its totality and in its particulars. It alludes to this matter when it states, "he is firmly established in all mine house" (Numbers 12:7); that is to say, [Moses] understood the existence of the entirety of my universe with a true and solid understanding—for incorrect opinions have no permanent existence. Thus, the perception of these matters is the attainment of God's attributes (may he be exalted), by means of which he (may he be exalted) can be known.

The proof that what was being promised was the knowledge of God's actions lies in the fact that the knowledge that was made known to him consisted unmistakably of attributes of action: "merciful and gracious, long-suffering and abundant in goodness," etc., (Exodus 34:6).

It has thus been made clear that the ways which Moses wished to know, and which were in fact brought to his knowledge, are the actions emanating from him (may he be exalted). Our Sages refer to them a *middot* (qualities), and speak of the thirteen *middot* of God. In their parlance this word is used to designate traits of personality ... The intention is not to suggest that traits of personality can really be applied to him, but rather that he performs actions that resemble the actions that among us mortals result from personality traits, such as psychological moods—but not that God is actually subject to psychological moods.

He confined himself to mentioning these three qualities, even though he had attained an understanding of all his goodness, that is to say, all his works, because these are the actions that emanate from before him (may he be exalted) with respect to providing people with life and leadership. This was the last object of his request, for the conclusion of his passage is: "that I may know thee, that I may find grace in thy sight, and consider that this nation is thy people" (Exodus 33:16)—whom I have to lead by means of actions in the performance of which I must emulate your own actions in governing them.

It has thus been demonstrated to you that "the ways" and "qualities" refer to the same thing; denoting the acts issuing from before God in the world. Whenever they perceive one of God's actions, they describe him (may he be exalted) using the attribute by means of which such an action is caused, and he is then designated by a noun that is derived from that action. For example, when we are perceiving his subtle guidance in the fashioning of embryos of living creatures, and in instilling abilities in them or in those who rear them after their births, which protect them from destruction and ruin, preserve them from injuries and benefit them in their necessary functions—such a deed would only arise among us as the outcome of a certain emotion and tenderness; and this is how God is said to be merciful ... It is not that God (may he be exalted) is really moved by emotion or tenderness, but rather he is being likened to similar acts that are performed by a father for his son as the result of tenderness, compassion and mere emotion. This effect issues from God toward those who are near to him not out of any emotion or change of attitude. Similarly, when we give something to a person to whom we are under no obligation to give them anything, this is referred to in our parlance as an act of grace . . . He (may he be exalted) brings into existence and guides beings who have no claim upon him to be brought into existence or to be guided. Therefore he is designated "gracious."

Similarly, we find among his actions toward mankind great calamities that befall some individuals and destroy them, or general phenomena that affect entire tribes or even entire regions, and cause children or even grandchildren to perish without sparing the women or children; such as landslides, earthquakes, deadly lightning storms, or when one nation attacks others in order to destroy them by the sword and blot out their traces, and many other similar actions, which one of us would not inflict on another unless we were motivated by fierce anger, intense hatred or a desire for revenge. Therefore, with respect to these actions he is called jealous, revengeful, wrathful, keeping anger (see Nahum 1:2); that is to say, actions similar to those which, when performed by us mortals, originate in certain emotional moods—in envy, vengeful-ness, deep-seated hatred or anger. In respect to him they occur in accordance with what those who are being punished actually deserve, and by no means as the result of any emotion. He is above any defect. Thus all divine actions, though they might bear a resemblance to actions that in humans are motivated by our passions and emotional moods—with respect to him (may he be exalted) they are not due to anything external to his essence.

It is also fitting that the ruler of a country, if he is a prophet, should emulate these qualities, and that such deeds on his part be performed on reflection and in accordance with what is just, not merely because he is driven by some emotion. And he should not give free reign to his rage, nor should he assign a role to his emotions, since all passions are bad. Instead, he ought to safeguard himself from them to the utmost of his ability. Thus he will be at times compassionate and merciful toward certain people, not out of graciousness or mercy alone, but in accordance with what they deserve. And at times he will be vengeful or wrathful toward certain individuals in keeping with what they deserve, and not out of simple anger. As when he decrees that a person must be executed by burning, not because he is impelled by any rage or anger, and out of consideration for the great benefit that will result for many people as the result of this deed . . .

Nevertheless, it is fitting that actions of love, pardon, pity, and graciousness should be performed by the ruler of the country more frequently than acts of punishment: seeing that all the "thirteen attri-butes" are attributes of mercy with the sole exception of "visiting the iniquity of the fathers upon the children" (Exodus 34:7) . . .

Behold, we have digressed far from the subject of this chapter, but we have explained why he limited himself to mentioning only these [thirteen] out of all his acts. It was because they are necessary for the good government of a country; for the chief objective of a man should be to emulate him (may he be exalted), as far as is possible; that is to say, to make our actions similar to his actions. Or as our Sages expressed it when expounding the verse "Ye shall be holy" (Leviticus 21:2): "Just as he is gracious, so shall you also be gracious. Just as he is compassionate, so too you should be compassionate."

The main point is that all attributes that are ascribed to God are attributes of his actions, but not that he possesses any qualities.

Comments

This passage from the *Guide of the Perplexed* presents the main statement of Maimonides' doctrine of attributes. An attribute is a descriptive adjective, a quality, and the use of attributes in connection with God constituted a major problem for the medieval philosophers. They reasoned that if more than one attribute can be applied to God, then this would violate the principle of divine oneness. According to the prevailing philosophical outlook, divine oneness meant that God was not composed of multiple elements (even conceptual divisions). Thus, it was inappropriate to describe God as, say, all-powerful, all-knowing and good because these were three different attributes. Furthermore, all the attributes are known to us by means of human languages, and human language is inherently incapable of describing the abstraction that is God. The specific attributes that are applied to God in the Bible often seem singularly inappropriate, evoking inconstant human emotions (such as compassion, jealousy or anger) that the philosophers would not consider ascribing to God.

Maimonides' starting point for this discussion is the biblical passage (Exodus 33–34) in which Moses pleads with God to forgive the Israelites for worshiping the golden calf. The passage appears to bring together all the most outrageously anthropomorphic descriptions of God that caused embarrassment to rationalist readers: the human Moses appears to be winning an argument with God; God is portrayed in terms of emotional character traits such as mercy and compassion, and in the end Moses is allowed to see God's "back parts," though not his face.

Maimonides explains the passage as a philosophical confrontation between Moses and God. In fact, he proves from here that philosophical contemplation about God is the most favored form of religious activity—more valued than conventional expressions of piety such as prayer and fasting (which he refers to here with a measure of perceptible disdain). This was, of course, a claim that would have been challenged by most traditional Jews.

In the biblical passage, Moses asked to know God's ways and God's essence. The "ways" are understood to be the "attributes of action," in the sense of the effects that God has on the world. The use of vocabulary taken from the realm of human personalities is nothing more than a convenient metaphor and does not imply that God possesses a changeable personality or emotional traits.

In Maimonides' version of the story, Moses was vouchsafed a complete knowledge and understanding of the scientific and metaphysical structures of the universe, the highest degree of intellectual knowledge ever attained by a mortal—thereby placing him a step above Aristotle.

Maimonides suggests that the particular attributes that God chose to reveal to Moses were determined by the context of the request, as part of Moses' plea for mercy and guidance for the Israelites after their fall from grace in the incident of the golden calf. The Bible's emphasis on "attributes of mercy" was, accordingly, not necessarily a metaphysically accurate description of God's most important attributes, but a selection of those traits that a political leader should strive hardest to emulate in order to inspire loyalty and good government from his subjects.

What Maimonides is in effect saying here is that the knowledge of God's actions that was divulged to Moses was not chosen because it is necessarily true, but because it is useful for a political leader.

This invites the question: can the same be said about everything else that the Bible tells us about God? Perhaps the theology of the Bible is not factual at all, but merely presents an image of God that is designed to serve the needs of the ruler? This is the implication that would eventually be drawn by Baruch (Benedict) Spinoza in his *Political-Theological Tractate*, and it is easy to understand how it would lead modern interpreters of Maimonides' philosophy to suspect that he had a secret agenda that was heretical and subversive.

The quoted passage deals almost entirely with the first of Moses' requests from God, the one related to God's "ways"; that is, the attributes of action. Elsewhere in the *Guide* Maimonides returns to the matter of "that I may know thee," which he expounded as an entreaty to be allowed to know God's essence. This is the request that was denied to Moses, and it furnishes the scriptural source for Maimonides' doctrine of "negative theology." In this manner Maimonides explains the enigmatic reply that God gave to Moses: "And it shall come to pass, while my glory passeth by, that I will put thee in a cleft of the rock, and will cover thee with my hand while I pass by. And I will take away mine hand, and thou shalt see my back parts: but my face shall not be seen." The "back parts" are the attributes of action, which humans are capable of perceiving through the study of natural science; however God's "face," his positive essence, remains unknowable even to Moses.

Moses Maimonides, Guide of the Perplexed 2:25

> Be aware that our reluctance to advocate a belief in the eternity of the universe does not stem from the fact that it is written in the Torah that

the universe was created. For the passages that suggest creation in time are not more numerous than the passages that indicate that God is corporeal. Furthermore, the gates of interpretation regarding a created universe are not closed or barred to us; on the contrary, we are perfectly capable of reinterpreting the texts just as we did when it came to denying God's corporeality. This might in fact have been much easier and we might have had an easier time explaining those texts in accordance with belief in the eternity of the universe, just as we interpreted various texts and proved that he (may he be exalted) is not corporeal.

However, two reasons impelled us not to do this and not to accept this view:

First, seeing that the incorporeality of God has been demonstrably proven, it is therefore obligatory to reinterpret any text whose literal sense appears to contradict scientific findings. However, the eternity of the universe has not been demonstrably proven. Consequently, it is not fitting to reject the scriptural texts and to reinterpret them on account of a mere theory when there are all sorts of reasons to favor the opposing theory. This is the first reason.

The second reason is that our faith in God's incorporeality does not destroy any of the foundations of the Torah, nor does it contradict the claims of any prophet. It is only the ignorant who believe that it contains a contradiction to the teaching of Scripture. However, in reality we have shown that this is not a contradiction—on the contrary, it is the true meaning of Scripture.

On the other hand, the doctrine of the eternity of the universe as Aristotle envisaged it is deterministic and allows for no changes in nature nor any deviations from the fixed path. It stands in fundamental contradiction to the Torah; it requires us to reject all miracles, and to deny all the promises and threats of the Torah, unless you also reinterpret the miracles, after the manner of the Muslim allegorists—but this would lead to absurd conclusions . . .

However, as long as the theory has not been proven irrefutably, since we do not lean toward this theory nor are we convinced at all by the other theory, we explain the scriptural texts literally and say that the Torah is teaching us something that we are unable to grasp, and miracles provide proof for the correctness of our view.

Comments

The question of whether the universe is eternal was perceived as perhaps the most serious conflict between science and revealed religion in medieval thought (analogous in many ways to the conflict between the Bible and Darwinian evolutionary theory among contemporary Christian fundamentalists). The opening verses of the Torah, as traditionally understood, imply that the universe did not exist until God created it through a series of declarations. Aristotelian science, on the other hand, argued that it is impossible even for God to create something out of nothing, and hence there must have been some sort of primordial matter that has existed from eternity (that is, since the infinite past) and that the creation process involved God shaping that pre-existent matter into a coherent universe.

In a previous discussion in the *Guide of the Perplexed*, Maimonides argued that Aristotle himself had been considerably more cautious and tentative in his approach to this question than was standardly believed. Furthermore, neither the biblical position of "creation out of nothing" nor the opposing doctrine of the eternity of the universe had been irrefutably proven.

In the present passage, Maimonides deals specifically with the alleged conflict between the Bible and science. His position is that in reality this is not a problem at all, since we are never bound to the literal meaning of Scripture. By this point in the *Guide*, Maimonides has already reinterpreted dozens of expressions that, if taken literally, would have suggested that God has a physical body ("corporeality") or human-like emotions. By comparison, it would be a very simple task to reinterpret the creation story in Genesis as referring to the reshaping of primordial matter rather than producing matter out of nothingness. The upshot of all this is that the question must ultimately be determined by solid scientific and philosophical criteria, not by invoking the Bible.

Given that science is unable to determine the question, Maimonides argues that there are serious reasons for preferring the doctrine of creation out of nothing as suggested by the literal text of the Bible. This view conforms better with the general spirit of biblical religion in which God is in full control of the creation and acts in accordance with wisdom and freedom. The Aristotelian God, on the other hand, is a mechanistic concept that is also subject to the inflexible determinism of cause-and-effect.

Maimonides concedes here that if science were to produce an irrefutable proof for the eternity of matter, he would accept it and reinterpret the Bible accordingly. However, we find that elsewhere in his philosophical writings he lays great stress on the doctrine of creation as a central component of Jewish theology, and even declares that a person who rejects that doctrine should be branded as a heretic.

Judah Halevi, *Kuzari*

Judah Halevi (c. 1075–1141) was a Spanish Jewish theologian, poet and physician. His theological masterpiece, the *Kuzari*, takes the literary form of a dialogue between the king of the Khazars and a Jewish rabbi. It is loosely based on an actual historical episode of a Turkic tribe in west Asia whose ruling classes adopted Judaism in the eighth or ninth century. The tenth-century Spanish Jewish courtier Hasdai Ibn Shaprut had initiated a correspondence with the Khazar monarch. Halevi made use of this event to fashion a theological dialogue in which the Khazar king, in his quest to find the best religion, consults with representatives of philosophy, Christianity and Islam, and finally with a rabbi who convinces him of the superiority of Judaism and proceeds to instruct him in its basic doctrines.

Although Halevi was fully adept in philosophical discourse, the thrust of his argument is essentially anti-philosophical. He claims that the theological claims of rationalist theology are flawed, and that the superiority of Judaism can be demonstrated more persuasively by means of historical proofs and miracles. In contrast to the general tendency of rationalist philosophy to stress truths that are universally true, and to portray Judaism as the purest version of that universal truth, Halevi advocates a very particularistic approach according to which the nation of Israel is endowed with a unique divine spark of holiness.

Judah Halevi, Kuzari 1:84–93[5]

The Rabbi:	. . . Since the Torah was given with such miraculous signs, it is incumbent upon all who see them to accept it, for no conceivable doubt can enter the minds of any of them that perhaps they were some act of magic or sleight-of-hand or a trick of the imagination. For, if the splitting of the sea and their passing through it were no more than a figment of their imagination, then so too, their departure from slavery and the deaths of their oppressors, and the taking of the Egyptians' spoils and the leaving of their wealth in their hands also only occurred in their imaginations—and a hypothesis like that is nothing more than the stubbornness of the heretics . . .
The Rabbi:	And after these things, when the Israelites arrived in the wilderness, a barren place, God caused bread to descend to them from the heavens each day, except for the Sabbath day. This bread was unlike any the world had ever known until that time—and they ate it for forty years.
The Khazar:	This sign cannot be refuted either: For the manna continued to come down for six hundred thousand men and all their entourage for forty years. And furthermore, the fact that the manna would come down for the six days of the week, but ceased on the Sabbath day, constitutes a proof that demands that all those who beheld it must agree to observe the Sabbath, upon seeing how a divine quality is attached to the Sabbath.
The Rabbi:	. . . The people did not receive these ten commandments from single individuals, nor from a prophet, but from God; only they did not possess the strength of Moses to withstand the power of the event. Henceforth the people believed that Moses held direct communication with God, that his words were not creations of his own mind, that prophecy did not

(as philosophers assume) burst forth in a refined soul, become united with the Active Intellect (also termed Holy Spirit or Gabriel) and be then inspired. They did not believe that Moses had seen a vision while sleeping, or that someone had spoken with him between sleeping and waking, so that he only heard the words in his imagination, but not with his ears; that he saw a phantom, and afterwards pretended that God had spoken with him. Faced with such an impressive experience, all notions of trickery vanished. The divine admonition was followed by the divine writing. For God inscribed these Ten Words on two tablets of precious stone and handed them to Moses. The people saw the divine writing, as they had heard the divine words. Moses made an ark in accordance with God's command, and built the tent over it. It remained among the Israelites for as long as prophecy lasted—that is to say, about nine hundred years, until the people became disobedient. Then the ark was hidden, and Nebuchadnezzar conquered and drove the Israelites into exile.

The Khazar: Should any one hear you relate that God spoke with your assembled multitude, and wrote tables for you, etc., he would be blamed for accusing you of holding the theory of anthropomorphism. You, on the other hand, are free from blame, because this grand and lofty spectacle, seen by thousands, cannot be denied. You are justified in rejecting [the charge of being] mere reasoning and speculation.

Comments

This exchange between the Jewish sage and the Khazar king consists largely of a straightforward retelling of the biblical story of the revelation on Mount Sinai and the giving of the Torah to the children of Israel. For the philosophers, such events were best viewed as symbolic accounts of an intellectual encounter between God and humans. For Judah Halevi, the exact opposite is the case: the importance of this event lies precisely in its historicity.

Halevi's rabbi is arguing that the historical claim underlying the revelation of the Torah at Mount Sinai is more credible than those of the rival theories or religions, in that it is founded on an event that was accompanied by manifest miracles, an event that was publicly witnessed by the entire Israelite nation consisting of hundreds of thousands of individuals, and subsequently verified by a consensus of tradition as well as by physical artifacts. Other religions were based on the visions and experiences of individual prophets, experiences that, by their nature, cannot be verified. Although the prophet Moses did of course take a more central part in the revelation of the Ten Commandments and the Torah at Mount Sinai, it was

God himself who spoke to the people with Moses only being brought in as an intermediary when the people could no longer withstand the intensely fearsome experience of divine communication.

For similar reasons Judah Halevi rejects the Aristotelian reinterpretation of prophecy as understood by philosophers such as Maimonides. The rationalists portrayed the prophets as accomplished philosophers, individuals who followed a regimen of intellectual self-improvement that led them to a stage of refined abstract thinking that allowed their "potential intellect" to link with the "Absolute Intellect," that is, the lowest of the "separate intelligences" emanating from God. This is what allows them to partake of a higher level of metaphysical knowledge, which is then communicated, via their faculty of imagination, to their community. In their attempts to harmonize these doctrines with the biblical traditions, the philosophers equated the Active Intellect with the scriptural images of the "Holy Spirit" (which is usually associated with prophetic revelation) or the angel Gabriel.

Halevi correctly shows that the Biblical text contains no hint that the prophet has undergone any such intellectual training. Quite the contrary, it is God who initiates the revelatory process, and the prophet is merely a passive receptacle. The vague kind of ecstatic mystical experience that accompanies philosophical meditation bears no resemblance to the clear and specific message that was broadcast to the Israelite people at Mount Sinai.

Judah Halevi, Kuzari 1:84–93 *(continued)*

The Rabbi: Heaven forbid that I should assume what is against sense and reason! The first of the Ten Commandments enjoins the belief in divine providence. The second commandment contains the prohibition of worshipping other gods, or the association of any being with God, the prohibition to represent him in statues, forms and images, or any personification of him. How should we not deem him exalted above any personification, since we do so with many of his creations, such as the human soul, which represents man's true essence. For that part of Moses which spoke to us, taught and guided us, was not his tongue, or heart, or brain. Those were only organs, whilst Moses himself is the intellectual, discriminating, incorporeal soul, not limited by place, neither too large, nor too small for any space in order to contain the images of all creatures.

    If we ascribe spiritual elements to it, how much more must we do so to the creator of all things? We must not, however, endeavor to reject the conclusions that are drawn from revelation. We say, then, that we do not know how the intention became corporealized and how there evolved a speech that struck our ear, nor what novel thing God created out of nothing, nor what existing thing he employed for the purpose.

He does not lack the power to do this. We say that he created the two tablets, engraved a text on them, in the same way as he created the heavens and the stars by means of his will alone. God desired it, and they became concrete as he wished it, engraved with the text of the Ten Commandments. We also assert that he divided the sea and formed it into two walls, which he caused to stand on the right and on the left of the people, for whom he made convenient wide roads and a smooth ground for them to walk on without any fear or trouble. This rending, constructing and arranging, are attributed to God, who required no tool or intermediary, as would be necessary for human toil. As the water stood at his command and shaped itself at his will, so the air that touched the prophet's ear assumed the form of sounds, which conveyed the matters that needed to be communicated by God to the prophet and the people.

The Khazar: This representation is satisfactory.

Comments

After belittling the importance of philosophical speculation as a source of religious authority, Halevi feels obliged to assert that the Torah should not be regarded as irrational or in opposition to the truths of science or philosophy. Like the most refined philosophical theology, the Ten Commandments proclaim the unity of God and forbid anthropomorphic representations of his image or nature. In fact, the prophetic faculty that was found in Moses was of a higher spiritual level than the mere intellect which is, after all, a function of the human body.

This raises the question of how God was able to communicate by means of audible speech, since speech is a physical faculty grounded in the biological makeup of the human body. Therefore Halevi explains that what Moses and others heard was a special audible entity that the omnipotent God created for the purpose.

Abraham Isaac Hakohen Kook

Rabbi Abraham Isaac Hakohen Kook (1865–1935) was born in Latvia and settled in the Land of Israel where he emerged as the most prominent Orthodox champion of the (largely secular) Zionist movement that was trying to create a Jewish national home. The British mandatory authorities appointed him to serve as the Palestine's first Ashkenazic Chief Rabbi. In his voluminous writings and in his activities, Rabbi Kook produced a remarkable synthesis of diverse streams in Jewish philosophy, mysticism and religion that absorbed contemporary European intellectual currents, especially those that were committed to a progressive understanding of history. Nurtured by traditional and kabbalistic eschatological imagery, Rabbi Kook was convinced that the Jewish people, in realizing their own national and spiritual renewals, were also spearheading an age of universal spiritual enlightenment.

Rabbi Abraham Isaac Hakohen Kook: Iggerot Ra'Ia"H 2:19

The theory of evolution

The theory of evolution, which is currently emerging triumphant, is in harmony with the kabbalistic mysteries of the universe, more so than any other philosophical theories.

Evolution, which follows a trajectory of improvement, posits an optimistic foundation to the world, for how is it possible to despair when we see that everything is evolving and progressing? When we penetrate to the essence of the foundation of progressive evolution, we find in it that the divine element is illuminated with absolute clarity, as it is precisely the Infinite [*Ein Sof*] that is bringing into actuality what is infinite in potential.

Evolution casts light on all the ways of the Lord. All of existence is progressively evolving, as can be discerned in segments of it; and this elevation is of a general as well as an individual character. It rises upward to the apex of the absolute Good. It is understood that the Good and the universal are joined together, and that reality is destined to reach that state when it will absorb in its entirety all the goodness that lies in its parts, and this is its universal elevation, that no individual detail will be excluded from it, no spark will be lost from the bundle, everything is prepared for the feast.

For this purpose it is necessary that the spirit be enhanced toward the supreme divine desire which is fashioned by means of faithful worship of the Lord.

Comments

Unlike many other modern traditionalists, Rabbi Kook was not terribly concerned about the contradictions between Charles Darwin's theory of biological evolution and the biblical account of creation. He was more impressed by the similarity between evolutionary theory and the generally optimistic dynamic of Jewish historical and eschatological thought, especially from the perspective of kabbalistic hermeneutics that deal with the deeper, hidden dynamics of creation and redemption. Properly understood, evolution presents us with a picture of a universe that is constantly improving itself until it reaches a state of perfection. That picture constitutes a reflection (in the realm of biology) of the Jewish mystical ideal of spiritual progress. Of course, in drawing this comparison, Kook was rejecting the impersonal, value-free character of the Darwinian theory.

Rabbi Abraham Isaac Hakohen Kook: from Ḥazon Ha-Ge'ulah

[From: The Resurrection of Israel]

Of immeasurable beauty is the ideal of the establishment of the chosen nation, a kingdom of priests and a holy people, from out of a nation that was immersed in a terrible enslavement, for whom the ancestral gems of its native stock illuminate its darkness. The ideal resides in the divine heights in the concealment of the mystery of its purity. It must take on substance, wrap itself up in a specific structure, with human beings who possess both good and bad urges, in societies that require sustenance and an economy, the cultivation of the soil and administration of a government. Their collective life must comprise everything, from the supreme apex of the pure of spirit and the most refined souls, down to the lowest depths of rough-hewn souls, who are destined for the humble activities of the lowliest aspects of life, bleary eyes of the flesh who have lost all their sparkle. And then the spiritual aspects are subjected to and become darkened by the gloom of life, which is replete with dungheaps and garbage; from this direction, humanity is able to influence its members in only a limited manner, as indignities exceed graciousness and nobility—lowly carnal wickedness and darkness, which is the source of the evil of liberalism.

When individual nationalism donned weekday profane garments that are as coarse as sackcloth, it also descended from its heights, and in Israel it became so faulty that it ceased to function altogether. And the only surviving remnant is the apex of the uppermost picture, in the hiding-place of the ideal of the establishment of the nation in the uppermost levels of the strength of its purity. From the heights of this strength, the waves of light can descend and return in the guise of resurrecting dewdrops, to restore the tottering structure to its original expansive breadth. This supreme celestial model has the potential to restore to life all the profane garments, when they draw nourishment from it.

However, if a person in that fallen and unsightly condition should decide to adhere only to the material forms of nationalism, without inner illumination from the primordial supernal light, he will quickly absorb the spirit of impurity, of pettiness and the sparks of wickedness, which will turn into a bitter fruit within the space of a few generations of historical development. This is the vision of nationalist evil that we are encountering.

Comments

The typically flowery language and convoluted syntax of Rabbi Kook's Hebrew make it difficult to provide a clear or precise translation of the text; however, the general argument is quite clear. He is contrasting his ideal of

Jewish nationalism, as he envisions its imminent restoration on Israel's native soil, with two other options that he rejects.

At one extreme is the typical Jewish pattern of life that developed during the era of exile, in which Judaism achieved only partial expression through spiritual, ritual and "religious" matters, but in which the ideals of the Torah were not being applied to the full range of social, political and economic issues, or addressing the simple, unscholarly masses.

At the other extreme is the purely secular brand of nationalism that is not inspired by the religious and ethical ideals of the Torah. This degenerates into a soulless, and possibly immoral, political ideology.

Rabbi Kook's vision is of a robust society that will be governed according to divine ideals, in which the Torah will provide guidance for all aspects of day-to-day life, and which will offer inspiration to all the nations of the world. This was the vision that he strove to instill in the Zionist movement of his own day.

6   Esoteric, mystical and kabbalistic texts

Mishnah Ḥagigah 2:1

The laws of incest may not be expounded before three persons,
   nor the account of the creation before two,
   nor the chariot before one
   unless the person is wise and able to understand on his own.
Anyone who meditates upon four things, it would be preferable for them if they had not come into the world:

what is above
what is below
what is before
and what is after.

And anyone who has no regard for the honor of their Creator, it would be preferable for them if they had not come into the world.

Comments

The Mishnah prohibits the public teaching of any of the topics mentioned here; instruction must be restricted to a limited number of students. The reasons for these restrictions are not stated, and they may not be the same for all the cases. As regards the laws of incest (presumably, the exposition of passages such as Leviticus Chapter 18 that contains a detailed list of relations whom it is forbidden to marry), the Talmud suggests that the nature of the topic might encourage inappropriate sexual thoughts among unsupervised students.

The "account of the creation" refers to the opening chapter of Genesis, and the worry is probably that it might lead to speculation concerning sensitive theological and cosmological questions about the creation process (such as, whether or not there existed some sort of preexistent primal matter out of which God fashioned the universe).

The account of the "chariot" consists of a tradition of expounding the opening chapters of Ezekiel, in which the prophet experienced a powerful and mysterious vision of angels in the form of a chariot that was drawn by fantastic beasts and which bore a throne on which was seated a human-like figure. This (along with other biblical passages such as Isaiah Chapter 6) contains the Bible's most graphic description of the highest heavenly realms. The author of this Mishnah may feel that such intimate familiarity with the divine should be discouraged because it is disrespectful of the "honor of their Creator." Other traditions (as you will read below) express a fear that involvement in such experiences could be perilous to one's sanity, faith, or even to one's life.

Tosefta *Ḥagigah* 2:2[1]

Once Rabban Yoḥanan ben Zakkai was riding on a donkey,
and Rabbi Eleazar ben 'Arakh was driving the donkey behind him.

He said to him: Rabbi, teach me one lesson in the account of the chariot.

He said to him: Have I not told you previously that the account of the chariot is not to be expounded before one person unless the person is wise and able to understand on his own?

He said to him: Hence I shall expound before you.

He said to him: Speak!

Rabbi Eleazar ben 'Arakh commenced expounding the account of the chariot.

Rabban Yoḥanan ben Zakkai alighted from the donkey and wrapped himself in his robe.

And the two of them seated themselves on a rock under an olive tree, while he expounded before him.

He stood up and kissed him on his head, and he said to him: Blessed is the Lord God of Israel who has given to our father Abraham such a one who knows how to expound and understand for the sake of the honor of his father in heaven. There are those who can expound beautifully but not fulfill beautifully; and those who can fulfill beautifully, but not expound beautifully. How fortunate are you, our father Abraham, that Eleazar ben 'Arakh issued from your loins, who knows how to understand and to expound for the sake of the honor of his father in heaven.

Babylonian Talmud *Ḥagigah* 14b

Our Rabbis taught:

Once Rabban Yoḥanan ben Zakkai was riding on a donkey,
and Rabbi Eleazar ben 'Arakh was driving the donkey behind him.

He said to him: Rabbi, teach me one lesson in the account of the chariot.

He said to him: Have I not told you previously that the Account of the Chariot is not expounded before one person unless the person is wise and able to understand on his own!

He said to him: Rabbi, permit me to say before you something which you taught me.

He said to him: Speak!

Immediately Rabban Yoḥanan ben Zakkai alighted from his donkey and wrapped himself up, and he seated himself on a rock under an olive tree.

He asked him: Rabbi, why did you alight from the donkey?

He said: Is it possible that you should be expounding on the account of the chariot, and the divine presence is among us, and the ministering angels are accompanying us—and I should be riding on a donkey!

Immediately, Rabbi Eleazar ben ʻArakh began the Account of the Chariot

and he expounded, and a flame descended from heaven and encompassed all the trees in the field. All broke out in song.

Which song did they utter?—"Praise the Lord from the earth, ye sea-monsters, and all deeps . . . fruitful trees and all cedars . . . Hallelujah" (Psalms 148:7, 9, 14).

An angel answered from the flame and said: This indeed is the account of the chariot!

Rabban Yoḥanan ben Zakkai stood up and kissed him on his head, and said to him: Blessed is the Lord God of Israel who has given to our father Abraham such a one who knows how to expound and understand for the sake of the honor of his father in heaven.

There are those who can expound beautifully but not fulfill beautifully; and those who can fulfill beautifully, but not expound beautifully. How fortunate are you, our father Abraham, that Eleazar ben ʻArakh issued from your loins.

And when these things were related before Rabbi Joshua, he and Rabbi Yosé the Priest were walking on the way.

They said: We too shall expound the account of the chariot.

Rabbi Joshua commenced his exposition.

And that day was a midsummer day. The heavens became filled with clouds, and there was an appearance like a rainbow in a cloud. And the ministering angels gathered together and came to see the rejoicing of the bride and bridegroom.

Rabbi Yosé the Priest went and related these things before Rabban Yoḥanan ben Zakkai.

And he said: Fortunate are you and fortunate are those who bore you, and fortunate are my eyes that have beheld this! Even you and I, in my dream, were reclining together on Mount Sinai, and a heavenly voice issued from the sky: Rise up to here, rise up to here! Great banquet halls and beautiful couches have been laid out for you, and you and your disciples and your disciples' disciples are assigned to the third section.

Comments

The two preceding texts are clearly alternate versions of the same original tradition and of the same event from the late first century. The Tosefta (edited in the early third century CE) is the earliest version and the Babylonian Talmud (finalized in the sixth or seventh century) is the latest. A comparison of the two texts provides us with an instructive example of how the traditions became expanded as they were transmitted and retold over the generations. The Tosefta tells a very cryptic story in which the content of Rabbi Eleazar's exposition is not revealed, and the praises of that exposition are known only from Rabban Yoḥanan's enthusiastic response that stresses Eleazar's concern for preserving God's "honor," likely by not elaborating the chariot vision in extensive detail.

The Talmud's version, on the other hand, is replete with supernatural and miraculous motifs: heavenly flames, angelic declarations and the sudden appearance of clouds and a rainbow in the summer sky. Thus, the later version is explicitly mystical in a way that cannot be said about the earlier one.

While academic historical scholars would normally give more credence to the shorter, earlier versions of such stories, it is clear that subsequent Jewish religious tradition accepted the elaborate account that was preserved in the authoritative Babylonian Talmud.

Tosefta Ḥagigah 2:3–4

Four entered the orchard: Ben 'Azzai and Ben Zoma and the Other and Rabbi 'Akiva.

One peeked and died.
One peeked and was injured.
One peeked and chopped down the plants.
And one went up safely and came down safely.

Ben Azzai peeked and died. Concerning him scripture says: "Precious in the sight of the Lord [is] the death of his saints" (Psalms 116:15).

Ben Zoma peeked and was injured. Concerning him scripture says: "Hast thou found honey? Eat so much as is sufficient for thee, lest thou be filled therewith, and vomit it" (Proverbs 25:16).

Elisha peeked and chopped down the plants. Concerning him scripture says: "Suffer not thy mouth to cause thy flesh to sin; neither say thou before the angel, that it was an error: wherefore should God be angry at thy voice, and destroy the work of thine hands?" (Ecclesiastes 5:5).

And Rabbi Akiva went up safely and came down safely. Concerning him scripture says: "Draw me, we will run after thee: the king hath brought me into his chambers: we will be glad and rejoice in thee, we will remember thy love more than wine: the upright love thee" (Song of Songs 1:4).

To what is this analogous?—To a king who owned an orchard, over which was built an upper chamber. What may a person do? He may peek, provided that his eye does not linger upon it.

Comments

This story, which is also found in an expanded version in the Babylonian Talmud, is an important source for the idea that the restrictions associated with the public teaching of the account of the chariot (as in the Mishnah cited above) were based on the fear that such involvements could prove spiritually dangerous and must be pursued very cautiously, as did Rabbi Akiva. The four rabbis were contemporaries (from the "generation of Yavneh" in the late first or early second century). It is not clear whether they were actually involved in some sort of shared enterprise, or whether the author of the text is comparing four independent and separate stories.

The image of entry into the orchard (or vineyard) is a parable, as stated later in the passage, for involvement in esoteric studies, portrayed as the eating of the king's fruits. The image implies that there is something illicit in the activity, as the protagonists have to climb a well to get into the protected garden, rather than openly walking in through the gate.

The Hebrew word for "orchard" is *pardes*, related to the English word "paradise" (from an original Persian word). Indeed, Rashi's commentary to the Talmud rendered the word as "Garden of Eden," the afterlife abode of the righteous according to rabbinic belief. Although that interpretation became the dominant one in later Jewish mystical discourse, it is hard to justify it according to ancient Hebrew usage.

The sources provide no precise explanation for the circumstances of Ben Azzai's death. On the other hand, the Talmud contains several stories, cryptic though they might be, suggesting that Ben Zoma's "injury" consisted of some sort of madness. The chopping down of the plants by "the Other" (still in keeping with the orchard parable) is a metaphor for heresy; talmudic literature speaks in elaborate detail of how Elisha ben Abuya became a heretic who rejected the fundamental beliefs of Judaism and the Torah, abandoned Jewish practice and became a collaborator with the Romans. For this reason, the rabbinic tradition stopped referring to him by name and employed instead the epithet "the Other."

"*Heikhalot*" mysticism

From Heikhalot Rabbati (MS Budapest 238)[2]

Said Rabbi Ishmael: When you come and stand at the entrance of the first palace, take hold of two seals in both your hands: One for Tutrusiai-Lord, and one for Soveria the prince of the countenance. Show that of Tutrusiai-Lord to those who are standing on the right. And that of

Soveria the prince of the countenance show to those who are standing on the left.

Immediately Rahaviel the prince, who is the chief of the entrance of the first palace and is in charge of the first palace, who stands to the right of the lintel, and with him Tohafiel the prince who stands to the left of the lintel, seize you, one from your right side and one from your left side, until they conduct you and hand you over and issue a warning about you to Tagriel the prince who is the chief of the second palace and stands to the right of the lintel, and with him is Matpiel the prince who stands to the left of the lintel.

And show them two seals: one of Ahriharon-Lord, and one of Uzhiya the prince of the countenance. That of Adriharon-Lord show to those who stand to the right; and that of Uzhiya the prince of the countenance show to those who stand on the left.

Immediately they seize you, one from your right and one from your left, until they lead you and hand you over and issue a warning about you to Shaburiel the prince who is the chief of the gate of the third palace and stands to the right of the lintel, and with him is Rasisiel the prince who stands to the left of the lintel . . .

. . . And show them two seals: One of Totraviel-Lord, and one of Zahapnuriai the prince of the countenance. That of Totraviel-Lord show to those who are standing to the right; and that of Zahapnuriai the prince of the countenance show to those who are standing at the left.

Immediately, they seize you and lead you, three princes in front of you and three princes behind you. And (perhaps) [as they go?].

Because the guards of the entrance of the sixth palace would destroy those who go down to the chariot; and not those who go down in the chariot without permission. And they command them and strike them and burn them and set others in their place. And also the others who stand in their stead, such is their manner, that they are not afraid, nor does it occur to them to say: Why are we being burned, and what benefit do we derive that we destroy those who go down to the chariot and not those who go down to the chariot without permission. And this is still the manner of the guardians of the entrance of the sixth palace . . .

. . . And we asked of him [Rabbi Ishmael]: What is the meaning of "those who go down to the chariot and not those who go down to the chariot"? And he said to us: These are people whom those who go down to the chariot would take, and have them stand over them, or they seat them in front of them, and tell them "Watch and see and listen and write everything that we say and everything that we hear from before the throne of glory." And those people are not worthy. For this reason the guardians of the sixth gate would injure them. Be careful to select suitable people; and they are from among the tested comrades.

When you come and stand at the entrance of the sixth palace, show three seals of the guardians of the entrance of the sixth palace: Two for Qaspiel the prince whose sword was unsheathed in his hand, and they would cause grief and there would issue from it lightning. And he would incite it against anyone who is not worthy to gaze upon the King and his throne. And no creature resists him. And his sword was unsheathed, calling and saying everything. And he stands at the right lintel . . .

And when the guardians of the entrance to the seventh palace would behold Romiel and Qaspiel and Gabriel coming before the wagon of that man who was deserving to go down to the chariot, they would cover their faces and sit, for they were incensed. And they stand and loosen the taut bows and return their gleaming swords to their sheaths. Nevertheless, it is necessary to show them the great seal, and the awesome crown Taram and Barmanogaiah and Ba'atpatish-Lord-God-of-Israel. And they would enter before his throne of glory, and take out for him all sorts of musical instruments and song, and they would make music, and come before him until they lift him up and seat him next to the Cherubs and next to the Ophanim and next to the Holy Living Things. And he beholds wonders and mighty things and pride and greatness, holiness and purity, terror, humility and uprightness at the same time.

Comments

The selections brought here, describing the ascents to the first two and last two "palaces," should suffice to convey the prevailing mood of the mystical ascents through the palaces. The paragraphs describing the lower palaces are almost all identical, with only the names of the angels varying. The meanings of these names are not easy to reconstruct, and it is generally assumed that the texts have become corrupted in the course of their transmission in manuscript. Like many ancient magical amulets and papyri, these names incorporate Hebrew, Greek and perhaps other linguistic elements. Thus, a name such as "Tutrusiai" is probably related to tetra, Greek for "four," perhaps as an allusion to the four-letter name of God (Tetragrammaton) or the fourfold creatures who drew Ezekiel's chariot. Qaspiel means "wrath of God," and "Romiel" "the elevation of God," and so forth. "Ba'atpatish" apparently means "the hammer struck," an interesting name for a gate-keeper. Those names in which I have translated the word "Lord" actually contain the Tetragrammaton, the four-letter divine name which Jews consider too holy to pronounce. The horrifying angels of the sixth level are actually temporary beings who are burned and replaced daily, in keeping with a talmudic belief. The angels who populate the seventh level are the same ones who appear in Ezekiel's chariot vision. To reach that level was the ultimate goal of the ascent.

It should be emphasized that within the broader context of Heikhalot Rabbati the ascent through the palaces is not depicted as a mystical quest for its own sake. Rather, it has an urgent purpose occasioned by reports of a terrible persecution that is about to befall the Jewish community, in which a group of celebrated and saintly teachers are about to be martyred at the hands of the Romans. (This framework story of the "Ten Imperial Martyrs" is loosely based on the events of the Hadrianic persecutions in the second century, though several of its particulars are not historically accurate.) In this connection, the Jewish sages are anxious to approach God in order to beseech him to cancel the decree, or at least to provide an explanation of why righteous people will be subjected to such an appalling fate. At the conclusion of the story, Rabbi Ishmael does not succeed in averting the decree.

In spite of the text's narrative framework, the story contains several fascinating indications of how these mystical journeys were conducted in real life. Of particular importance is the statement about "those who go down to the chariot and not those who go down to the chariot." From that paragraph we can apparently infer that the mystics were organized into fellowships of "comrades," circles of devotees in which experienced masters were grouped together with their disciples. As the mystic entered his trance (this appears to be what was happening on the visible plane), trained disciples were assigned to carefully record what the mystic was saying, as well as the words that the mystic was hearing from the throne of glory! The role of the secretary is viewed as an extremely momentous responsibility, and requires moral and spiritual qualifications that are comparable to those of the actual mystics. It is reasonable to suppose that the notes that were recorded by those mystical secretaries provided the original basis for what was later organized into the Heikhalot literature.

Kabbalah and the symbolism of the ten *sefirot*

It is impossible to understand kabbalistic texts such as the *Bahir*, the *Zohar* or the teachings of Isaac Luria without first introducing ourselves to the defining feature of the Kabbalah, the doctrine of the ten *sefirot* (singular: *sefirah*). In the *Bahir* as in other classic kabbalistic works, the *sefirot* are not discussed explicitly, and the word makes only the rarest of appearances. The structure and symbolism of the *sefirot* are, however, presupposed, and the ostensible midrashic exposition seems like a chaotic and unconnected joining together of biblical quotations, until we fill in the intricate associations and symbolic motifs that relate them to the system of *sefirot*.

The *sefirot* have names taken from familiar descriptions of God that appear frequently in the Bible, liturgy and other traditional texts, names such as: Wise, Understanding, Glorious, Just, and so forth. However, in non-kabbalistic discourse, these words are mere adjectives that describe God. In the kabbalistic usage, on the other hand, each *sefirah* is a distinct

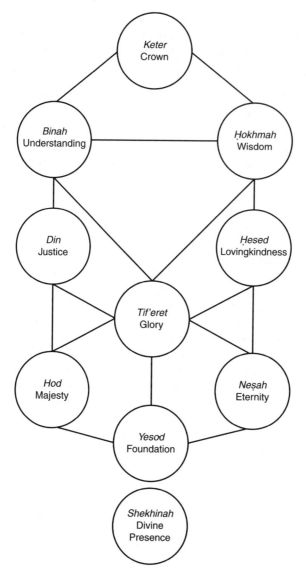

Figure 6.1 The ten *sefirot*.

and separate metaphysical entity that is capable of interacting with the other *sefirot* or with the world. For the kabbalist, virtually every word in the Bible may be identified with one or other of the *sefirot*. Innocent-looking nouns such as "water," "silver" or "hand" are all candidates for this kind of interpretation. The upshot of this method is that, though the kabbalist and non-kabbalist are reading precisely the same scripture, they are understanding it in completely different ways. For the kabbalist, the Bible is nothing less than a carefully coded account of the metaphysical unfolding of the universe.

Thus, names of God are assigned to different *sefirot*. Other symbolic motifs involve male and female, parents and children, mercy and justice. The *sefirot* are also perceived as constituting a series of channels through which divine benevolence flows down to the earthly world and through which mortals can influence the celestial realms.

There are many terms and elements in the kabbalistic symbolism that originated in biblical and rabbinic writings. For example, the tension between the loving, compassionate God and the fearsome God of justice and vengeance is integral to the Bible; and rabbinic literature created a special conceptual vocabulary in order to distinguish between God's "standard of justice" and "standard of mercy." Unique to the kabbalistic symbolic structures is its fascination with erotic and sexual imagery. This aspect sets it apart from virtually every other version of traditional Judaism from the Bible onwards, where God is depicted almost without exception in masculine language, though to be sure, the rationalists insisted that none of this language should be understood literally when applied to an incorporeal deity. Kabbalistic imagery depicts a group of *sefirot* as constituting a single male figure whose core is the *sefirah* "Tif'eret" who is usually portrayed as a king, prince or bridegroom. The object of his affections is the tenth *sefirah*, the Shekhinah, who appears as a princess. The romantic longing between the prince and princess is never consummated, a tragic situation that serves as a celestial reflection of the state of disorientation and exile in which medieval Jews found themselves, an anomalous existence defined by their exile from their homeland and their inability to worship in the proper manner at the Jerusalem Temple.

The term "Shekhinah" [presence] is derived from the rabbinic vocabulary, where it was employed initially as an abstract noun that reflected how the omnipresent God, whose glory fills the universe, could nevertheless be associated with specific localities, such as the Temple or a community of worshippers or students of Torah. Talmudic and midrashic sources, maintaining a respectful distance between God and the created world, preferred to employ a circumlocution, speaking of God's presence (rather than God himself) dwelling or acting in the world. Although the Hebrew word "Shekhinah" is grammatically feminine (all Hebrew nouns must be either masculine or feminine), this fact did not usually affect the metaphoric usage of the term in rabbinic sources.

The kabbalistic Shekhinah incorporated several motifs from biblical and rabbinic religion. The ancient prophets often described the covenant between God and the Jewish people as a marriage, with God as the husband and Israel as the wife. A sensuous volume of love poetry, the Song of Songs, was included in the Hebrew Bible because it was interpreted as such a metaphor. The imagery of the Song of Songs, understood as an account of the turbulent relationship between God and the Shekhinah, figures prominently in the writings of the kabbalists.

Sefer Ha-Bahir

The *Sefer ha-Bahir* ("book of brightness") was known to many medievals as "the Midrash of Rabbi Nehunya ben ha-Kanah," and indeed this brief and enigmatic volume imitates the features of a midrashic exposition from the talmudic era. In the manner of ancient rabbinic works, it assembles teachings in the names of diverse rabbis. There was a real Rabbi Nehunya who is cited in the Mishnah and Talmud, but the words ascribed to him in the *Bahir* are clearly pseudepigraphic. It is the earliest known kabbalistic work in the sense that it is based on the doctrine of the ten *sefirot*. Although there are some tantalizing hints that elements of the *Bahir*'s teachings can be traced or linked to similar trends in Jewish and non-Jewish religious milieus, it is as yet impossible to speak with any degree of certainty about its sources or influences.

Sefer Ha-Bahir *34ff.*[3]

> Rabbi Berakhiah's disciples asked him: Let us present our words before you.
> He did not give them permission.
> On another occasion he gave them permission. And he did what he did in order to test them, as to whether they had the proper concentration [or: whether they could come to the correct interpretation by themselves].
> One day he tested them. He said to them: Let me hear your wisdom.
> They commenced and said:
> "In the beginning" (Genesis 1:1)—One.
> "For the spirit should fail before me, and the souls which I have made" (Isaiah 57:16).
> "The *peleg* of God, which is full of water" (Psalms 65:10).
> What is the *peleg* of God?—Thus did you teach us, our master, that the Holy One took from the primordial waters and divided them, and placed half of them in the firmament and half of them in the ocean. This is what is written "the *peleg* of God, which is full of water" [*peleg* means "divide"]. And it is by means of them that a person learns Torah, as the master has said: by virtue of acts of lovingkindness a person learns Torah; as it says "Ho, every one that thirsteth, come ye to the waters, and he that hath no money; come ye, buy, and eat; yea, come, buy wine and milk without money and without price" (Isaiah 55:1).
> Another interpretation: He that hath no money, go to him, because he has money; as it is written "The silver is mine, and the gold is mine" (Haggai 2:8).

What is "The silver is mine, and the gold is mine"?—This can be illustrated through a parable about a king who had two treasures, one of silver and one of gold. He placed the silver one in his right hand and the gold one in his left. He said: this will be readily available for spending.

He acts mildly, and he will cleave to the poor and lead them mildly. This is what is written: "Thy right hand, O Lord, is become glorious in power" (Exodus 15:6). And if he is satisfied with his lot, then it is good. And if he is not, then: "thy right hand, O Lord, hath dashed in pieces the enemy."

What is "thy right hand, O Lord, hath dashed in pieces the enemy"?— He said to him: this is gold, as it is written "the silver is mine, and the gold is mine."

And why is gold called *ZaHaB*?—Because in it are included three qualities:

[1] The masculine [*Zakhar*], which is the *Z*;

[2] the soul [*Neshamah*], which is *H*. And the soul has five names: spirit, living, single, soul, life. [The Hebrew letter *H* has the numerological value of five.] And what is its function?—The *H* serves as a throne for the *Z*; as it is written "for he that is higher than the highest guardeth" (Ecclesiastes 5:7).

[3] And *B* is their existence, as you say "In the beginning" [Hebrew: *bereshit*] (Genesis 1:1). And what is its function here? It may be illustrated by means of a parable about a king who had a daughter who was good and fair and pleasant and perfect, and he gave her in marriage to a prince, and he dressed her and placed a crown upon her and placed ornaments upon her and gave her to him for an immense sum.

Is it possible for this king to remain apart from his daughter? You say: No.

Is it possible for him to remain constantly with her all day? You say: No.

What is the solution?—He placed a window between himself and her, and at any time that the daughter needed her father, or the father needed his daughter, they would communicate through the window. This is what is written "The king's daughter is all glorious within; her clothing is of wrought gold" (Psalms 45:14).

COMMENTS

The external narrative structure of this passage resembles that of a typical talmudic exchange between a master and his disciples. There was an actual Rabbi Berakhiah who was cited frequently in midrashic literature as a prominent homilist; however, the figure of that name who appears in the

Sefer Ha-Bahir is clearly offering teachings that would not have been imagined by the original Rabbi Berakhiah.

The concern that the students should be self-motivated and capable of pursuing their studies independently is reminiscent of the conditions set by the Talmud for transmitting "chapter headings" of the account of the chariot to select individual students.

The content of this exposition strikes us as rather incoherent. While the untrained reader might sense some logical connections and verbal affinities between the various biblical quotations and parables that are being strung together, it is impossible to arrive at any meaningful understanding of the discourse without prior knowledge of the symbolic system that is being simultaneously presupposed and delineated.

The three verses that are cited by the disciples at the beginning of their discourse are understood as allusions to three distinct manifestations of the divine "*sefirot*." The Hebrew word *bereshit*, the opening word of the Torah, normally translated as an adverbial phrase "in the beginning" or "when at first," was read by the kabbalists as a noun referring to the *sefirah* of Wisdom (*Ḥokhmah*), based on the phrase "*The fear of the Lord is the beginning of wisdom*" in Proverbs 9:10. The "soul" in the Isaiah verse was understood as the *sefirah* of Understanding (*Binah*). The *peleg* of God in the Psalms verse was understood to refer to the *sefirah* of lovingkindness (*Ḥesed*), or to the metaphysical division of reality between poles of Lovingkindness and strict Justice (the *sefirah* of *Din* or *Gevurah*). What we have here is a remarkable reading of the biblical creation story in which the words of the Hebrew text are not referring to the creation of the *physical* world, but rather to the emanation of metaphysical powers that issue from the unknowable God.

With this basic symbolic structure in mind, we may now proceed to explain how the *Bahir* expounded the Psalms verse. The unusual expression "*peleg* of God," usually understood as a river, is interpreted here according to a different meaning of the Hebrew root: divide. Similarly, the word "God," which is the usual English rendering of the Hebrew *Elohim*, is associated in kabbalistic symbolism with the *sefirah* of Understanding.

Accordingly, the *Bahir* is describing how the primordial "waters" of the divine creative powers flowed down from Wisdom and through Understanding into Lovingkindness, from which they were subsequently divided among two lower *sefirot* that are represented as the "firmament" and the "ocean." The *sefirah* of Lovingkindness brings generosity and abundance into the lower realms. One of the central motifs of kabbalistic symbolism is that the channels through which the divine "waters" flow must be kept in a state of harmonious union, which is achieved by following a pious religious life. Otherwise, sin causes the channels to become broken and clogged, obstructing the flow of the beneficial influences down to our world. One of the benefits of the divine Lovingkindness is that it gives humans the spiritual insight necessary for a proper understanding of the Torah. This lesson is derived from Isaiah 55:1 in which (according to an old rabbinic interpretation) water is used as an image for religious teaching.

Isaiah's imagery of purchasing food and drink with money (in Hebrew, the word for money is the same as the one for silver) leads the *Bahir* to an exposition of the verse in Haggai. The discussion was apparently sparked by the unstated question of why silver is mentioned before gold in the verse though it is less valuable. Underlying the solution is the symbolic identification of silver with the *sefirah* of Lovingkindness and gold with that of divine Judgment. The point is illustrated, as happens so often in the *Bahir*, with the help of a parable. The parable, a simple fable in which the relationships between the characters are employed in order to convey more general truths, is one of the favorite literary and didactic devices of midrashic literature. The great majority of the midrashic parables are about kings, who always represent God; while the people of Israel are portrayed as the king's wife, beloved, son or daughter. The *Bahir*'s parable is thus fully consistent with its attempt to imitate an ancient rabbinic text.

If we accept these premises (and, it might be argued by the kabbalists, *only* if we accept them), then the priority of silver over gold makes eminent sense. The silver coinage of Lovingkindness provides "ready cash" which God can bestow freely and readily upon the needy of the world. The gold, on the other hand, symbolizes the principle of Justice, and is stored away from the hands of the deserving.

Since the right arm is identified in the kabbalistic symbolism with generosity and lovingkindness, a difficulty is posed by Exodus 15:6 when it speaks of the Lord's right hand dashing the enemy in pieces. This does not fit our expectations of supreme benevolence! The precise meaning of the *Bahir* text is obscure here, but most commentators understand it to be saying that the dashing to pieces is not performed by the *sefirah* of Lovingkindness, but by a different *sefirah*, the *Shekhinah* (see below), which can also be referred to occasionally as the "right hand." The severe punishment is meted out to people who fail to acknowledge their gratitude for the favors that God has bestowed upon them.

Having introduced the topic of the *Shekhinah*, the Divine Presence in our world, the *Bahir* proceeds to expound how the imagery of gold is applied both to it and to the *sefirah* of *Din*. In general, the *Shekhinah* is the receptacle that absorbs the influences that flow through from the upper *sefirot* (it occupies the bottommost rung in the hierarchy); and therefore it "mirrors" several symbols that belong primarily to those higher *sefirot*.

The exposition of the three consonants that make up the Hebrew word for gold demonstrates how the very word alludes to the multiple facets that coalesce in the *Shekhinah*.

The first letter, Z, is the initial of *zakhar*, the Hebrew word for masculine. While the *Shekhinah* is in fact a feminine principle, it stands in a romantic relationship with the *sefirah* of *Tif'eret* (Beauty or Glory), personified as a prince. In fact, the imagery of *Tif'eret* is usually extended to a constellation of seven lower *sefirot* that are depicted as a single symbolic entity. Since the Hebrew letter *Z* has the numerological value of seven, this is fully appropriate.

The second letter in the Hebrew word for gold, the *H*, is described as an allusion to the *sefirah* Understanding (*Binah*) which is often symbolized as the mother of the *Shekhinah*. In standard kabbalistic imagery, Understanding is identified with the letter *H*, the second of the four letters of the Tetragrammaton (the four-letter biblical name of God). However, the present exposition is based on a different association, namely the numerological value of the *H*, which is five. This evokes the idea of the soul which, according to an ancient rabbinic tradition, is composed of five distinct elements (as derived from the different words by which it is designated in the Bible). The soul is believed to fall within the domain of *Binah*.

The last letter of *Zahab*, the *B*, represents the *sefirah* of Wisdom. It is the first letter of the word *Bereshit*, the opening word of the Hebrew Bible, which the kabbalists regarded as an epithet for Wisdom, as we noted previously.

The parable about the king and his married daughter expresses in touching and delicately anthropomorphic terms the special role of the *Shekhinah* in kabbalistic religiosity and theology, as a being that is at once part of God and part of the lower world. Having sent his presence into the world, Wisdom cannot exercise direct control over the community of Israel which is personified in the *Shekhinah*. His loving concern for his daughter does not permit Wisdom to separate himself completely from the *Shekhinah* and Israel, even as the *Shekhinah* cannot survive unless she can communicate with her father. The solution is to maintain the relationship at a mature and autonomous distance through a "window"; that is, through the intermediary of the upper *sefirot*.

The *Zohar*

The *Zohar* ("brilliance," "enlightenment") emerged as the most popular and influential work of the Kabbalah. Like the *Bahir*, it adopts the format of an ancient midrashic compendium composed in Aramaic, and consists chiefly of ingenious expositions of biblical passages according to the hermeneutical system of the ten *sefirot*. The most prominent teacher in the *Zohar* is Rabbi Simeon ben Yohai, who appears as the charismatic spiritual master of a circle of kabbalistic rabbis who travel about the holy land regaling one another with their insights into the mysteries of the Torah. Notwithstanding its claims of ancient origin, there is little doubt that it was written in the thirteenth century by Rabbi Moses de Leon of Guadalajara, Spain, perhaps with the assistance of a circle of collaborators.

From Zohar 1:246b[4]

> "Naphtali is a hind let loose: he giveth goodly words" (Genesis 49:21).
> This is what is written: "and thy speech is comely" (Song of Songs 4:3).
> For the voice conveys the speech, and there is no voice without speech.
> And that voice is let loose from a deep place that is above, and it is let
> loose from before him in order to convey the speech. For there is no
> voice without speech and no speech without voice.

COMMENTS

Jacob's son Naphtali is interpreted here as a symbol for the unity of the *sefirot*
Tif'eret and the *Shekhinah*. This is derived from the fact that the wording of
Jacob's blessing employs both masculine and feminine language ("two sides")
with reference to him. While the main verb "he giveth" is, as expected, masculine, the verse also speaks of Naphtali as a "hind," a female deer.

The Bible's images of "letting loose" and "giving words" lead the *Zohar*
to an intriguing discourse comparing the subtle relationships between the
sefirot and those between voice (or sound) and speech. Voice is the general
power that is actualized in specific acts of speech. Just as speech cannot exist
except as an instance of voice, so it is true that voice has no real existence
until it is given specific expression as speech. Likewise in the metaphysical
realms, though the *Shekhinah* is emanated from the higher *sefirot*, those
sefirot influence the lower world only after they have been channeled through
the *Shekhinah*. The interdependence of the *Shekhinah* and *Tif'eret* is like
that between voice and speech.

From Zohar 1:246b (continued)

> And this is a general principle that is in need of a particular instance,
> and an instance that is in need of a general principle.

COMMENTS

The *Zohar* posits an analogy between this theoretical model and a well-
known rule of talmudic legal hermeneutics that refers to (as exceptions to
the normal procedures for interpreting general and specific expressions in
the Torah) "a general principle that is in need of a particular instance, and
an instance that is in need of a general principle"; that is to say, where
neither the general expression nor the specific instance have any meaning
without the other. The *Zohar*'s analogy is not at all inappropriate.

From Zohar 1:246b (continued)

> And this voice issues from the south and it heads westward.

COMMENTS

The passage describes how the "voice" emanates from the "south," *Ḥesed*. In Hebrew, the directions are charted in relation to the east (facing the sunrise), so that "south" is the same as the right side, the side of compassion and maleness. It then flows through *Tif'eret* to the "west," the *Shekhinah*.

From Zohar 1:246b (continued)

It inherits two sides.

And this is what is written (Deuteronomy 33:23): "And of Naphtali he said, O Naphtali, satisfied with favor, and full with the blessing of the Lord: possess thou the west and the south."

Male above and female below.

For this reason: "Naphtali is a hind let loose"—Female below.

And similarly, male above, as it is written: "he giveth goodly words"— It is written "he giveth" and not "she giveth."

Come see: Thought is the beginning of all. And because it is Thought, it is within, concealed and unknown.

When this Thought spread outward, it came to the place where the spirit dwells.

And when it reached that place it was called Understanding. And this one is not as concealed as the previous one, even though it is concealed.

This spirit spread outward and brought forth a voice that is blended of fire and water and wind [or: spirit], which are north and south and east.

This voice is the totality of all the other powers.

And this voice conveys the speech and pronounces the word correctly, because the voice is sent from the place of the spirit and comes to convey the word, to pronounce proper things.

COMMENTS

After expounding the actualization of the voice through the lower *sefirot*, the passage reverts to the origins of that voice in the higher *sefirot*. It began as a secret and undifferentiated entity deep within Thought (Wisdom), and began to unfold itself in the guise of Understanding. "The place where the spirit dwells" is a kabbalistic symbol for the *sefirah* Understanding, based on Genesis 1:2: "*And the spirit of God moved upon the face of the waters.*" There the voice remained only slightly less concealed than it had been in Wisdom. At this state it was still only thought, and had not yet become perceptible as sound or voice.

It is only when it arrives at a lower level that the thought/voice, like the *sefirot* themselves, differentiates itself into a form of expression. This is the level that has been channeled into *Din, Ḥesed* and *Tif'eret*, symbolized respectively as Fire, Water and Wind; or as North, South and East.

From Zohar 1:246b *(continued)*

And if you should meditate on the levels, [you will note that] Thought is the same as Understanding, which is the same as voice, which is the same as speech; and they are all one.

And Thought is the beginning of all.

And there was no separation. Rather, it was all a unity, and a single bond, which is real Thought, which is bound to Nothingness and is never ever separated.

And this is "one Lord, and his name one" (Zechariah 14:9).

COMMENTS

In a very profound summary of the process, the *Zohar* declares that there is no real difference between the differentiated speech that is produced at the culmination of the metaphysical speech process and the ultimate unity of divine thought from which it originated. The sacred utterances that issue from or through the *Shekhinah* partake of the mysterious oneness of divine thought. The apparent differences between the higher and lower manifestations exist only from the limited human perspective, but not in absolute reality.

In fact, the origin of the divine speech could even be traced back to a state prior to Thought/Wisdom, to the mysterious first *sefirah*, known as *Keter*, the Supreme Crown. The kabbalistic symbolism refers to this *sefirah* as *Ayin*: Nothingness. The expression is taken from the vocabulary of the philosophers, who employed it mostly when discussing the doctrine of "creation out of nothingness." Whereas for the philosophers, the term referred to total absence, emptiness or non-being, the kabbalistic Nothingness is the highest state of ultimate reality, prior even to absolute unity.

Sefer Ha-Zohar 3:25b

Rabbi Aḥa was walking on the road, when Rabbi Ḥiyya and Rabbi Yosé happened upon him at the same time.

Said Rabbi Aḥa: The three of us are surely destined to receive the *Shekhinah*.

They joined company and went.

Said Rabbi Aḥa: Let each one of us say something in connection with the Torah, and let us proceed.

COMMENTS

The introductory lines of this passage are typical of the literary narratives that abound in the *Zohar* in which the fictitious rabbis roam about their mythical Israeli landscape, delighting one another with their inspired expositions of the esoteric meanings of biblical texts. Following a talmudic tradition, the itinerant sages believed that the Divine Presence (the *Shekhinah*) adhered to sites where words of Torah were being expounded.

Sefer Ha-Zohar 3:25b (continued)

Rabbi Ḥiyya began and said: "*Har'ifu* [Drop down], ye heavens, from above, etc." (Isaiah 45: 8).

This verse embodies the mystery of Wisdom, which I have learned from the Holy Lamp [=Rabbi Simeon ben Yoḥai].

"*Har'ifu*, ye heavens, from above"—What is *har'ifu*?

—It is as you say (Deuteronomy 32:2) "My doctrine shall drop [*tir'af*] as the rain." And it is in connection with the rain, which is the sustenance of all things, that it says this.

And therefore the eyes of the entire world look to the Holy One for nourishment, because he provides food to all and nourishes all; as you say (Psalms 145:15) "The eyes of all wait upon thee; [and thou givest them their bread in due season]."

And if you should state that the matter is dependent upon the place that is called "heavens"—behold, we have learned that the matter does not depend on merit [*zekhuta*]. And with regards to merit, have we not interpreted it to mean "charity"? And the Aramaic rendering of "charity" is *zekhuta*. And *zekhuta* and charity are the same thing.

Yet here it says "*Har'ifu*, ye heavens"!

COMMENTS

Rabbi Ḥiyya's discourse expounds Isaiah 45:8 where the prophet's metaphoric portrayal of righteousness and divine inspiration raining down upon the world provides a convenient occasion to explore the familiar kabbalistic themes of benevolent divine influences cascading through the celestial realms until they reach our earthly world.

The rare Hebrew verb *har'ifu* is explained, by means of a comparison with the use of the same root in Deuteronomy 32:2, as referring to rainfall. This prompts some observations about the human dependence on divine bounty for our nourishment. So far, the ideas and their associative connections remain quite conventional and have no distinctively kabbalistic slant.

However, we soon discover that several of the innocent-looking expressions are in reality being employed as symbols and code-words for the various *sefirot*. Thus, "heavens" here is referring not to the physical sky from which the rains fall, but to the *sefirah* of *Tif'eret* and the constellation of lower *sefirot* that it epitomizes. This in fact poses a difficulty for Rabbi Ḥiyya, since an established tradition asserts that the provision of divine favors does not depend on merit, and the word "merit" is believed to be an equivalent to charity, which in turn is equated with *Tif'eret*!

Sefer Ha-Zohar 3:25b (continued)

It is written "from above." Literally: "from Above": Namely, it comes from the Ancient Holy One, and not from the one that is called "Heavens," which is called "merit," but literally: "from Above."

COMMENTS

The conundrum is resolved by proposing a different way of reading the verse. "From above" should not be seen as a modifier of "the heavens," but rather it indicates an additional level. Thus, the verse teaches that the sustaining nourishment is triggered by the uppermost *sefirot*, the ones that are situated above the "heavens." It is they that cause the "heavens" to release the gifts.

Sefer Ha-Zohar 3:25b (continued)

"And let the skies pour down righteousness" (Isaiah, *ibid.*)
    For when heaven receives nourishment from above, from that elevated place that dwells above it, then "the skies pour down righteousness."
    What are "the skies [*shehaqim*]"—The place where they grind manna for the righteous.
    And who are they?—Eternity [*Nesah*] and Majesty [*Hod*], who assuredly grind manna for the righteous.

COMMENTS

Expounding the continuation of the verse from Isaiah, the *Zohar* explains that the word denoting "skies" also must be understood as a reference to *sefirot*. In this case, the identification is with *Nesah* and *Hod*, two of the lower *sefirot* (the seventh and eighth). The identification of that level with "the place where they grind manna" appears to be based on a subtle word-play since the Hebrew word for "grind" is *shahaq*, from the same root that was used here for "skies" (though the Hebrew word is not actually mentioned in this Aramaic text). At any rate, we have now added another station to the route traveled by the divine blessing: from *Tif'eret* it now descends through *Nesah* and *Hod*.

Sefer Ha-Zohar 3:25b (continued)

For whom?—For that place that is called "the Righteous One."
    For behold, they grind the manna which is referred to as "from above," and all that good is contained within them, in order to give it to the level of the Righteous One.

Comments

Having introduced the idea that the manna is prepared *for the righteous*, the *Zohar* now observes that the word "righteous" is referring to the ninth *sefirah*, Foundation (*Yesod*). Indeed, the names "Righteous" and "Foundation" are used interchangeably throughout kabbalistic literature to identify this *sefirah*, based on the verse (Proverbs 10:25): "the righteous is an everlasting foundation."

Sefer Ha-Zohar 3:25b (continued)

Who are the righteous, such that Righteousness will be blessed through their pouring down, and therefore they grind manna for the righteous?

Who are the righteous?—This is the Righteous One and Righteousness: Joseph and Rachel, who are called the Righteous Ones when they join together.

Comments

The final beneficiary of this nourishment is the *Shekhinah*, the tenth *sefirah*, also known as "Righteousness" (as distinct from "the Righteous One"). *Yesod* is often portrayed as the channel through which divine creative force is poured into the *Shekhinah*. When the *sefirot* are imagined in terms of human imagery, this idea is expressed by equating Yesod with the male sexual organ. The *Zohar* identifies *Yesod* and the *Shekhinah* by the biblical figures of Joseph (who is often designated in rabbinic literature as "the righteous") and Rachel.

Sefer Ha-Zohar 3:25b (continued)

And these grind manna for the righteous ones—Really! And concerning this: "the skies pour down righteousness."

And thus, "let the earth open"—below.

"And let them bring forth salvation"—to the children of the world.

"And let righteousness spring up together"—may all the mercies and all the good that is in the world be plentiful, and may people's sustenance be found in the world. Then joy will be added to joy, and all the worlds will be blessed.

Said Rabbi Aḥa: If I had come only to hear this, then it would have been worth it!

Comments

After expounding the verse from Isaiah, the discourse concludes with an inspiring prayer that the world should enjoy the benefits of God's generous blessings. Although the blessing in question is understood to allude to spiritual gifts, there is no *prima facie* reason to assume that it does not extend as well to more material expressions of divine bounty. Such upbeat prayers for a happy future are a standard feature of conventional midrashic homilies.

The Ra'aya Meheimana *and* Tikkunei Ha-Zohar

An unknown Spanish author in the late thirteenth or early fourteenth century composed supplements to the *Zohar*, known as the *Ra'aya Meheimana* (the Faithful Shepherd) and *Sefer ha-Tikkunim*, or *Tikkunei Ha-Zohar* (the Garments of the *Zohar*), which were subsequently included in the standard editions of the *Zohar*. The "faithful shepherd" of the title is Moses who appears alongside Rabbi Simeon ben Yohai and other sages, to expound the esoteric meanings of the 613 commandment of the Torah. The *Tikkunei ha-Zohar* interprets the beginning of the book of Genesis. Both these works argue aggressively for the superiority of the kabbalistic approach to Judaism, and are animated by the strong belief that the spread of Kabbalah and the *Zohar* is a crucial condition for the imminent redemption.

From Ra'aya Meheimana *(Zohar 3:28a)*[5]

> Thus shall it be done in order to test Israel at the final redemption. This is what is written (Daniel 12:10) "Many shall be purified and made white and tried." For they are from the side of goodness and can withstand the test.
>
> "But the wicked shall do wickedly" They are from the side of evil, and concerning them will be fulfilled (Ezekiel 13:9) *"neither shall they enter into the land of Israel"*; and he will put them to death.
>
> "But the wise shall understand" From the side of Understanding [*Binah*] which is the Tree of Life. Because of them it is said (Daniel 12:3) "And they that be wise shall shine as the brightness of the firmament"— in this book of yours, which is the book of the *Zohar*, from the illumination of the celestial Mother, Repentance.
>
> For these there is no need for a test. And because Israel are destined to taste from the Tree of Life, which is this book of the *Zohar*, through it they will emerge from the exile in mercy, and it shall be fulfilled for them (Deuteronomy 32:12) "So the Lord alone did lead him, and there was no strange god with him."
>
> And the Tree of Good and Evil, which consists of prohibition and permission, defilement and purity, shall not hold sway over Israel any longer, since their sustenance will be only from the side of the Tree of Life, which has no objection from the side of Evil, nor any disagreement from the spirit of impurity; as it is written (Zechariah 13:2) "I will cause . . . the unclean spirit to pass out of the land."

And the scholars will not derive their sustenance from the ignorant folk, but rather from the side of Goodness, in that they will eat what is pure, what is fit and permissible; and not from the mixed multitude, who eat what is impure, unfit, forbidden; for they are impure, since they defile themselves with menstruating women, with maidservants, with gentiles and harlots. Because they are the children of Lilith, who is a menstruating woman, a maidservant, a heathen, a harlot, they return to their roots. And regarding them it is said (Isaiah 14:29) "for out of the serpent's root shall come forth a cockatrice."

And while the Tree of Good and Evil rules, which is the profanity of purity and the profanity of impurity, those sages who resemble Sabbaths and festivals have only what those profane ones give them; such as the Sabbath day, which has only what they prepare for it on weekdays.

And at the time when the Tree of Life rules, the Tree of Good and Evil is subjugated, and the ignorant folk have only what the scholars give to them, and they will be subjugated to them as if they did not exist in the world.

And similarly, with regard to what is forbidden or permissible, impure or pure, these shall not pass from the ignorant; for from their perspective the only difference between exile and the messianic age is the subjection to foreign kingdoms. For they do not taste of the Tree of Life, and they are in need of Mishnahs on matters of what is prohibited or permitted, impure or pure.

Instead, they will be degraded before the scholars, like darkness before light. For the mixed multitude, the ignorant people, are in darkness. And they are not called "Israel," but rather they are slaves who are sold to Israel. And this is because they are like beasts.

COMMENTS

The current passage is attached to an exposition that was purportedly preached before Moses by the prophet Elijah, on the text of Numbers 5:11–31. The exposition outlines the procedures for testing a wife accused of adultery. The author compares that test with the test that will be applied in the days of the messianic redemption in order to separate the righteous from the wicked.

The expression "the wise" is employed in this passage to designate the kabbalists, in contrast to "the ignorant." The latter constitute a group that might include anyone who is not a kabbalist, even those who have attained mastery of the other works of the conventional Jewish religious curriculum.

The main symbolism of this passage is based on the two trees in the Garden of Eden story in Genesis. According to that story, Adam and Eve partook of the tree of knowledge of good and evil, and were afterwards expelled from the garden in order to prevent them from eating the fruit of a second tree, the tree of life. As understood by our passage, the Torah that is studied by most Jews according to its normal, outward sense is being equated with the tree of knowledge of good and evil. It represents a world of moral and religious contrasts in which goodness, purity and sanctity are in a constant struggle against the forces of evil, defilement and profanity. This Torah is valid in our unredeemed state, while we are banished from Paradise, and Israel is exiled from the holy land. In the age of the final redemption, however, Israel will be restored to the Torah of the tree of life in which all conflicts shall be overcome, and evil and impurity will be eliminated from the world. At that time there will no longer be a need for the laws and precepts that serve in the war against evil.

The passage mentions some typical features of talmudic argumentation, employing terms such as "objection" and "disagreement" (used in the Talmud when rabbis take opposite sides in a debate and one of them raises difficulties or contradictory proof-texts to challenge his colleague's opinion). In the unconventional view of the *Ra'aya Meheimana*, the foundation of talmudic debate derives from the realms of impurity, and will be rendered obsolete in the redeemed world.

According to the imagery of the *sefirot*, the tree of knowledge of good and evil is associated with the *Shekhinah*, the lowest *sefirah*, whereas the tree of life derives from the superior level of Understanding (also symbolized as Repentance).

Traditional Jewish eschatology, as depicted in the quote from Daniel 12:10, teaches that the redemption will be preceded by terrible wars and cataclysms, one of whose purposes will be to purify the people, to refine them by removing every last trace of evil. Our passage makes the bold claim that the wise men, namely the kabbalistic scholars, will be exempted from the sufferings of that cataclysm because they have already achieved a state of spiritual perfection. The instrument for reaching this exalted state is none other than the *Zohar*, which the author of the *Ra'aya Meheimana* ascribes here to Moses himself. The study of the *Zohar* will play a decisive role in bringing to a close the era of Jewish exile.

The passage goes on to comment on the social status of scholars in the Jewish community. It regards it a deplorable state of affairs that the kabbalists are not economically self-sufficient, but must rely on the magnanimity of ignorant Jews—that is to say, of those otherwise pious individuals who have not been initiated into the mysteries of the Kabbalah. The passage expresses an attitude of elitist resentment as it heaps upon those unenlightened wretches the full range of satanic imagery and accuses them bitterly of the most heinous of religious transgressions. Among other things, it identifies them with the "mixed multitude," the band of non-Israelite camp-followers who accompanied the Israelites out of Egypt and whom the rabbis blamed for many of the tragedies that befell the people during their wanderings in the desert. For the Kabbalah, the mixed multitude represents the demonic hosts of evil, the spawn of the arch-demoness Lilith.

In our author's vision of the redemption, the tables will ultimately be turned, and it will then be the unenlightened who will turn desperately to the kabbalists for crumbs of spirituality, reversing the situation that prevails in the author's time when the kabbalists must humble themselves before their ignorant benefactors for their scraps of material sustenance.

Abraham Abulafia

The medieval rationalist doctrine, as taught by Maimonides and others, held that the state of prophecy was a step beyond philosophical enlightenment and could only be achieved after mastering a rigorous curriculum of scientific and metaphysical studies. After transcending the limitations of material discourse, the philosopher learns to contemplate the abstract concepts that are eternally true—chief among these, of course, is the contemplation of a God who is removed from all matter or physicality. It is only after purifying the intellect in this manner that a person (and only a very rare person at that!) can merge his intellect with the divine "Active Intellect" and receive supernatural communications that are mediated by means of the faculty of imagination. The medieval Jewish philosophers equated this state with that of the biblical prophets.

The thirteenth-century Spanish mystical thinker Abraham Abulafia subscribed to the basic premises of Maimonides' theory of prophecy; however, he proposed a different and more accessible path for achieving it. In Abulafia's system, there is no need to pursue an intellectually demanding course of study in order to refine one's abstract conceptual thinking. The same state can be achieved by *cleansing* one's mind of the clutter of trivial and confusing thoughts.

Abraham Abulafia, Sefer Hayei ha-'Olam ha-Ba[6]

"Prepare to meet thy God, O Israel" (Amos 4:12)! Prepare yourself to unify your heart and cleanse your body. Choose yourself a special place where your voice will not be audible to any other person. Remain solitary and separate from anyone else, alone. Sit in one place in a room or an upper chamber, and do not reveal your secret to any person. If possible, do it during the day in the house, even if you can only do it a little bit. Nevertheless, it is preferable to do it at night.

Be careful to void your thoughts of all worldly vanities at the time when you are readying yourself to speak to your creator and you desire him to teach you his great power.

Wrap yourself in your prayer shawl, and place *tefillin* on your head and arm, so that you will be full of fear and awe before the divine presence that is with you at that time.

Clean your garments, and if possible let all your garments be white, since all this helps you very much to focus on love and fear.

If it is nighttime, kindle many lamps until they light up your eyes very intensely. Afterwards, take hold of ink, a pen and a tablet, and they will serve as a testimony for you that you have come to perform the worship of the Lord your God with joyfulness and with gladness of heart.

Now begin to combine the letters, the few with the many, to transform them and to rearrange them quickly until your heart becomes warm through their rearrangement.

And you shall find new understandings in them that you were never able to achieve previously by means of a human tradition, and you did not grasp them through rational analysis.

At this point you are ready to receive the influence that is bestowed upon you. It inspires you with a continuing sequence of words.

Prepare your truest thoughts to picture the blessed Lord and his supreme angels, to picture them in your heart as if they were humans standing or sitting around you, and you are among them like an emissary whom the king and his servants want to send. Be prepared to listen to the message that issues from their mouths, whether it is from the king or from his servants.

After you have visualized all this, prepare your mind and your heart to understand from your thoughts the many matters to which you are brought by the letters that you are contemplating. Meditate upon their totality and upon their parts, as a person who is being told a parable or a riddle or a dream, or is pondering a book of wisdom concerning a matter whose profundity exceeds his comprehension.

Find an interpretation for what you are hearing, to the best of your ability, and in accordance with your understanding of it apply it to yourself, as well as others, with respect to everything that they are telling you. And all this will happen to you after you have cast aside the tablet from your hand and the stylus from your fingers; or after they fall down by themselves on account of all your thoughts.

And be aware that as long as the intense intellectual energy remains powerful with you, your outer limbs and inner organs will become weak, and your entire body will begin to rage in an exceedingly mighty storm, until you think that you are going to surely die at this time, because your soul is becoming separated from your body on account of its great joyfulness in its understanding and in its ability to discern what you have discerned. And you will prefer death over life because of your awareness that death affects the body alone. It is for this reason that the soul experiences eternal resurrection.

. . . Make yourself ready as I have told you, and direct your heart and soul, and strengthen your rational thoughts. The initial step will be to utter with complete concentration and with a proper melody that is beautiful and pleasant, enunciating the true vowels for each and every letter of the following divine name: *VH"V, YL"Y, SY"T, 'L"M, MH"Sh,*

LL"H—six names from among the holy names; in eighteen breaths, until you reach the final one which is the name *MV"M*; if the inspiration does not force you to pause between them. For we possess a tradition that the influence comes upon a perfect individual when he reaches the conclusion of the first verse, after he has pronounced the twenty-four names . . .

At that point you will behold the image of a youth [*na'a"r*] or the image of a *shakh*, since in the language of Ishmael *sheikh* means elder [*zaqen*], which alludes to Metatron. He is also a youth, and he also is named Enoch.

Comments

This text offers a precise and systematic set of instructions on how to ascend to the spiritual state wherein one becomes receptive to the divine "influences" of prophetic inspiration. The recipe includes symbolic purification (clean body and white garments, and so forth), removal of all distractions, and the use of symbolic objects (the prayer shawl and *tefillin* ["phylacteries"]) to promote consciousness of the divine presence.

Central to the process is the random permutation of Hebrew letters. This produces a physical excitement (warming of the heart) that leads to an outpouring of uncontrolled speech. Abulafia claims that these random words are actually prophetic, issuing from a supernatural inspiration. Although they might initially appear nonsensical, sufficient meditation will elicit from them a profound meaning. The trance-like state involves a draining of physical energy from one's body.

An important element in the mystical technique is the mechanical combining of the letters that make up God's seventy-two-letter mystical name. This name, very popular among medieval Jewish mystics and magicians, was formed by juxtaposing three verses from the Torah (Exodus 14:19–21) that are made up of seventy-two Hebrew letters apiece, writing the second verse backwards, and then "slicing up" the resulting text into seventy-two groups of three letters consisting of one letter from each verse.

According to Abulafia, meditation on the seventy-two-letter name will bring about a vision of Metatron. In ancient Jewish mystical tradition, Metatron, the "prince of the divine presence," is the most exalted spiritual being except for God himself, and is the human-like form that was beheld in prophetic visions. The Bible (Genesis 4:24) states that "Enoch walked with God: and he was not; for God took him." According to the early Apocalyptic tradition, God transformed Enoch into the supreme angelic being Metatron. Thus, one of the greatest accomplishments to which a mystic can aspire is to reach the spiritual level at which one beholds Metatron. This would be analogous to the visions experienced by Moses, Isaiah and Ezekiel in the Bible.

The Kabbalah of Rabbi Isaac Luria

This brief passage is taken from the *Eṣ Ḥayyim* by Rabbi Ḥayyim Vital which came to be accepted as the most authoritative statement of the kabbal-istic doctrines of Rabbi Isaac Luria. Luria himself did not write any treatises of his own, claiming that the ideas came to him in such a dynamic torrent that he was unable to organize them.

It is more than likely that you will be beset by a feeling of confused help-lessness as you are confronted by the elaborately intricate set of concepts and obscure terms that often presuppose knowledge of complex processes in the uppermost metaphysical and cosmological realms. This obsession with detail is typical of the Lurianic Kabbalah. At every stage, the author tries to map out the mystical topography in minute precision, with special reference to the most sublime levels of the spiritual universe, the areas that lie above the realm of the *sefirot* and which gave birth to it, areas which were not discussed very much in the *Zohar*.

This selection relates to one of the most influential themes in Lurianic cosmology, the metaphysical event known as the "shattering of the vessels." Viewed broadly, the Lurianic creation process began when the *Ein Sof* ["Infinite"], the essential and unknowable aspect of God who had hitherto permeated the whole of reality, chose to contract himself [*ṣimṣum*] from a portion of the universe in order to make room for the existence something other than himself upon which he could radiate his blessed light. For this purpose, he generated "vessels" that were supposed to receive and contain the light. In the end, the vessels that were created proved unable to receive the divine light, causing them to shatter.

Ḥayyim Vital Eṣ Ḥayyim 2 Heikhal 2:4:11:8

> After the aspect of Restoration [*Tiqqun*] has been explained briefly, let us return to the explanation of the above-mentioned sequence of degrees, namely: back-to-back, back-to-front, front-to-back and front-to-front. Indeed before there existed any Restoration whatsoever in all the emanation, even within the Ancient of Days—now with the issuing of the lights of Father and Mother they entered into their vessels when they were still in the secret state of Dots/Points [*Nequdim*]. As was noted, they were back-to-back because it was known that Father and Mother stand on two sides of the Long-faced One [*Arikh Anpin*]—this one in his Lovingkindness [*Ḥesed*] and this one in his Might [*Din*]. And inasmuch as Father and Mother were face-to-face, then the light of the countenance of the Long-faced One would descend and be drawn in a direct manner midway between the face of the Father and the face of the Mother, and it illuminated both of them. Now, when they were still within the secret of the Point [*Nequdah*] without Restoration (thus it has already been explained by us), this caused the shattering of the

vessels because when there was as yet no Restoration, the light would come without any screen, and behold they were great un-screened lights, and then the vessels were unable to contain it, and they were neutralized. After the Restoration the lesser light came through Screens so that the lower vessels were able to bear it as well.

Comments

The emanation of the light took place in three stages of gradually decreasing orders of spirituality, which are referred to as "streaked, speckled and spotted" (based on Genesis 30:39). The separation of the lights into distinct *sefirot* and vessels took place at the second level, designated in Luria's system as the world of Dots or Points (*Nequdim*).

The earliest and most sublime stage in this process was that of the Primordial Man [*Adam Qadmon*], the actual light that descended from the *Ein Sof* after the *şimşum*. The Primordial Man contained the initial, unstable versions of the divine qualities that would later be configured into the ten *sefirot*. The vessels were fashioned using elements of divine Might/Justice [*Din*].

The vessels that were related to the lower *sefirot* were not strong enough to contain the light, resulting in the catastrophic shattering of those vessels. The result was a chaotic confusion of the original divine lights and of the sherds [*kelippot*] that remained from the broken vessels which became the basis for the existence of evil in our world. From the human perspective, this situation calls for a Restoration [*tiqqun*] of the divine sparks by freeing them from the sherds and elevating them to their primordial state of holiness, by means of the observance of the commandments of the Torah.

The Restoration process that followed the Shattering of the Vessels included a reconfiguration of the *sefirot* into more carefully defined entities that were strong enough to serve as "screens" to mediate and soften the divine light.

Within the structure of the Primordial Man, the highest Sefirah, *Keter* (Crown) is referred to as the "Long-faced (or: Patient) One." The upper portion of Keter is designated *Atiq Yomin* [Ancient of Days; see Daniel 7:9] and is considered the most secret of the divine "aspects" [*parşufin*] and the source out of which all the other *parşufin* were constructed. From the Long-faced One the light subdivides into the Father and Mother, as Luria designates the *sefirot* of Wisdom [*Hokhmah*] and Understanding [*Binah*] respectively. From them begins the basic differentiation between Right (governed by lovingkindness) and Left (governed by strict justice). The relationship between the Father and Mother exists on four distinct levels ranging from the most intimate, face-to-face, to the more distant back-to-back.

Ḥayyim Vital Eş Ḥayyim 2 Heikhal 2:4:11:8 (continued)

And behold, when there did not yet exist any Restoration, even in the realms of Creation and Fashioning, there was a great and diverse light that was not screened. In this manner, if the Father and Mother were face-to-face, as the light of the Long-faced One was drawn between them (as noted) by way of his chest, they were unable to receive it at all because the natures of the faces are purer and brighter and more delicate than their backs. So the light was absorbed, and penetrated deeply into them, and it was impossible that they should be capable of containing it. So they also were shattered and dropped downward, after the manner of the Short-faced One [*Ze'ir*] and his Female. And they suffered actual death, God forbid, and therefore they remained back-to-back.

Comments

"The realms of Creation and Fashioning" The lowest of the four worlds according to kabbalistic cosmology. These two are, respectively, the realms of the angels and of the material world.

 "Faces" configurations of the ten *sefirot* into sub-groupings.

 "The Short-faced One [*Ze'ir*]" The seven *sefirot* below Wisdom and Understanding that are configured as a single masculine figure, *Ze'ir Anpin*.

 "His Female" The *sefirah* of *Malkhut*, the Divine Presence / *Shekhinah* is depicted in kabbalistic imagery as a princess, the female beloved.

 The vessels that received the intense "face-to-face" light were totally shattered. The Shattering of the Vessels is referred to in Lurianic Kabbalah as the "death of the kings" using imagery derived from Genesis Chapter 36: "And these are the kings that reigned in the land of Edom, before there reigned any king over the children of Israel" (verse 31).

Ḥayyim Vital Eṣ Ḥayyim 2 Heikhal 2:4:11:8 *(continued)*

And then, as the light of the countenance of the Long-faced One was drawn out by way of his chest and it was drawn and entered between the two backs of Father and Mother which are much thicker and grosser than the aspect of "faces"—then that light was not absorbed nor did it penetrate deeply into them, because it [the light] is of a spiritual essence while they [the sherds] are dark and gross. For this reason all that penetrated into them was a faint light which they were able to contain. Therefore at the beginning, the Father and Mother stood back-to-back, and accordingly they did not die like the other kings who did actually die. And they descended into the world of creation [*B'ri'ah*].

Comments

The vessels that received the light in a "diluted" version were able to withstand it because their coarser substance did not actually absorb the light.

Rabbi Joseph Caro's *Maggid Meisharim*

Rabbi Joseph ben Ephraim Caro (1488–1575) figures elsewhere in this book as the author of the *Shulḥan 'Arukh* and the most prominent authority on Jewish religious law in the early modern era. He was also an accomplished kabbalist, an important member of the mystical circle that assembled in Safed in the Galilee. Through much of his life, Caro received messages from a "*maggid*," a supernatural voice. Caro's angelic *maggid* is depicted as a personification of the Mishnah who spoke through his mouth in ecstatic moments. The contents of these messages, which often consisted of moral exhortations or criticisms, personal guidance or foretelling of future events, were recorded in a mystical diary that was published under the title *Maggid Meisharim* ("declarer of things that are right" based on Isaiah 45:19).

Rabbi Joseph Caro, Maggid Meisharim

A chastisement that he chastised him as a father to his son:

On the eve of the Sabbath, Iyyar 27 when the designated reading was "in the wilderness of Sinai" [the beginning of Numbers], I ate only a minimal amount, and the same applies to my drinking, and I reviewed Mishnah passages in the early part of the night, then I slept until daylight. When I awakened, the sun was shining upon the earth, and I was very upset, noting how I had not arisen while it was still dark so that the speech would come upon me as it normally does.

Nevertheless I began to read the Mishnah. I read five chapters, and as I was still reading the Mishnah texts, a voice began to pound inside my mouth, intoning on its own. It opened by saying: May the Lord be with you in all the paths that you take; and in everything that you have done and that you shall do the Lord will bring you success, as long as you cleave continually to me and to my awe and to my Torah and my Mishnahs—not as you did tonight. Even though you sanctified yourself in your eating and in your drinking, nevertheless you slept the sleep of the sluggard, for "as the door turneth upon his hinges, so doth the slothful upon his bed" (Proverbs 26:14). You did not awaken to read the Mishnah as is your fine custom. For this it would have been fitting that I abandon you and forsake you, now that you have added to the power of Samael and the serpent and the evil inclination by virtue of the sleep that you indulged in until daylight.

Comments

"Samael and the serpent and the evil inclination" Samael is identified in rabbinic and kabbalistic lore as the principal demon, identified with Satan as well as with the evil inclination. In all these roles, he entices humans to sin, and then acts as a prosecutor to accuse us in the heavenly court.

Rabbi Joseph Caro, **Maggid Meisharim** *(continued)*

However, owing to the merit of the six orders of the Mishnah that you have memorized, and through the merit of all those ascetic practices and acts of self-denial that you have performed in the past, and which you continue still today, they have concurred in the celestial academy that I should return to speak to you as before, and that I should not abandon you or forsake you. And thus have I done, as you now behold that I am speaking with you even as a man might speak to his friend. Your own eyes can see that in several generations no other person has achieved this great height, only a small and select group. Therefore, my son, listen carefully to what I shall command you: to occupy yourself continually in my Torah by day and by night without interruption, and without letting your thoughts be distracted by any worldly matters—nothing but words of Torah and my awe and my Mishnah.

After this I slept for about half an hour, and when I awakened I was upset at how the speech had been interrupted on account of my sleeping. So I read from the Mishnah, and then "the voice of my beloved" began to pound in my mouth saying: You should know that the Holy One and the entire celestial academy send you greetings, and they have sent me to you in order to notify you of the deeds of the Holy One that are all founded on providence.

Comments

In the sample that is translated here, we catch a precious glimpse of the austere regimen that Caro followed in order to induce his revelations. He would severely limit his food intake and deprive himself of sleep, devoting all his waking hours to religious study, focusing especially on the study of the Mishnah. The *maggid* expresses itself in the guise of a powerful voice pounding inside Caro's mouth and speaks as the rabbi's conscience. While he criticizes him when he has not lived up to his demanding spiritual expectations, at the same time he also offers reassurance that his efforts are not in vain, and reinforces his self-image regarding his exceptional moral stature.

"the voice of my beloved" The expression comes from the Song of Songs (2:8; 5:2).

"celestial academy" Rabbinic lore portrays God as being occupied in talmudic study and debate in an academy that is modeled after a rabbinic yeshivah, in the company of the great Jewish sages and biblical heroes who have passed on to the next world.

7 Moralistic and ethical writings

Mishnah *Avot* chapter 4

The following section is taken from the tractate *Avot* in the Mishnah. The title translates as "fathers" and derives from the tractate's opening section that enumerates the great sages who transmitted the Torah (presumably, the oral tradition) from Moses until the time when *Avot* was compiled. To each of those figures the Mishnah attaches maxims and words of wisdom that they were accustomed to say. These sayings are a valuable source for reconstructing the values and beliefs of early rabbinic Judaism.

By far the greatest proportion of the Mishneh as a whole is devoted to topics in Jewish law, halakhah; and it was discussed in that connection in previous sections of this book. *Avot* is unique among the tractates that comprise the Mishnah in that it deals with Aggadah, themes of moral and theological guidance, rather than with the technical discussions of religious law that occupy the rest of the Mishnah. It is a popular text in its own right, and many communities follow the custom of studying chapters from it on Sabbath afternoons, especially during the spring and summer seasons. In English the tractate *Avot* is often referred to as "the Chapters of the Fathers" or "the Ethics of the Fathers."

Mishnah Avot *chapter 4*

[1] Ben Zoma says: Who is wise? One who learns from every person; as it says (Psalms 119:99): "From all my teachers I have gained understanding."

Comments

Note that the standard translation of the verse in Psalms means something quite different. The translation adopted here reflects the usage by Ben Zoma.

Mishnah **Avot** *chapter 4 (continued)*

[1] Who is mighty?—One who conquers his desire; as it says (Proverbs 16:32): "He who is slow to anger is better than the mighty, and he who rules his spirit than he who takes a city."

Who is wealthy?—One who is content with his lot; as it says (Psalms 128:2): "When you eat the labor of your hands, you shall be happy, and it shall be well with you."

"You shall be happy"—in this world;

"and it shall be well with you"—in the next world."

Comments

The **"next world"** can refer either to the afterlife or to the redeemed world after the coming of the messiah when, according to normative rabbinic belief, the dead will be resurrected.

Mishnah **Avot** *chapter 4 (continued)*

Who is honored?—One who honors others; as it says (I Samuel 2:30): "for those who honor me I will honor, and those who despise me shall be lightly esteemed."

[2] Ben Azzai says: Hasten to a minor precept just as to a major one; and flee from transgression. For one precept leads to another precept and one transgression leads to another transgression. For the recompense for a precept is the precept itself, and the recompense for a transgression is the transgression.

Comments

"Precept" in Hebrew: *"miṣvah,"* commandment, generally considered to be the principal virtue according to the Jewish religious outlook.

The rabbis were often reluctant to suggest that some commandments are more important than others, although a gradation of that sort is implicit, for example, in the relative severity of the punishments that are attached to transgression of different precepts.

Ben Azzai seems to be saying here that people should not observe the commandments or lead virtuous lives because of their fear of punishment, or because they hope to be rewarded for their righteous behavior. Instead, one should observe the commandments for their own sake. There are many passages in Jewish religious literature that express the opposite view, stressing the rewards and punishments that await people in the ultimate divine judgment.

Mishnah Avot *chapter 4 (continued)*

[3] He used to say: Do not be contemptuous of anyone; and do not dismiss any possibility. For you will not find a person who does not have his hour, nor will you find any thing that does not have its place.

Comments

The passage is somewhat obscure. The interpretation reflected in this translation seems to be saying that one should have faith in the positive potential of all people, even when such confidence is not warranted by the observable facts, since anything is possible.

Mishnah Avot *chapter 4 (continued)*

[4] Rabbi Levitas of Yavneh says: Be very, very humble of spirit, because the ultimate destiny of humans is the worm.

Rabbi Yoḥanan ben Beroqa says: Whoever profanes the name of Heaven secretly will have punishment exacted from him publicly. No distinction is made between unintentional and intentional action when it comes to the profanation of God's name.

[5] His son Rabbi Ishmael says: When a person learns in order to teach, they give him the opportunity to learn and to teach. And when a person learns in order to do, they give him the opportunity to learn and to teach to observe and to do.

Rabbi Zadok says: Do not make them into a crown for self-aggrandizement, or a spade to dig with.

Comments

As is evident from the context and from the continuation of the passage, "them" in paragraph #5 is referring to the words of Torah.

Rabbi Zadok is stressing that mastery of the Torah is a religious value that should be sought for its own sake, and not for ulterior motives, such as to earn a living from it or to enjoy the prestige that attaches to a scholarly reputation. This ideal has not always been strictly observed in practice. Even in Jewish communities that cultivate a professional rabbinate (the classic instance of using the Torah as a "spade to dig with"), it is common to word the rabbi's contract in such a way that the rabbi is not receiving his salary for his expertise in the words of the Torah, but as compensation for other factors, such as the claims on his time.

Mishnah Avot *chapter 4 (continued)*

And thus was Hillel accustomed to say: One who makes use of the crown will be removed.

From this you have learned that anyone who benefits from the words of the Torah is removing his life from the world.

[6] Rabbi Yosé says: Whoever honors the Torah will himself be honored by others. And whoever has dishonored the Torah is himself dishonored by others.

Baḥya Ibn Paquda

We have made the acquaintance of the eleventh-century Rabbi Baḥya Ibn Paquda and his treatise *The Duties of the Heart* as one of the most prominent examples of medieval Jewish Neoplatonic philosophy. *The Duties of the Heart* was also a practical guide to pious living, setting down a detailed discipline of virtue and morality in accordance with Jewish teachings and philosophical moral principles. The following excerpt is typical of Baḥya's penchant for systematic classification.

Baḥya Ibn Paquda, The Duties of the Heart

The Torah divides human actions into three categories: commands, prohibitions and permitted things.

There are three types of commands:

One of these types consists of "commands of the heart." This refers to things that may be done by means of sincere conviction, such as the belief that God is one, insofar as one believes in him wholeheartedly and with complete faith and devotion, and is eager to obey his precepts and to believe the words of his prophets and his Torah, to fear him and keep his commandments, to consider his wonders and appreciate his goodness, and so many other qualities that it would take too long to relate them.

The second category consists of commandments that relate jointly to the heart and the limbs, such as the sincere correspondence between what one says and what one feels, or the reading and study of the text of the Torah, or prayer, fasting and charity, refraining from work on sabbaths and festivals, or fashioning a *sukkah* and *lulav* and ritual tassels, and similar matters.

Comments

"sukkah" The temporary booth or tabernacle in which Jews are supposed to dwell during the Feast of Tabernacles as a commemoration of the wanderings of the Israelites in the desert when they left Egypt (Leviticus 23:42–43).

"lulav" The palm frond that is taken on the Feast of Tabernacles (Leviticus 23:40).

"ritual tassels" *ṣiṣit*; as commanded in Numbers 15:38.

Baḥya Ibn Paquda, The Duties of the Heart *(continued)*

Prohibitions can also be subdivided into two categories: the first consists of duties of the heart, while the second consists of duties of the limbs.

The prohibitions that pertain to the "duties of the heart" include secretly equating the Creator with something else; hypocrisy, desiring to act in defiance of what God has forbidden; pride, arrogance and haughtiness, abusiveness, deriding the prophets or those whose tongues utter the words of God, despising goodness and virtuous people, or being dissatisfied with philosophical wisdom; or envy and malice toward others, and resenting the Creator's decrees—and many similar vices.

Comments

"equating the Creator with something else" Baḥya here has adopted a theological principle normally associated with Islam according to which "*shirq*"—ascribing divine status to other beings—is deemed the gravest of sins. It extends to the Christian belief in Jesus's divinity which makes him a "partner" of God.

Baḥya Ibn Paquda, The Duties of the Heart *(continued)*

The category of prohibitions related to "obligations of the limbs" includes: openly equating God with something else, false oaths, dishonesty, gossiping, eating prohibited foods, illicit sexual relations, murder, and many more deeds of this kind.

The permissible actions can be divided into three categories: the required, the excessive and the deficient.

Required actions consist of things that are essential for human survival, such as nourishment through food and drink, clothing and shelter, and speech insofar as it is necessary for conducting one's affairs, activities and commerce, the exercising of all sorts of bodily movements. A person should indulge these things as necessary, for purposes of the appropriate administering of his affairs; as it is stated in the scriptures (Psalms 112:5): "A good man shows favor, and lends: he will guide his affairs with discretion."

The second category, which is more common, is when we go beyond the bounds of the essential and indulge in superfluous luxuries, such as excessive eating and drinking. The wise man has already admonished us concerning this when he said (Proverbs 23:20): "Be not among wine-bibbers, among riotous eaters of flesh."

Comments

"the wise man" King Solomon, traditionally believed to be the author of the biblical books of Proverbs, Ecclesiastes and Song of Songs.

Baḥya Ibn Paquda, The Duties of the Heart *(continued)*

The same applies to one who is unnecessarily extravagant with respect to dress or domicile, or in unrestrained speaking when there is a strong likelihood that one will be led to stumble on account of inappropriate comments; as the wise man wrote (Proverbs 10:19): "In the multitude of words there wants not sin: but he that refrains his lips is wise."

This category also includes overindulgence in sexual relations, regarding which he has said (Proverbs 29:3): "he that keeps company with harlots spends his substance"; and (Proverbs 31:3): "Give not your strength to women." And with regard to a king it specifies (Deuteronomy 17:17): "Neither shall he multiply wives to himself." The category also includes immoderate exertions for purposes of acquiring property and wealth, regarding which it says (Proverbs 23:4): "Labor not to be rich: cease from your own wisdom." And concerning a king it states (Deuteronomy 17:17): "Neither shall he greatly multiply to himself silver and gold." All those things that we mentioned previously with respect to the maintaining and enjoying of the physical body may ultimately become reprehensible because they can lead to the transgressing of prohibitions imposed on us by the Creator.

The third category of permitted things is the "deficient." This refers to people who refrain from reaching the state of full satisfaction in eating, drinking, dress or speech, or in activities related to nourishment and the like. It can be subdivided into two types: it can either be an expression of piety, or of worldly considerations.

Insofar as it is motivated by piety and the desire to use it as a means for coming closer to God by means of self-denial, it is laudable and will be rewarded; as the wise man wrote (Ecclesiastes 7:4): "The heart of the wise is in the house of mourning; but the heart of fools is in the house of mirth."

If, however, he is motivated by worldly interests, meaning that he refrains from excesses because he wishes thereby to increase or augment his possessions and for that reason he consumes less than his proper share of nourishment, then such conduct is objectionable, because this person is acting immoderately and causing harm to his body, and this is a consequence of his worldliness. Some wise men have quipped that a person who withdraws from the world because of his love of the world is comparable to one who uses straw to extinguish a fire.

At any rate, when it comes to talking and sleeping, brevity is certainly more praiseworthy.

As regards talking, this is because silence is ultimately better, as the wise man wrote (Ecclesiastes 5:2): "Be not rash with your mouth, and let not your heart be hasty to utter any thing before God: for God is in heaven, and you on earth: therefore let your words be few."

And concerning sleep, it is as he stated in Proverbs (6:10–11]):
"A little sleep, a little slumber, a little folding of the hands to sleep
[so shall your poverty come as one that travels, and your want as an
armed man].

The *Book of the Pious*

The *Book of the Pious* [*Sefer Ḥasidim*] is considered to be the quintessential
product of the religious outlook known as German Pietism (*Ḥasidut
Ashkenaz*], an approach to Judaism that flourished in central Europe in
the twelfth and thirteenth centuries. German pietism was an eclectic
blend of moralistic, mystical and devotional ideals that aspired to produce a
spiritual elite that combined strict standards of traditional observance and
scholarship with an ascetic ethic and a heightened sense of unceasing devotion to God, even to the point of martyrdom. The *Book of the Pious* is
a collective work whose principal author was Rabbi Judah ben Samuel
of Regensburg (1140–1217). It has the character of a kind of scrapbook
of short observations on diverse topics, including fascinating homilies,
folklore and stories. The author's Hebrew style is at times notoriously
rambling and garbled, and this will at times be reflected in the English
translation.

The passage selected for translation here is from a section dealing with
religious education. It includes some remarkable insights into the develop-
mental psychology of children, as well as information about the curriculum
and schools of the time.

The Book of the Pious[1]

[819] "And Joab sent messengers to David, and said, I have fought
against Rabbah, and have taken the city of waters. Now therefore
gather the rest of the people together, and encamp against the city,
and take it: lest I take the city, and it be called after my name"
(2 Samuel 12:27–28). Therefore a student whose master has authorized
him to issue rulings, in a case when the master does not have the time
to investigate the question in detail or to sit in judgement or to involve
himself in some matter that is generally regarded as important—
whereas the student has studied it in detail and is fully prepared
and competent to deal with it—the student should merely say to his
master "this is my opinion, based on such-and-such an argument."
However, he should leave the final decision to the master in order that
his master's name should be attached to it. The student should not
reason, "I shall issue the final ruling so that I can get the credit for it.
For it is written (Song of Songs 7:10): "Moving gently the lips of
sleepers." Instead, he should leave his master to issue the final ruling
of respect for his master. Furthermore, the declarations will have a

greater impact and be more readily received if they are issued in the name of a prominent authority. We also find that Rav Judah and Rava used to say, "Rabbi Jonathan forbade" in order to lend greater authority to their rulings.

Comments

In the biblical story, King David's general Joab had all but conquered the Ammonite capital Rabbah, but refrained from completing the campaign in order to urge David to strike the final blows and thereby claim the credit for the victory. The author of this passage in the *Book of the Pious* infers from this that this is an advisable policy for rabbinical students when dealing with their teachers. Even when the disciple is fully competent to issue a ruling on a question of religious law, they should not do so in categorical terms, but merely make a polite suggestion and allow the senior rabbi to make the final ruling. Aside from indicating respectful deference to one's master and restraining the student's pride, this policy has the practical advantage of lending stronger authority to the ruling, making it more likely that it will in fact be obeyed.

The Book of the Pious *(continued)*

[820] "The fear of the Lord is the beginning of wisdom" (Psalms 111:10).

"The fear of the Lord is the beginning of knowledge, but fools despise wisdom and instruction" (Proverbs 1:7).

"The fear of the Lord is the beginning of wisdom, and the knowledge of the holy ones is understanding" (Proverbs 9:10).

We see, then, that there are three verses. It is also written "Wisdom is the principal thing; therefore get wisdom, and in all your getting, get understanding" (Proverbs 4:7). From the beginning, when a person hires a teacher for his son, he should investigate with respect to the subject that he is going to be learning; for instance, if his children will be learning Bible, whereas the teacher is an expert in Talmud but is utterly ignorant in Bible which is the subject that his children require and in which he is supposed to be knowledgable.

Comments

The Bible's threefold repetition of the link between the fear of God and the acquisition of wisdom is expounded here as a mandate to take special care in choosing and hiring teachers for one's children. If nothing else, the teacher should have competence in the particular subject that he will be teaching. The need to state this point implies that (at least in the author's judgment) many teachers were not suitably trained in the areas of their pedagogic responsibilities.

The Book of the Pious *(continued)*

"In all your getting, get understanding." He ought to have a teacher; even if all that he has is a bare reading knowledge of the letters, he should understand what it is that he is learning. And when he is learning the Bible, he should understand it when he comes to read texts that speak of the fear of Heaven, such as giving honor to the Torah. And he will learn that the Creator is in Heaven, and he is the one who is generous and sustaining. And he will show him that God is in Heaven. And as he gets older, he will teach him that there is a Gehenna and a Paradise. For the hearts of children are like those of adults when they are dreaming who believe that it is all real; in this way children will give credence to everything that you tell them before they are corrupted by bad companions.

The three verses correspond to the three stages of: Scripture, Mishnah and Talmud. The three verses were written in order to indicate that his son and daughter will grow up with the ability to comprehend according to their appropriate level. For then [in ancient times] there would have been a teacher for Scripture, a teacher for Mishnah and a teacher for Talmud; whereas now the three are: one for Torah, one for the Prophets and one for Talmud.

Comments

Note the author's awareness that the standard curriculum of his own community has undergone changes since earlier generations. Whereas once children were expected to study the entire Bible as well as the Mishnah and Talmud, in his own days they limited themselves to the five books of the Torah and the Prophets (perhaps only those sections that are read in conjunction with the liturgical Torah reading cycle) and the Talmud. The Mishnah has been conspicuously excluded as a separate subject of study in the schools. In fact, later generations of German Jews would come to focus exclusively on the study of the Babylonian Talmud, arguing that some familiarity with the Bible and Mishnah could be acquired by virtue of the quotations in the Talmud.

The Book of the Pious *(continued)*

And it says that all the rabbis should be God-fearing, for anyone who does not learn first to fear God will have no success afterwards in teaching his children.

And there are three teachers: (1) the father and mother; (2) the teacher and instructor; and (3) the companions.

Comments

The text of the preceding passage is probably corrupt, and the translation is somewhat conjectural.

The Book of the Pious *(continued)*

And there are three initial stages: (1) until reaching puberty, prior to the age of fourteen while he still has no sexual desire; (2) until he marries; (3) and from marriage until he has children.

At the beginning he should have a God-fearing teacher and companion, to keep him from becoming a glutton or a drunkard or from profaning the Sabbath. And he should also have a good teacher and a good companion in order to caution him against women; and after he gets married, to caution him regarding her period of menstrual impurity, to keep him from transferring objects from his hand to hers, even bread; and when he has children, to caution him concerning stealing, and to urge him and his offspring to devote themselves to the Torah.

Comments

The German Jewish pietists, like other medieval moralists, often understood moral discipline as consisting largely of a struggle between the spirit and the body, especially against sexual temptation. This was reflected in their attitudes toward menstrual impurity. Although biblical and talmudic law placed restrictions on sexual relations and other forms of familiar contact with a woman during her menstrual period, the pietists expanded those restrictions considerably.

The discourses of Rabbi Nissim ben Reuben of Gerona

Rabbi Nissim ben Reuben of Gerona (c. 1310–c. 1375) was a prominent fourteenth-century Catalonian scholar whose literary production reflects the full range of rabbinic activities of the era. He is best known for his commentary on Rabbi Isaac Alfasi's law code, which has been printed alongside most editions of the code. He also contributed to the genres of *piyyut*, responsa, Talmud and Bible commentaries and other genre of Jewish literature.

The current passage is from a collection of twelve sermons (*Derashot*) to the book of Genesis.

Rabbi Nissim of Gerona, from discourse #8

[Scriptural text:] "And he said, Hear now my words: If there be a prophet among you, I the Lord will make myself known unto him in a vision, and will speak unto him in a dream" (Numbers 12:6).

[Discourse:] God, may he be exalted, wanted to chastise Aaron and Miriam for speaking against Moses, as it is written "And Miriam and Aaron spake against Moses because of the Ethiopian woman whom he had married: for he had married an Ethiopian woman" (12:1). He informed them that, although their intentions had been pious, they had acted wrongly in criticizing him.

Indeed, as regards the fact that they were inspired to speak to him only now and not previously—I believe that it was because until now it was on account of Moses' being too busy with the governing of the Israelites, and since he was devoting all his time to the performance of a religious duty, he was therefore exempt from performing other precepts. It was for this reason that they had given him the benefit of the doubt up until now. However, now that he beseeched the Almighty to let others share with him in the responsibilities of leadership, so that he no longer needed to do it all by himself, and he brought in with him seventy men from the elders of Israel—now they felt that he was obligated to perform this precept. It was for this reason that they approached him now.

Indeed, even though their intentions were for the sake of Heaven, they were guilty of a transgression; because they discussed the matter among themselves, but did not ask Moses what his motives were. And also because they considered their own prophetic powers to be on the same level as his prophecy, and they did not treat him with the appropriate respect. "And they said, Hath the Lord indeed spoken only by Moses? hath he not spoken also by us?" The Almighty replied to them that Moses had acted properly, whereas they had sinned toward him. And God informed them that there was an immense difference between their prophetic status and Moses' prophecy, and on account of that difference he was justified in separating himself from his wife, as we shall explain.

This is what it means when it states "Hear *na* my words" (in verse 6). The rabbis stated in the *Sifré*: " 'Hear *na* my words." The word *na* implies an entreaty. And does this not follow logically: If he who called the world into existence spoke beseechingly, can we not infer all the more so that creatures of flesh and blood should act in the same manner!?"

This request demands an explanation. For if they sinned and the Almighty was castigating them for it, does their dignity not warrant that he should spell out their crime before punishing them? "Open rebuke is better than secret love" (Proverbs 27:5), and for this reason he did not need to speak imploringly.

The most reasonable explanation, in my opinion, appears to be that the prophetic vision was very difficult for them to bear and contrary to their nature, since they were not prepared to experience prophecy at any moment as Moses was. Rather, they had to make themselves ready prior to receiving God's word. And this message came upon them with suddenness, as it says: "And the Lord spoke suddenly, etc." (Numbers 12:7). Moses did not find any difficulty whatsoever with this, because he was prepared to receive prophecy at all times, and there was nothing in his body that stood against this and opposed the sudden coming of prophecy upon him. However, the cases of Aaron and Miriam were not like this. For this reason, you will find that it is very difficult for them when prophecy comes upon them suddenly, because when a person's nature is suddenly transformed from one extreme to another, the person becomes panicked and upset. The situation of Aaron and Miriam is comparable to that of a person who is sitting in gloom and darkness for an extended period. If they are suddenly taken into a strong light, they will immediately lose their sight and panic.

The Holy One does not make unreasonable demands upon his creatures, and he now had to approach them in this way suddenly, in order to notify them that Moses had acted properly, whereas they had erred in speaking to him; since because he was constantly in a receptive state for prophecy he therefore had to maintain preparedness at all times. For this reason, he spoke to them in a conciliatory manner, which is courteous and imploring, as the Sages put it. This was in order to avoid their being shocked when God was revealed to them so suddenly.

Comments

Like most Jewish sermons, this one expounds a passage from the biblical text that is being read in the synagogue on the present occasion. The story that is recounted in Numbers Chapter 12 speaks of how Aaron and Miriam criticized their brother Moses "because of the Ethiopian woman whom he had married." Whatever its original meaning might have been, the rabbis of the Midrash explained this passage as referring to Moses' wife Zipporah, whose conjugal needs had been neglected while Moses was preoccupied with his vocation as prophet and leader of his people. Moses' elder siblings reproached him for this dereliction of a domestic duty, and were then castigated by God. Miriam was punished severely by being stricken with leprosy.

It is typical of such homilies to begin by noting difficulties in the biblical passage. In the present instance, some of the problems that Rabbi Nissim points out are:

- Since Moses' marital problems had presumably been in evidence since the beginning of his calling, what prompted Aaron and Miriam to raise the issue at this late juncture in the narrative?
- If Aaron and Miriam were sincerely concerned for Zipporah's welfare, why did God take them to task or punish them for their protest?
- If Aaron and Miriam were acting out of line, then why does the Sifré (an early midrashic compendium) explain that God addressed them in polite, beseeching tones?

Rabbi Nissim's discourse answers all these questions, and more. The major thrust of his words is a lengthy theological analysis of the phenomenon of prophecy, in the spirit of Maimonides (the full discussion has been excluded from the current sample text).

In the current passage, we see a mixing of exegetical concerns (that is, an attempt to produce a coherent reading of the scriptural passage) and some simple moral lessons that can be derived from the story; for example, that when you are displeased by a person's behavior, it is preferable to approach the person directly, rather than talking behind their back.

In spite of the academic and theoretical nature of the topic, which is typical of Spanish Jewish sermons, Rabbi Nissim attempts to formulate it in terms that are understandable to his audience. Note for example the analogy that he draws between an unexpected prophetic experience and exposure to a sudden glare of light.

The memoirs of Glueckel of Hameln

Glueckel [or Glikl] (1646–1724) was married twice to Jewish merchants in Germany, and in addition to her duties as a wife and as the mother of fourteen children, she took an active role in her husbands' business enterprises and continued to administer them after their deaths. Her autobiographical memoir composed in Yiddish offers us a rare and fascinating glimpse into the daily lives of Jewish women in her society, including countless intimate details of the sort that would not be recorded in the standard genres of official religious literature composed by male rabbis. In addition to the meticulous chronicling of her life and that of her family, Glueckel intersperses her memoir with numerous passages of moral instruction addressed to her children. These draw from the traditional Hebrew moralistic texts, and probably reflect the values and conventions of popular vernacular works and sermons addressed to women.

The Memoirs of Glueckel of Hameln[2]

> How shall I give fitting praise and thanks to my creator for all the kindness that he bestows upon us though we can claim no merit of our own? . . . If only we were capable, miserable sinful human beings that we are, of appreciating the great mercies by which the great Creator fashioned us from a lump of clay into human beings, and made us capable of recognizing his great and awesome holy name so that we may serve our Creator with all our heart!
>
> Indeed, my beloved children, behold what a sinful human would do in order to obtain the favor of a king who is nothing but flesh and blood, who is here today and tomorrow in the grave, and nobody knows how long that king of flesh and blood will live from whom they receive the favors, nor how long the recipient of the favors will live. And what

indeed are the favors that he receives from a king of flesh and blood? He can appoint him an important personage, he can arrange for him to receive much money. But all this is momentary and does not last forever. And even if he can possess it until the day of his death, still all this is as nothing because bitter death causes everything to be forgotten, and all his wealth and honor are of no use to him "and no one has power in the day of death" (Ecclesiastes 8:8). Man knows this, but nonetheless he thinks that he should serve the king of flesh and blood diligently in order receive ephemeral benefits. How much more should we be thinking day and night about how we ought to serve the Holy One blessed be he, the King of kings of kings who is living and eternal—for he is the one from whom all those favors that we receive from the king of flesh and blood really originate! And it is the Omnipresent, may he be blessed, who gives everything to mortal kings and who implants in their hearts the inclination to be gracious to whomever his holy will wants, for "the king's heart is in the hand of the Lord" (Proverbs 21:1), and gifts from a king of flesh and blood are as naught in comparison with what the Omnipresent, may he be blessed, grants to those who fear him; namely eternal life, which has no measurement and no bounds and never perishes.

Therefore, my children, the beloved of my heart, take comfort and be patient in your times of suffering, and serve the almighty God with all your hearts when things are going badly for you, God forbid, just as when things go well for you. For even when we feel that the burden that the great God is imposing upon us is too heavy, to the point that we find it almost unbearable—we must nevertheless know that the great God never imposes upon his servants burdens that are too weighty for us to bear. Happy is the man upon whom God imposes something, whether on him or on his children, and he accepts it all with good grace and patience. Therefore I too beseech my creator to but grant me the necessary patience. Furthermore, anything that befalls us in this world that is contrary to our desires comes as retribution for our deeds, and consequently it behooves us to bear it also with patience. Just as one should offer blessings for good things, so should we offer blessings for bad things. A loyal servant of a king of flesh and blood will risk life and limb for the sake of his master, even though his master can only reward him with wealth and financial benefits during this fleeting time which, as I have already mentioned, will last we know not how long. But the reward that comes from our God lasts until eternity. Indeed, exactly as he exists eternally, so too are his great mercies eternal.

Rabbi Moses Hayyim Luzzatto, *The Path of the Upright*

Rabbi Moses ben Hayyim Luzzatto (1707–1746) was a charismatic and brilliant Italian scholar whose commitment to Kabbalah and to active messianic pursuits provoked an intense controversy leading to his excommunication. His ethical treatise *Mesillat Yesharim* (*Path of the Upright*) is in most respects a conventional representative of the genre, delineating a course of life that can eventually make the devotee worthy of receiving the prophetic spirit. Like medieval works of its kind, it stresses a discipline to overcome the temptations of the flesh, the cultivation of humility and other virtuous personality traits, and the imbuing of rituals with profound spiritual significance. The treatise has maintained a continuing popularity.

Rabbi Moses Hayyim Luzzatto, The Path of the Upright, Chapter 23: on the ways to acquire humility and to distance oneself from its shortcomings

There are two factors that accustom a person to humility: habit and contemplation.

"Habit" refers to when a person habituates himself gradually to acting in a humble manner as we have noted previously, by sitting in open spaces and always walking on the sidelines, and by wearing modest clothing—that is to say: respectable but not ornate. For when he accustoms himself to such conduct, the quality of humility will enter his heart by degrees until it establishes itself there properly. Since the nature of the human heart tends toward being overbearing and proud, it is difficult to eradicate this natural tendency entirely. It is only by means of outward actions that are under his control that he can gradually cultivate the internal quality over which he wields less control. This is consistent with what we have explained regarding the quality of eagerness, and all this is subsumed under the dictum of our sages of blessed memory (*Berakhot* 17a): "A person should always be cunning in fear"; this means that he should seek stratagems against his natural inclination until he overcomes it.

However, "contemplation" relates to various matters. One of them is what was mentioned in the words of Akavia ben Mehalalel [Avot 3:1]: "Know from whence you came—from a putrid drop. And know to where you are going—to a place of dust and worms and maggots. And know before whom you will eventually give an accounting—before the King of kings of kings, the Holy One (may he be blessed)." For indeed, all these factors serve as a countermeasure to pride and they promote humility, for once a person considers the worthlessness of his material substance and the lowliness of his origin, he will no longer have any desire at all to be overbearing. Rather, he will tend toward shame and humiliation.

To what may this be compared? To a swineherd who became a monarch. Whenever he recalls his early days it is impossible for him to be proud. By the same token, when one considers that at the end of all his glory he will revert to dust and maggots, all the more so will his pride be overpowered and he will mute the fanfare of his arrogance. For what is the point of all his goodness and grandeur, when it will end in a shameful and lowly state! And when a person goes on to consider and imagine in his heart the moment when he will approach the great court of the celestial host; when he envisages himself standing in judgment before the King of kings of kings, the Holy One (may he be blessed) who is holy and pure to the ultimate degree of holiness and purity, in the council of the holy ones who minister to his might, the mighty ones who do his bidding, who are entirely without blemish; whereas he is standing before them in all his imperfection, lowly and despised by virtue of his character, impure and filthy by virtue of his deeds. Will he be able to lift his head? Is he capable of uttering words? And when they ask him "where is your mouth? Where are your pride and your honor that bore you aloft in your world?"—what will he be able to answer, and what can he reply to this rebuke?

It is therefore clear that if a person were to imagine this true situation for even a moment in its full and vivid reality, then his pride would immediately evaporate never to return.

The second aspect [of contemplation] relates to the vagaries of time and its manifold variations. For it is easy for a wealthy person to be reduced to poverty, for a ruler to become a slave, for a distinguished person to fall into disgrace. If it is so easy for him to plunge into a deplorable state, then how can he ever become arrogant regarding his present situation when he can never be sure of its permanence? How many strains of illnesses might (God forbid!) afflict a person compelling him to offer supplications for assistance and for a slight easing of his plight? How much suffering (God forbid!) might come upon him, forcing him to come begging to people to whom he previously would not have given the time of day, imploring them to rescue him from his predicament? These are things that we all witness on a daily basis, and they are sufficient to remove all traces of pride from the human heart and to clothe him in humility and meekness.

Furthermore, when a person contemplates how deeply he is indebted to the Almighty, and how much he is still in arrears and how negligent he is about it, he will assuredly feel shame and not pride, he will be mortified and his heart will not be haughty. And thus does it say (Jeremiah 31:18): "I have surely heard Ephraim's moaning: [You disciplined me like an unruly calf, and I have been disciplined. Restore me, and I will return]."

Regarding all these things he should frequently contemplate in order to acknowledge the imperfection of the human intellect, and realize how numerous are its errors and falsehoods and that errors are more common than true knowledge.

Therefore he should be in constant fear of this danger, and he should be willing to learn at all times from any person and to always heed their counsel, rather than stumble. This is what our sages had in mind when they stated (Avot 4:1): "Who is wise?—He who learns from all people." In a similar vein it states (*Berakhot* 32b): "A lion does not roar after consuming a basket of straw, but only after a basket of meat."

Ḥasidic stories

From Shivḥei Ha-Besht *(the praises of the Ba'al Shem Tov)*[3]

Rabbi Israel ben Eliezer Ba'al Shem Tov (1698–1760) was the founder of the movement known as Ḥasidism that arose in eastern Europe in the second half of the eighteenth century. His title (often shortened into the acronym "Besht") means "the good master of the name." "Master of the name" was a term used to designate kabbalistic practitioners who were believed to be capable of healing and other miraculous acts by means of mystical manipulations of the holy names of God. The ideology of Ḥasidism was in many ways a reaction to the scholarly ideals that dominated mainstream Judaism. Ḥasidism stressed the importance of simple piety, joyful trust in a loving God and intensely personal prayer.

There is little reliable historical information about the Ba'al Shem Tov. The most influential collection of stories about him was the *Shivḥei Ha-Besht* (Berdichev, 1815), a compendium of hagiographic legends and folktales. Current historical research has demonstrated that the portrait of the Ba'al Shem Tov contained in this work is completely unreliable, that it includes many prototypical legends that were originally told about other figures, and that it contradicts data obtained from more reliable documents. Nevertheless, it continues to exert an influence in Ḥasidic circles as the definitive biography of the movement's founder.

The Ba'al Shem Tov and the Frog

And some say: It once happened that the Rabbi entered into a deep trance and was walking in this meditative state for three days and three nights, while entirely unaware of this. Afterwards, he realized that he was in a great desert, very far from his home, and he was completely amazed that he had wandered into such a desert. Clearly this was no meaningless happenstance.

In the meantime, a frog came before him that was so gigantic that he was almost unable to recognize what kind of creature it was. He asked him: "Who are you?"; to which he replied that he was a rabbinic scholar who had been reincarnated into this frog.

The Ba'al Shem Tov said: "You are a rabbinic scholar!"

And by means of this utterance he elevated him very much.

Now he recounted to him that he had been undergoing the reincarnation process for five hundred years, notwithstanding that Rabbi Isaac

Luria (may his righteous and holy memory be a blessing) repaired all the souls; nevertheless, owing to the seriousness of his transgressions, they kept him wandering through a place that is not frequented by people so that they would not restore him.

He asked him what his crime had been.

And he answered: Once he had belittled the practice of ritual hand-washing, in that he did not wash his hands properly. Then Satan indicted him, to which they replied that he should not be charged for a single transgression. However, since one transgression leads to another, if you succeed in causing him to stumble regarding another transgression, then the current one will also be counted against him. However, if he were to remember the Lord and repent, then he would be exonerated of this one as well.

So he tempted him with one transgression, but he slipped and failed the test. And this was repeated twice and three times until he had transgressed almost the entire Torah. The verdict was to reject him in such a way that his repentance would not be accepted.

In spite of all this, if he were to pound on the gates of repentance they would have accepted him, as is well known, since a heavenly voice once issued announcing "Return, O backsliding children" (Jeremiah 3:14)—except Aḥer! But this was a punishment for his sin in order to push him away. However, if he were to press hard and repent, they would receive him, for there is nothing that stands in the way of repentance. But Satan enticed him and he became a great drunkard, until he had no more time to contemplate and repent, and he transgressed every single sin. And because his first sin had been his belittling of hand-washing, therefore when he died he was reincarnated into a frog, which is always in water, and he was to be relegated to a place that is not frequented by human beings; for if a Jew were to pass by, or if he were to recite some blessing or think a virtuous thought, that might "take out the precious from the vile" (Jeremiah 15:19).

And the Ba'al Shem Tov created a repair for his soul and elevated it until the frog remained a lifeless corpse.

COMMENTS

The motifs of talking animals and of humans being transformed into frogs have more in common with folk literature than with any normative Jewish religious traditions. In this story, those motifs are combined with several beliefs and values that are characteristic of Judaism or Kabbalah. The conventional Jewish concepts include: the rabbinic institution of ritual washing of the hands; the belief in the human capacity for repentance; and the depiction of Satan as a prosecuting attorney in the heavenly court who tries to entice people into sin. Kabbalistic and Ḥasidic themes include: meditative trances; the Lurianic goal of "repairing" or "restoring" sinful souls

[*Tiqqun*]; and the belief that imperfect souls are subjected to cycles of repeated reincarnations until they are purified enough to enjoy their final rest.

"Aḥer" ["the other one"] was an epithet attached to the first-century Rabbi Elisha ben Abuya who became the Talmud's paradigmatic heretic. The Talmud relates that Elisha abandoned hope of ever repenting when he heard a heavenly voice proclaiming that his sin was so terrible that his repentance would not be accepted. From this it is inferred that in all other cases, sincere repentance has the power to obtain forgiveness; even though the sinners might have been told otherwise in order to test the strength of their determination.

The Tales of Rabbi Naḥman of Bratslav

Rabbi Naḥman of Bratslav was the great-grandson of the Ba'al Shem Tov, a prominent, enigmatic and tempestuous leader of the Ḥasidic movement. He was tormented through much of his life by doubts and struggles with his "evil urge"; and his distinctive brand of spirituality encouraged solitary wanderings in the countryside where he would conduct intimate conversations with God. Naḥman's claim to leadership was frequently accompanied by his dismissal of older and more revered leaders of the movement, and it appears that he saw himself as a potential messiah, or at least as one who would help usher in the redemption.

Rabbi Naḥman's "*Sippurei Ma'asiyyot*" (Tales) consist of thirteen symbolic stories that he told to his followers toward the end of his life. They were published in 1815 in Yiddish and Hebrew. They employ conventional motifs from folk literature to convey the author's ideals of redemption, leadership and other spiritual issues. The stories continue to occupy an important place in the curriculum and rituals of the sect that he founded.

The Tale of the Lost Princess

> Once there was a king who had six sons and one daughter. That daughter was very important in his eyes, and he was exceedingly fond of her, and he would dote on her very much. Once he was meeting together with her on a certain day, and he became angry with her, until he blurted out "May the Not-Good take you away!". That night, she retired to her chamber, and when morning came they did not know where she was. Her father was very troubled and went out to search for her hither and yon. The viceroy of the kingdom, moved by what he saw of the king's great sorrow, arose and asked to be provided with an attendant, a horse and money for his expenses, and he went out to look for her.
>
> He searched for her intensively for a very long time until he found her. [Now he tells how he searched for her until he found her.]

He was going to and fro for a long time in the deserts and in the fields and in the forests, searching for her for a very long time. As he was traveling through the desert, he saw a certain path on the side. He deliberated: "inasmuch as I have been going for such a long time in the desert and yet I am unable to find her, I will follow that trail and perhaps I will reach an inhabited place." He went on for a long time, and afterwards he saw a castle around which were posted several troops. The castle was fine-looking, tidy and well-ordered with the troops, and he feared that the troops might not permit him to enter. He thought to himself: I will go ahead and try. He left the horse and proceeded toward the castle, and they left him alone and they did not detain him at all. He kept going continually from room to room, until he arrived at a certain chamber, where he saw a king sitting with his crown, and with him were several troops and there were some musicians with instruments before him. Everything there was perfectly fine and beautiful, and neither the king nor anyone who was present asked him anything at all. He saw there fine dainties and delicacies, and he stayed there and ate. Then he went and lay down in a corner to see what would happen there.

He beheld how the king commanded to have the queen brought in. They went to bring her, and there was a great commotion and much rejoicing and the musicians were playing when they brought in the queen and offered her a throne and seated her next to him. She was the princess, and the viceroy saw her and recognized her.

Afterwards, the queen peered and saw that someone was lying in the corner, and she recognized him. She arose from her throne and approached him, and touched him and asked him: "Do you recognize me?"

He answered her: "Yes, I recognize you. You are the lost princess." Then he asked her, "How did you come to this place?"

She replied: "It was because my father blurted out that utterance; and indeed, this place, is not a good one."

So he told her that her father was exceedingly sad, and that he had been searching for her many years. He asked her, "How might I be able to take you out of here?"

She said to him, "It is impossible for you to take me out, unless you choose a place and then dwell there for one year, and for that entire year you will yearn for me to take me out, and in every free moment you will do nothing but yearn and pray and hope to bring me out. And you will afflict yourself, and on the last day of that year you will not sleep for a full day."

So he went and did this. And at the conclusion of the year, he fasted and did not sleep, and then he arose and went there. He saw a tree upon which were growing very lovely fruits. They were very appealing to his eyes, so he stayed there and ate.

As soon as he had eaten the apple, he fell and was overcome by sleep, and he slept for a very long time. Then the servant was trying to awaken him, but he would not wake up at all. Afterwards he did wake up from his slumber and he asked the servant "Where in the world am I?" So the servant told him the story and said to him "You have been asleep for a very long time, for several years now, and I have been sustaining myself with the fruits."

He was exceedingly grieved, and then he went there and found her and she was very upset. She said to him, "If you had come here on that day, you would have brought me out of there. But on account of that one day you missed out. Indeed, it is very difficult to not eat, especially on the last day, when the evil urge becomes most powerful.

So go now and choose yourself a place, and again stay there for a year. On the last day you shall be permitted to eat, as long as you do not sleep. Do not drink wine, so that you will not sleep, because the important thing is sleeping."

He went and did this. On the last day he was on his way there, when he saw a flowing spring with a red hue and the aroma of wine. He asked the servant: "Do you see that this is a spring, and it ought to have water, but its appearance is red and its aroma is of wine?" So he went and tasted from the spring, and immediately he fell asleep for several years, up to seven years.

There were many troops traveling behind them with their possessions. The servant hid himself from the troops. Afterwards there rode by an ornate chariot in which the princess was seated. She stopped near him, alighted and sat beside him. She recognized him and was shaking him vigorously, but he did not awaken. She began to castigate him, for the numerous efforts and great difficulties he had undergone for so many years in order to rescue her; but on account of that one day when he could have rescued her—it was all lost. She wept bitterly for this, for it is most pitiful for him and for her, that she must remain there for such a long time and she was unable to leave.

Then she took a kerchief from atop her head, and she wrote on it in tears, and she left it with him. She stood up and seated herself in her chariot, and set off from there.

Afterwards, he awakened and asked the servant, "Where in the world am I?" He related the whole story to him, about the soldiers who were passing by and the halting of the chariot, and that she was weeping for him and screaming that it is most pitiful for him and for her. Meanwhile he peeked and noticed that the kerchief was lying nearby. He asked "Where did this come from?" He replied that she had written on it with tears.

He took it and lifted it up facing the sun, and he began to discern letters. He read what was written there: all her plaints and her outcry, and that at the moment she was not at the castle; and that he should seek out a mountain of gold and a castle of pearls, "and there you shall find me." He left the servant behind and went by himself to seek her.

For several years he continued to search for her, and he considered in his mind that there certainly is a mountain of gold or castle of pearls in some inhabited place; for he was conversant with the map of the world. "Therefore I shall go into the deserts." So he went to seek her in the deserts for many, many years.

Later he saw a very large man, who was so large that he was not human at all. The man was carrying a huge tree, such as could not be found in any inhabited place. The man asked him, "Who are you?"

He replied, "I am a man [Adam]."

He was astonished and said, "I have been in the desert for such a long time, and yet I have never seen a man here." Then he told him the whole story of how he was seeking a mountain of gold and a castle of pearls.

He said to him, "Obviously, it does not exist at all." And he put him off telling him that he had been trying to distract him by telling him nonsense, for certainly no such a thing exists.

He began to weep bitterly, for it certainly had to exist somewhere. But the other one put him off saying that no doubt they had been telling him nonsense. But the viceroy insisted that it certainly did exist.

The strange man said to him, "In my opinion it is nonsense, but since you are so insistent, I am placing you in authority over all the beasts. For your sake I shall call to all the beasts, because they roam throughout the world and perhaps one of them knows something about the mountain and the castle."

He summoned them all, from the smallest to the largest, all the beasts, and asked them; and they all replied that they had not seen them.

He said to him, "You see that they were telling you nonsense. If you are ready to listen, then turn back, for you will certainly not find it, because it does not exist."

But he kept imploring him saying that it certainly does exist.

He said to him, "Behold, my brother is in the desert and he is in charge of all the birds. Perhaps they know because they fly in the heights of the air, and maybe they have spotted the mountain and the castle. Go to him and tell him that I sent you to him."

He went for several years in search of him, and again he found a very large man who was also carrying a huge tree. The giant also asked him, and the viceroy told him the whole story, saying that his brother had sent him to him. But this man also put him off saying that it certainly did not exist. But the viceroy also implored him.

He answered, "Behold I am in charge of all the birds. I shall summon them, perhaps they know."

He summoned all the birds and asked them all, from the smallest to the greatest. They replied that they did not know of the mountain and the fortress.

He said to him, "Do you not see that they certainly do not exist! Take my advice and turn back, for it certainly does not exist." But he kept imploring him saying that it certainly does exist.

He said to him, "Farther on in the desert is my brother who is in charge of all the winds. They roam about the world and perhaps they know."

He went for many, many years searching, and came upon a great man and asked him. He repeated to him the whole story, and he too put him off, and he also kept imploring him. The third man said to the viceroy, that for his sake he would summon all the winds and he could ask them. He summoned them, and all the winds came, and he asked them all, but not a single one of them knew anything about that mountain and castle.

He said to him, "Do you not see that they were telling you nonsense?"

He began to weep bitterly and said, "I know that they exist for sure." Meanwhile he saw that one more wind had arrived. The one in charge was angry at him. "Why did you arrive late? Did I not decree that all the winds must come, so why did you not come with them?"

He replied, "I was delayed because I had to carry a princess to a mountain of gold and a castle of pearls."

He was very happy and the one in charge asked the wind, "What are the things that are deemed precious there?"

He said to him that everything there is very precious.

The one in charge of the winds said, "Seeing as you have been seeking her for such a long time, and how many efforts you have undergone, perhaps you will now be prevented from going because of insufficient funds. Therefore I am giving you a vessel, and when you place your hand inside it you will receive coins from it." Then he commanded the wind to carry him there.

A stormy wind came and carried him there, bringing him to the gate. There were troops stationed there who did not allow him to enter the city. He extended his hand into the vessel, took out coins and bribed them, and then entered the city. The city was beautiful. He went to a lord and purchased provisions because he would have to sojourn there, since he would require considerable intelligence and wisdom in order to rescue her.

[He did not tell how he rescued her. But in the end he did rescue her.]

COMMENTS

Although it is not possible in this context to discuss all the obscure details of this story (such as the significance of the three "giants"), the main themes are quite clear. The "princess," as always in kabbalistic literature, represents the *Shekhinah*, the lowest of the ten *sefirot* who represents God's presence in our world; her six "older brothers" represent the constellation of the six *sefirot* above the *Shekhinah*—"*Ze'ir Anpin*" (the Short-faced One) in the Lurianic terminology. The separation of the princess from her father is the classic kabbalistic metaphor (especially in Lurianic Kabbalah) for the inter-connected exiles of the *Shekhinah* and of the Jewish people. The rescue of the princess and her restoration to her home are, accordingly, symbols for the ultimate redemption.

The role of the viceroy in the tale is complex and ambiguous. At one level it represents the persistent Jewish hope, against constant discouragement and all the evidence to the contrary, that the redemption is in fact an imminent possibility; and what is delaying it is the weakness of the human spirit that keeps missing out on the opportunities that are provided for it. On other levels, however, the viceroy represents the responsibilities that are thrust on the shoulders of the true Hasidic leader, the *zaddik*, who is charged with helping to prepare his flock for redemption. It is very likely that we should read into this story the frustrations and self-doubts of Rabbi Naḥman himself who failed in his desperate determination to bring about the messianic era.

The tale does not really have an ending—nothing more than a reassurance by the author or editor that the princess will eventually be found and rescued and that there will be a "happy ending." While this might reflect something as banal as the fact that Rabbi Naḥman ran out of time when telling the story to his followers, it can also be interpreted as an indication that the story's final chapter, as it were, awaits completion in the (imminent) future.

From Mif'alot Ẓaddiqim

The following two tales are translated from a collection entitled *Mif'alot Ẓaddiqim* (the deeds of the righteous) published in Lvov (Lemberg) in 1856.

Tale from Mif'alot Ẓaddiqim

It happened once that one of the disciples of the "great tamarisk," the preacher Rabbi [Dov Baer] of Mezhirech was returning from a visit to his teacher, and he passed through the town of Karlin. He happened to enter the town at night and he was most eager to meet with the righteous Rabbi Aaron of blessed memory who dwelt in that town. So he went in the darkness of the night and knocked on the rabbi's window, saying "Aaron, Aaron, open up for me!"

The righteous rabbi, who was sitting deep in study, answered "Who are you?"; to which the disciple said "[It is] I"—presuming that he would certainly recognize him by his voice.

But the rabbi was silent and did not reply to him, nor did he open the door for him.

And when he knocked on the window yet a second time and a third time without receiving a reply, and the disciple said to him "Aaron, why do you not want to open for me?" he answered as follows: "Who is the one who is able to say 'I'? As it were, only the Holy One himself would have been able to say 'I' and nobody else."

The disciple thought to himself: If so, then I have not learned anything from my master. So he turned around to go back at once to his teacher.

COMMENTS

The lesson of Rabbi Aaron's comment is that no human being can properly regard himself as an "I"—as an independent, autonomous subject. That is a status that is unique to God, the subject and creator of the universe. The interpretation alludes to the opening word of the Ten Commandments (Exodus 20:2): "I [am the Lord your God]." The Hebrew text of the tale employs the same unusual word for "I" as in the verse: "anokhi"—though it appears unlikely that the participants were actually conducting their conversation in Hebrew.

Several of the motifs in this tale are typical of Ḥasidic stories; including: the master's strange behavior that astonishes and disturbs the observer or disciple until it is explained; and the stressing of the fact that true religious learning consists not of mastering texts or performing rituals, but of subtle spiritual values that can only be experienced through personal observation of a righteous teacher.

Tale from Mif'alot Ẓaddiqim

The righteous holy master, etc. Rabbi Elimelech (also known as Rabbi Melech) of Lyzhansk was once accompanied by a certain rustic whose son-in-law was very learned and pious, and occupied himself day and night in Torah and worship without any interruption. The son-in-law did not wish to travel to the rabbi because he imagined that the rabbi would pose questions to him about the Talmud and its commentaries in order to evaluate his character; and perhaps he would be unable to answer and would be humiliated. Eventually, however, owing to his overwhelming efforts to study diligently and to meditate on the Torah day and night, he achieved mastery of "the sea of the Talmud," the law codes and true wisdom; and it occurred to him that he should now travel to the rabbi, for he estimated that there was no possibility of his being unable to produce any answer to the rabbi's question, for he was not deficient in even the most obscure details.

So he said to his father-in-law, "it is now the proper time and occasion to journey to visit the rabbi." When his father-in-law heard this, he rejoiced greatly and was very grateful to God for giving him the merit of bringing his son-in-law under the wings of the divine presence [Shekhinah] and finding shelter in the rabbi's shade. He forthwith harnessed his wagon and they traveled together to his holy master.

As they were treading on the rabbi's doorstep, Rabbi Elimelech approached and greeted the rustic father-in-law, but he offered no greeting to the son-in-law. He merely turned his back to him and asked him directly: "Young man, what does the Lord say?" The son-in-law was overcome with much fear and trembling, and all the hair on his body bristled because he had no idea how to respond, nor did he understand the meaning of the question. In their astonishment at the rabbi's words, the son-in-law and his father-in-law remained standing in their places; and afterwards they journeyed back to their home in a state of depression.

The young man sat silently and regretted his journey, saying "who compelled or forced me to undertake the journey? Whatever happened happened."

Later, on the holy Sabbath day, as he was seated at the table with the rabbi for the Sabbath meal immediately following the recitation of the blessing over the bread, the rabbi turned to the young man and asked him again: "What does the Lord say?" And thus, on each and every Sabbath the rabbi would continue to ask him "What does the Lord say?"

It happened at the conclusion of the Sabbath, when they came before the rabbi to take their leave from him and to return home safely, the rabbi asked him once again, "Young man, what does the Lord say?" and he remained silent and did not answer in his perplexity at not understanding the meaning of the words.

The holy rabbi now said to him, "It is written (Jeremiah 23:24): 'Can anyone hide himself in secret places?'— It means that even if a person should perform only good deeds and in secret, which is certainly a fine thing—'So I'—as long as he is saying and thinking in his mind 'I am learned and righteous and upright'—'shall not see him'—I cannot bear to look at such a person—'says the Lord'—This is what the Lord says."

COMMENTS

This tale is very similar in its spirit to the previous one. It is built around the tension between "conventional" Jewish religious learning and the personal, spiritual sensitivity that is the ideal of the Ḥasidic masters. In conventional Jewish society, the learned son-in-law would be held in greater esteem than his rustic and unlettered father-in-law; and the son-in-law, unfamiliar with Ḥasidic values, expects Rabbi Elimelech to judge him by the standards of rabbinic scholarship. After bringing himself to a state of considerable scholarly accomplishment, Elimelech dumfounds him by asking him a simple question that he is totally unequipped to answer, or even to understand.

On a straightforward "textual" level, the correct understanding of Rabbi Elimelech's question lay in the fact that it was actually a quotation from Jeremiah. In typical Ḥasidic fashion, Rabbi Elimelech read the verse in an unconventional and disconnected manner. The word "I" is not the subject of the verb "shall not see," but rather the object: God is declaring I cannot bear to look at a person with a strong sense of "I"—what we would now call an "ego." (Technically, this farfetched reading is possible in the Hebrew because, as an inflected language, the grammatical subject is implied by the verb form, and the pronoun is written for extra emphasis.)

But it is not sufficient to understand the verse in a theoretical manner. Evidently, subjecting the son-in-law to the extended process of personal humiliation—that is, the actual undermining of his pride and egotism—was an essential precondition for the true internalizing of the rabbi's lesson.

Ḥasidic teachings: Rabbi Elimelech of Lyzhansk

Elimelech of Lyzhansk (1717–1787) was one of the powerful spiritual leaders in the third generation of Ḥasidism. He was a disciple of the Ba'al Shem Tov's successor Dov Baer of Mezhirech, and spent his early years wandering and leading a very ascetic life. In 1772 he settled in Lyzhansk in Galicia, where he established an influential center of Ḥasidic activity. In his life, thought and writings he paid particular attention to defining the role of the "ẓaddik" (righteous man) who was to serve as an intermediary between God and the common Jews. The ẓaddik bears a heavy responsibility, according to Rabbi Elimelech; his failings and subsequent repentance perform an eschatological function in bringing about redemption in accordance with the Lurianic doctrine of the "elevation of the sparks."

His *No'am Elimelech* is a collection of homiletical expositions on the Bible. Like several Ḥasidic works of the genre, it makes frequent use of unlikely interpretations and audacious word-plays on the words of the scriptural text.

Rabbi Elimelech of Lyzhansk, No'am Elimelech *to Deuteronomy*[4]

> "[Behold, I set before you today a blessing and a curse:] the blessing, if you listen to the commandments of the Lord your God (Deuteronomy 11:27).
>
> This can be interpreted with the help of a parable. A man who had been suffering from an illness, God forbid, was cured. Afterwards, at each and every moment he will be attentive and alert to find out whether he might be having (God forbid) a relapse of that disease.
>
> This, then, is the moral of the parable: Every person ought to be listening to himself at every moment, to be attentive to whether he is fulfilling his obligation in performing the commandments of the Lord; to notice whether there might arise, God forbid, something inappropriate. This is the meaning of "the blessing, if you listen." The blessing for a person consists of the fact that you are listening to [the commandments, etc.]; as noted, that you must listen and be alert constantly, even as you are carrying out his commandments (may his name be exalted), to note whether something is lacking in them.
>
> "And the curse, if you do not listen" (verse 28)—This means: if you do not guard yourselves as noted.

Therefore, a person must watch constantly and be vigilant for himself at all times, that this will be a blessing for him and for his descendants forever.

Comments

Like many Ḥasidic homilies, this one takes bold liberties with the plain meaning of the text in order to elicit its distinctive message. Taken in its original context, the biblical passage beginning with Deuteronomy 11:26 means something like: Behold, I am setting before you today a blessing and a curse. The blessing will apply if you obey the commandments of the Lord, whereas the curse will apply if you do not obey the commandments. Specific blessings and curses are set out in detail later on in the book.

Rabbi Elimelech reads the text differently, so that the blessing consists of listening to the commandments and the curse consists of not listening. God has allowed humans the opportunity of monitoring the level of their religious observance in order to make them aware whether or not they are achieving their full spiritual potential. It is typical of Ḥasidism that the goal of religious life is not merely to observe the laws (which can be achieved in a cold, mechanical way), but to strive to fulfill them to the highest, most conscientious degree.

The message is made vivid with the help of a parable. A person who has recovered from a disease is doubly alert to any irregularities in his physical state. Similarly, fallible human beings who have sinned should be especially sensitive to the symptoms of spiritual weakness.

Timeline of Jewish religious texts and authors

Author, Person or Work	from	until
Hillel the Elder	c. 30 BCE	10 CE
Yavneh generations: Rabban Yoḥanan ben Zakkai, Rabbi Eliezer, Rabban Gamaliel, Rabbi Joshua, Ben Azzai, Rabbi Levitas of Yavneh, Rabbi Yoḥanan ben Beroqa, Rabbi Zadok, Rabbi Eleazar ben ʿArakh	c. 70	c. 130
Usha generation: Rabbis Meir, Judah, Nehemiah, Yosé, etc.	c. 135	c. 180
Mishnah	c. 50 CE	c. 220
Tosefta		c. 230
Mekhilta deRabbi Ishmael		c. 250
First generation of Amoraim: Rabbi Joshua ben Levi, Rav (Abba Arika), Samuel, Mar Ukva, Rav Assi, etc.	c. 220	c. 250
Second generation of Amoraim: Rabbi Yoḥanan, Rav Huna, etc.	c. 250	c. 280
Third generation of Amoraim: Rabbi Isaac, Rav Nahman, Rabbah bar Nahmani, etc.	c. 280	c. 310
Fourth generation of Amoraim: Abayé, Rava, etc.	c. 310	c. 340
Fifth generation of Amoraim: Rav Pappa, etc.	c. 340	c. 380
Sixth generation of Amoraim: Rav Ashi, Mart Zuṭra, etc.	c. 380	c. 430
Pesiqta deRav Kahana		5th century
Babylonian Talmud	c. 200	c. 600
Yannai	6th century?	7th century?
Amram Gaon		died 875
Heikhalot literature		dates unknown; between 3rd and 10th centuries
Saadiah ben Joseph al-Fayyumi Gaon	882	942

Hananel ben Hushiel		died 1055–1056
Bahya ben Joseph Ibn Paquda		late 11th century
Rashi: Rabbi Solomon ben Isaac of Troyes	1041	1105
Judah ben Samuel Halevi	c. 1075	1141
Abraham ben Meir Ibn Ezra	1089	1164
Jacob ben Meir Tam	c. 1100	c. 1171
Samuel ben Meir	c. 1085	c. 1174
Moses ben Maimon (Maimonides, Rambam)	1138	1204
Rabbi Isaac ben Abraham	late 12th century	early 13th century
Sefer Ha-Bahir		early 13th century
Eleazar the son of Judah ben Rabbi Kalonymos	c. 1165	c. 1230
Hezekiah ben Manoah		mid-13th century
Moses ben Naḥman (Naḥmanides, Ramban)	1194	1270
Abraham ben Samuel Abulafia	1240	c. 1295
Meir Ha-Kohen of Rothenburg, author of *Hagahot Maimoniot*		end of 13th century
Tosafot	c. 1100	c. 1300
Zohar	c. 1270	c. 1300
Ra'aya Meheimana	c. 1290	c. 1310
Jacob ben Asher	c. 1270	1340
Nissim of Gerona	c. 1310	c. 1375
Israel Isserlein	1390	1460
Don Isaac ben Judah Abrabanel	1437	1508
Moses Isserles	c. 1530	1572
Isaac Luria (ARI)	1534	1572
Joseph Caro	1488	1575
Ḥayyim ben Joseph Vital	1543	1620
Glueckel of Hameln	1646	1724
Moses Hayyim Luzzatto	1707	1746
Israel ben Eliezer Ba'al Shem Tov	1698	1760
Dov Baer of Mezhirech		died 1772
Aaron ben Jacob of Karlin	1736	1772
Elimelech of Lyzhansk	1717	1787
Naḥman ben Simḥah of Bratslav	1772	1810
Israel Lipschutz	1782	1860
Jacob Zevi Meklenburg	1785	1865
Israel Meir Ha-Kohen Kagan	1838	1933
Abraham Isaac Hakohen Kook	1865	1935

Glossary

Aaron The older brother of Moses and the first high priest. All subsequent Jewish priests (*kohanim*) claim to be patrilineal descendants of Aaron (Aaronides).

Abraham The ancestor of the Hebrews. According to the story in the Torah, God was impressed with Abraham's faith, and made a covenant with him and his descendants.

Account of creation An esoteric tradition of expounding the biblical creation story. The Mishnah forbids teaching this publicly.

Account of the chariot An esoteric tradition of expounding Ezekiel's vision of a chariot composed of angelic beings. The Mishnah forbade public dissemination of this mystical discipline.

Aggadah (English adjective: aggadic) The component of the oral tradition that is not concerned with the technical study of religious law. It consists largely of homiletical expositions of the Bible.

Agudat Israel An association representing the interests of traditionalist Orthodox ("haredi") groups.

Agunah An "anchored woman"; one who is unable to remarry because she cannot obtain a divorce from her first husband, or because his death cannot be satisfactorily established.

Amidah "The standing [prayer]" another name for the Eighteen Benedictions, which is recited while standing.

Amora A rabbi from the third to seventh centuries, whose views are cited in the Talmud or contemporary rabbinic works.

Aninut The initial and most intense stage of grieving, from the moment of the death until the burial.

Apocalypse A popular genre of ancient Jewish literature, especially during the Roman era, in which the hero, usually a figure from the Bible, receives a graphically symbolic vision of a catastrophic future when God will overthrow the forces of evil and institute his kingdom on earth.

Apocrypha One of the works that were included in the Greek corpus of Jewish scriptures, but not in the Hebrew Bible.

Aramaic A Semitic language similar to Hebrew that was spoken by Jews during the Second Temple era, especially in the Galilee and Babylonia.

Aravah Willow, one of the "four species" that is carried during the rituals on the feast of Tabernacles (Sukkot).

Ashkenaz The Hebrew name for Germany, used to refer to Jewish communities that originated in central Europe, or to the Jews of Christian Europe in general.

'*Asiyyah* Hebrew: "action"—the last of the four worlds according to kabbalistic teaching, the one that converges with the physical world.

Attributes of action In the thought of Maimonides, these are descriptions of God that are to be understood metaphorically, as analogous to the frame of mind that would have produced a certain result if a similar effect has been produced by a human being.

Avot/Pirkei Avot A tractate in the Mishnah consisting of adages and other non-halakhic traditions. It opens by describing the sequence of transmitting the Torah from Moses via the "fathers of the world" until their own time.

Azilut Hebrew: "emanation"—the third of the four planes of reality according to the Kabbalah.

Ba'al Shem "Master of the name"—a practitioner of magic and healing by means of the kabbalistic manipulation of the names of God.

Bad urge In rabbinic homilies, the aspect of the human personality that seduces people to sin. It is equated with the sexual urge, and therefore is essential for human survival.

Bahir The earliest known document containing the teachings of the Kabbalah, the symbolism of the ten *sefirot*. It first appeared in the twelfth century in Provence, and takes the form of a pseudepigraphic rabbinic midrashic exposition whose main protagonist is Rabbi Nehunya ben ha-Kanah.

Bar Kokhba, Simeon Leader of a failed Jewish revolt against Rome between 132 and 135 CE. Rabbi Akiva and others believed he was the messiah.

Bar mitzvah "Subject to the commandments"—a Jewish male who has reached the age when he is legally responsible under Jewish religious law; equated with the attainment of puberty, which is assumed to have occurred by the age of thirteen years and one day.

Bat mitzvah "Subject to the commandments"—a Jewish female who has reached the age when she is legally responsible under Jewish religious law; equated with the attainment of puberty, which is assumed to have occurred by the age of twelve years and one day.

Bat qol (Hebrew: "daughter of a voice") A divine voice or omen, as recounted in ancient rabbinic lore.

Beit keneset \ be kenishta "House of assembly," the Hebrew and Aramaic terms for synagogue.

Beit Ya'akov A network of Orthodox schools for girls founded by Sara Schnirer in 1917.

Berakhah A blessing, a liturgical formula beginning "Blessed are you, God . . .".

Beri'ah   Hebrew: "creation"—the third of the four planes of reality according to the Kabbalah; the realm of the highest angels.

Berit milah   "The covenant of circumcision," the ritual circumcision performed on Jewish males, usually on the eighth day of their lives; or as part of a religious conversion procedure.

Bimah   The elevated platform of a synagogue, used principally for the reading of the Torah.

Bi'ur   A commentary and German translation of the Bible (in Hebrew letters) by Moses Mendelssohn.

B'nei Akiva   The youth movement of the Mizrachi religious Zionist movement.

Breaking of the Vessels   In the kabbalistic teachings of Rabbi Isaac Luria, the myth that explains the origins of evil in the universe, caused when the vessels created by God to receive the divine light were unable to contain it and shattered, leaving a mixture of holy sparks and evil shards.

Cairo Genizah   A repository for discarded documents in a synagogue in Fustat (Cairo), Egypt that preserved hundreds of thousands of texts from the early medieval era, and is a key resource for the study of Jewish society, literature and religion.

Canaan   The name for the land of Israel prior to its conquest by Joshua.

Canaanites   The peoples who inhabited the land of Israel prior to its conquest by the Israelites.

Central Conference of American Rabbis   The association of rabbis affiliated with the American Reform movement.

Chair of Elijah   A chair that is customarily set aside for the biblical prophet Elijah at circumcision ceremonies.

Chariot mysticism   See "account of the chariot."

Children of darkness   Those who do not follow God's ways, according to the teachings of the Qumran documents.

Children of light   Those who faithfully follow God's true law, according to the teachings of the Qumran documents.

Columbus Platform   A policy statement issued by American Reform Judaism in 1937, expressing more traditional positions on certain issues.

Committee on Law and Standards   The body of Conservative Judaism that makes policy decisions on major questions of Jewish religious law.

Conservative movement   The American incarnation of Positive-Historical Judaism, espousing an approach that tries to accommodate modern values within the structures of traditional Jewish law.

Conversos   Jews who converted to Christianity under compulsion during the time of the Spanish Inquisition.

Council of Torah Sages   An assembly of rabbis who have supreme authority over decisions of the Agudat Israel movement.

Covenant   In Jewish belief, a mutual agreement that defines the relationship between God and the people of Israel. Hebrew: *Berit*.

Daniel A book included in the *Ketuvim* section of the Bible, purporting to tell the story of the namesake hero, a Jew who lived during the Babylonian exile and was able to interpret apocalyptic visions of the future.

Day of Atonement Annual holy day designated by the Torah for forgiveness and atonement of sins. It falls on the tenth day of the seventh month, Tishri, and is observed through fasting and prayer.

Dead Sea scrolls A library of ancient Jewish texts written during the Second Temple era discovered in caves near Khirbet Qumran in the Judean desert.

Derash Interpretations that follow the methods of rabbinic midrash.

Devekut "Cleaving"—the Ḥasidic ideal of maintaining uninterrupted consciousness of God, especially during prayer.

Diaspora The Jewish communities scattered outside the land of Israel.

Divided Monarchy In biblical history, the era during which Israel was divided into two states: the northern ten tribes of Israel, and the southern kingdom of Judah.

Doenmeh A sect of adherents of Shabbetai Zevi, they accepted Islam while secretly maintaining their faith in Shabbetai Zevi's eventual reappearance.

Eighteen Benedictions The central prayer of the rabbinic liturgy, whose original structure consisted of a sequence of eighteen blessings (*berakhot*) of praise, petition and thanksgiving. The current version contains nineteen blessings.

Ein-Sof Hebrew: "The Infinite"—in the Kabbalah, the most exalted level of the godhead, entirely beyond the grasp of human understanding.

Emancipation The extending of citizenship and civil rights to Jews in modern societies.

Enlightenment The movement calling for adapting Jewish culture and religion so as to facilitate participation in modern society.

Epicurean In rabbinic terminology, the most common designation for a heretic, presumably referring to the Greek philosopher Epicurus who denied God's active involvement with the created world.

Erez Yisra'el Hebrew: "the land of Israel"—the historic Jewish homeland.

Erusin Hebrew: "betrothal"—a formal stage in the Jewish marriage process, in which the couple are legally bound to one another but do not yet live together.

Essenes A Second Temple Jewish movement that removed itself from Jerusalem and inhabited separate communities where they observed their distinctive standards of piety and purity. Most scholars identify them as the authors of the Dead Sea scrolls from Qumran.

Etrog A citron; the "fruit of a goodly tree" that is included among the "four species" used in the rituals of the feast of Tabernacles.

Exodus The second book of the Torah, describing the enslavement of the Hebrew from Egypt, their miraculous liberation (exodus) by God, and the receiving of the Torah at Mount Sinai.

Ez Ḥayyim   The kabbalistic compendium by Rabbi Hayyim Vital containing his version of the teachings of Rabbi Isaac Luria.

Ezra-Nehemiah   A book in the *Ketuvim* section of the Hebrew Bible (now usually divided into two books) that describes the return of the Jews to Jerusalem following the Babylonian exile.

Fifteenth of Shevat   A date in the winter used for measuring the ages of fruit trees for purposes of various agricultural regulations. Mainly among the kabbalists and Zionists it has taken on the status of a holiday celebrating the land of Israel and its produce.

Four species   Plants that are carried in ritual processions on the feast of Tabernacles as commanded in the Torah. Rabbinic tradition identifies the species as: date-palm frond (*lulav*); citron (*etrog*); myrtle branches (*hadas*); willow branches (*aravah*).

Gaon (plural: *Geonim*; English adjective: geonic)   From a Hebrew word meaning "pride"; the title given to the heads of talmudic academies, especially in Babylonia, after the talmudic era.

Galilee   The northern district of the land of Israel. It became the center of Jewish religious and communal life in the second century CE following the decline of Judea.

Garden of Eden   The paradise in which the first man and woman were placed until they were banished for their disobedience. In traditional Jewish thought, the term is used to designate the abode of the righteous in the afterlife. Hebrew: "Gan Eden."

Gehinnom   A notorious and cursed site of heathen child sacrifice in biblical times, it later became identified with the place where sinners suffer torments in the afterlife.

Genesis Rabbah   A work of aggadic midrash on the book of Genesis.

Genizah   A repository for discarded sacred texts, which according to Jewish law may not be actively destroyed.

German pietism   Hebrew: "*Ḥasidut Ashkenaz*"; an influential mystical and moralistic ideology that arose in the Rhineland in the twelfth and thirteenth centuries.

Get   A Jewish bill of divorce.

Gezerah shavah   A method of midrashic exegesis in which analogies are drawn based on the appearance of a similar expression in two biblical passages.

Ghetto   A neighborhood in which Jews were forced to live. The term was probably taken from the restricted Jewish quarter of Venice, established in 1516, that was situated near a foundry (getto).

Gilgul   Reincarnation or metempsychosis into a different body in the next life, according to the doctrines of the Kabbalah.

Gog and Magog, war of   A catastrophic war described in the book of Ezekiel (chapters 38–39) in his vision of the end of days. This war became a standard component of Jewish eschatology.

Golah or *galut*   Exile, the state of removal from the homeland as punishment for sins.

Golden Age of Spanish Jewry   A blossoming of Jewish cultural and religious creativity in Spain, especially during the eleventh century.

Good urge   In rabbinic homilies, the aspect of the human personality that tends toward virtue and obedience to God.

Great Revolt   The failed uprising against Rome in 66–73 CE that culminated in the destruction of the second Temple in the year 70.

Guide of the Perplexed   The philosophical masterpiece by Moses Maimonides in which he attempted to reconcile traditional Jewish beliefs with Aristotelian science and philosophy.

Gush Emunim   Hebrew: "bloc of the faithful"—an Israeli religious and political movement that is concerned with maintaining Jewish settlement in territories acquired in the 1967 Six-Day War.

Hadas   Hebrew: "myrtle"—one of the "four species" carried in processions on the feast of Tabernacles.

Haggadah   Hebrew: "telling"—the liturgy for the traditional Passover night meal (*seder*) in which the liberation of the Hebrews from Egyptian slavery is recounted. The reciting of the haggadah is seen as the fulfillment of the precept (Exodus 13:8) "And you shall tell your son on that day."

Hagiographa   Greek for "holy writings"—see "Ketuvim."

Halakhah   The component of the Jewish oral tradition that deals with matters of law.

Hallah   A portion of dough that must be set aside and given to a priest according to Torah law. In colloquial usage, it has come to designate an ornamental loaf of bread eaten on the Sabbath or festivals.

Hanukkah   The "feast of Dedication" commemorating the purification of the Jerusalem Temple after it had been used for pagan worship during Antiochus IV's persecutions. The holiday lasts eight days in the winter and is celebrated by lighting lamps every night.

Hareidi   Hebrew for "those who tremble"—a term used to described the most conservative type of traditionalist Jews in terms of their dress, observance, devotion to full-time religious study and insulation from the modern world.

Hasid   From a Hebrew word meaning "pious," the term has been applied to several Jewish pietistic ideologies through history, particularly to the movement established by Rabbi Israel Baal Shem Tov in the eighteenth century that advocated a popular mystical devotion based on serving God in joy.

Hasidut Ashkenaz   See: "German pietism."

Haskalah   The Hebrew name for the "Enlightenment."

Hasmoneans   The priestly family who led a successful revolt against the Hellenistic persecutions of Antiochus IV, and subsequently established themselves as the political and priestly leaders of Judea.

Havdalah   Hebrew for "separation"—a ceremony marking the conclusion of the Sabbath or festival.

Havurah   Hebrew for "fellowship"—a name used for various Jewish communal groupings through history, particularly the Havurat Shalom, an American movement of small, non-institutional communities and prayer groups that prominent in the 1960s and 1970s.

Hebrew   The Semitic language in which most of the Jewish Bible is composed, as is most subsequent Jewish religious literature. A revived, modernized version of Hebrew is the spoken language in the state of Israel.

Hebrew Bible   The sacred scriptures of the Jews, traditionally believed to have originated in divine revelation or inspiration. In old Jewish sources it is referred to as *Miqra* ("that which is read aloud"). According to the conventional classification, the Hebrew Bible is divided into three sections: Torah, *Nevi'im* (Prophets) and *Ketuvim* (Hagiographa), comprising twenty-four books.

Heder   Hebrew for "room"—used to designate the traditional European Jewish elementary schools that were often criticized for their primitive pedagogy.

Heikhalot   Hebrew for "palaces"; a genre of Hebrew mystical literature involving the ascent through multiple levels of palaces that are guarded by angels.

Herem   A ban of excommunication or ostracism, the most effective sanction for enforcing the authority of the rabbi and communal institutions in pre-modern Jewish society.

Hesder   Hebrew for "arrangement"—an option that allows religious soldiers in Israel to combine religious study with their military service.

Hevra kaddisha   Aramaic for "holy society"—a voluntary burial society.

Ḥiddushim   Hebrew for "new things"—used to designate critical comments on the Talmud or other rabbinic works.

Hitlahavut   Hebrew for "bursting into flame"—the Ḥasidic ideal of religious ecstasy or fervor, especially in prayer.

Holocaust   Originally a Greek term for a burnt sacrificial offering; standardly used to refer to the murder of millions of Jews by the Nazis and their collaborators during World War II. See: "Shoah."

Holy cherub   In the mysticism of the German pietists, a manifestation of divine glory.

Ḥuppah   Canopy under which Jewish wedding ceremonies are conducted, symbolizing the household now shared by the newly married couple.

Israel

- The name given to the biblical patriarch Jacob after wrestling with a mysterious being in Genesis 32:28: "for you have striven with God and with men and have prevailed."
- The entire nation descended from Jacob and his twelve sons ("children of Israel"; "Israelites").

- During the era of the divided monarchy, Israel was the northern kingdom consisting of ten tribes.
- In Jewish texts written in Hebrew, Jews almost invariably refer to themselves as "Israel."
- The modern Jewish state founded in 1948.

Jerusalem Talmud A commentary on the Mishnah compiled from the discussions of rabbis from the third to fifth centuries in the land of Israel. (This title is not quite accurate, since Jerusalem did not really exist at that time.)

Jewish Renewal A contemporary Jewish religious movement that incorporates elements of Ḥasidism, Kabbalah, meditation and various New Age concepts.

Job A book in the Ketuvim section of the Hebrew Bible that explores issues of theodicy and suffering in the framework of a story about a man named Job who is tested by God with terrible afflictions.

Kabbalah A medieval system of Jewish esoteric teaching based on the doctrine of the ten *sefirot*. Kabbalah includes a theological or theosophic theory about the relationship between the divinity and the created world, as well as a symbolic exegetical system for reading the Bible.

Kach An illegal ultra-nationalist religious movement in Israel founded by Meir Kahane and advocating the removal of Arabs from Israel.

Kaddish A prayer consisting of praises of God that is recited at the conclusions of units of the liturgy or of religious study. Since the Middle Ages it has been customary for mourners to lead certain instances of the Kaddish during the first eleven months after the death or on the Yahrtzeit.

Kalam A Muslim school of theology that influenced Jewish thinkers, it applied rational methods to the analysis and clarification of religious beliefs.

Karaites A movement that arose in the Middle Ages, whose adherents reject the rabbinic oral tradition and acknowledge only the authority of the Bible.

Kavod Hebrew: "[Divine] glory"—a spiritual force that serves as the intermediary between God and the created universe in the mystical speculations of the Ḥasidei Ashkenaz movement. See "holy Cherub."

Kedushah Hebrew: "sanctification"—the third section of the Eighteen Benedictions prayer (see "*Amidah*"). When recited in a congregational setting it incorporates verses from the chariot visions of Ezekiel and Isaiah.

Kelippot Hebrew: "husks" or "shards"—in the kabbalistic doctrine of Rabbi Isaac Luria, these are the remains of the shattered vessels that could not contain the divine light. They are the metaphysical source of evil in the world.

Kerovah An elaborate form of liturgical poetry designed to accompany the recitation of the *Amidah* prayer.

Ketubbah A Jewish marriage contract, whose main purpose is to guarantee the support of the wife in the event of divorce or widowhood. It also outlines the couple's mutual obligations during the marriage.

Ketuvim Hebrew: "(sacred) writings"—see "Hagiographa."

Khazars A seminomadic Turkic nation whose royalty and nobility converted to Judaism in the late eighth or early ninth century.

Kiddush Hebrew: "sanctification"—a liturgical ceremony, usually recited over a cup of wine, inaugurating the Sabbath or a festival.

Kiddushin Hebrew: "sanctifications"—a term for betrothal. See "*erusin.*"

Kohen (singular), *kohanim* (plural) A priest. In Judaism, all priests are patrilineal descendants of Aaron, Moses' brother, who was designated the first high priest.

Kol Nidrei Aramaic: "All the vows"—a ceremony for the cancellation of vows, recited before the evening service of the Day of Atonement.

Kolel An institution for advanced talmudic studies for married students.

Kosher Hebrew (according to Ashkenazic pronunciation): "fit"—colloquially applied to foods that are prepared according to the Jewish dietary regulation.

Kvater (masculine), *kvaterins* (feminine) Yiddish: "godfather"—an individual who is honored by being asked to carry the baby in to a circumcision.

Law of Return A law passed by the Israeli parliament in 1951 recognizing all Jews as Israeli expatriates and allowing them automatic citizenship.

Levirate marriage A biblical law requiring a childless widow to marry her late husband's brother, or to undergo a ritual ceremony of release.

Levites One of the twelve tribes of Israel, descended from Jacob's son Levi. The Levites were designated a holy tribe without a territory, and were to be supported by tithes.

Leviticus Rabbah A work of aggadic midrash on the book of Leviticus.

Lilith In folklore and kabbalistic traditions, a female demon, usually the queen of the demons, who threatens newborn infants.

Logos Greek: "word" or "reason"—in the philosophy of Philo of Alexandria, the rational principle of the universe that serves as an intermediary between God and the physical world.

Lulav The green, closed frond of a date palm. It is one of the "four species" taken in the ritual processions of the feast of Tabernacles.

Lurianic Kabbalah The interpretation of the Kabbalah taught by Rabbi Isaac Luria in sixteenth-century Safed.

Maccabee Epithet attached to Judah son of Mattathias, the first military leader of the Hasmonean uprising against the Hellenistic forces. The word means "hammer" and may refer to his might, or perhaps to a physical feature. The books about the uprising were titled "Maccabees."

Malkhuyyot Hebrew: "kingship"—the theme of the first section of the Additional Service for Rosh Hashanah, stressing the theme of God's absolute sovereignty over the universe.

Maror   Hebrew: "bitter herb"—a required food at the Passover seder, symbolizing the bitterness of the slavery in Egypt.

Marranos   A derogatory term for Conversos—probably from a word meaning "pigs."

Mashiaḥ   Hebrew: "anointed one"—a legitimate king or priest who has been installed through the biblical ceremony of anointing the head with olive oil. As an eschatological concept, it refers to the future restoration of the legitimate Davidic monarchy and Zadokite priesthood.

Masorti movement   Hebrew: "traditional"—the name used by Conservative Judaism in Israel and some other localities.

Massekhet   Hebrew: "tractate"—a section of the Mishnah or Talmud, usually dealing with a specific topic. Tractates are divided up into chapters, and several chapters make up an order (*seder*).

Matrilineal descent   The rule in rabbinic law that counts as Jewish a person who is born of a Jewish mother.

Matzah   Unleavened bread, eaten on Passover to recall how the Israelites left Egypt in haste and their dough did not have time to rise.

Megillah   Hebrew: "scroll"—especially the scroll of the book of Esther that is read ritually on Purim.

Merkabah **mysticism**   Hebrew: "chariot"—an esoteric mystical discipline based primarily on the prophet Ezekiel's vision of a chariot composed of angelic beings bearing a mysterious human-like figure.

Messiah   Widespread English rendering of "*Mashiaḥ.*"

Messiah son of Joseph   In some Jewish eschatological scenarios, a figure who will try to redeem Israel but will fall before achieving his mission. The ultimate messiah will be from the house of David.

Midrash   Rabbinic teachings related to the Bible.

Mikveh   A pool of water used for purification.

Min   In rabbinic literature, a heretic.

Minor Prophets   A volume in the *Nevi'im* section of the Bible containing twelve shorter works that are treated as a single book.

Mishnah   From a Hebrew root meaning "to recite from memory."

- The title of an authoritative collection of Jewish oral traditions, mostly of legal matters, and organized by subject; compiled by Rabbi Judah the Prince in the early third century CE.
- An individual unit or paragraph in the Mishnah.
- The genre consisting of oral teachings that are not connected to scripture.

Mishneh Torah   Hebrew: "second Law"—the Hebrew term that is rendered in Greek as "Deuteronomy" (the book in the Torah consisting of Moses' review of his life). The title was adopted to designate Maimonides' comprehensive code of Jewish law.

Mizrachi movement   Hebrew abbreviation for "spiritual center"—religious Zionist movement.

Mohel   One who performs circumcisions.

Moriah   The location of the mountain where Abraham was commanded to sacrifice his son; traditionally identified with the Temple Mount in Jerusalem.

Musaf   Hebrew: "additional"—the additional sacrifices offered on Sabbath and festivals; by analogy, the additional prayer services on those days.

Nasi   Hebrew: "prince"—title given to the communal and judicial head or patriarch of the Palestinian Jewish community.

Navi   Hebrew: "prophet"—one who was chosen to deliver messages from God.

Negative theology   In Maimonides' philosophy: the belief that the use of attributes in the Bible does not convey positive information about God, but serves to deny any deficiencies.

Neo-Orthodoxy   The interpretation of traditional Judaism associated with Rabbi Samson Raphael Hirsch, advocating active involvement with modern Western culture.

Neoplatonism   A philosophical approach based on the teachings of Plato and Plotinus that stresses the existence of the transcendent One from which emanated the diversity of the material world.

Neturei Karta   Aramaic: "guardians of the city"—a traditionalist religious movement that virulently opposes Zionism.

Nevi'im   Hebrew: "prophets" (see "*Navi*")—the second division in the Jewish classification of the Bible.

New Christians   Jews who converted to Christianity at the time of the Spanish Inquisition.

Niddah   A menstruating woman, or one who has not become purified of the impurity caused by menstruation.

Ninth of Av   The date of an annual day of fasting and mourning for the destruction of the two Jerusalem Temples and several other national catastrophes.

Noachide commandments   Seven moral and religious obligations that are considered binding on all of humanity (all of whom are descendants of Noah).

Odes to Zion   Poignant Hebrew poems about Jerusalem authored by Judah Halevy.

Old Testament   The Christian term for the Hebrew Bible.

Omer   Hebrew: "sheaf"—a sheaf of barley offered up on the second day of Passover, thereby beginning a count of seven weeks until Shavuot, the Feast of Weeks. By extension, the term is used to refer to the process of counting the seven weeks, and to the period during which the counting takes place.

Orthodox Union   The main organization of modern or centrist Orthodox congregations in America.

Orthodoxy   The modern Jewish movement that advocates traditional Judaism.

Other Side   Aramaic: *"Sitra Ahra"*—in the Kabbalah, the realm of evil.

Palestine   The name given by the Romans to the land of Israel.

Palestinian Talmud   See "Jerusalem Talmud."

Passover   Hebrew: *"Pesah"*—the springtime festival commemorating the liberation of the Israelites from slavery in Egypt. The name is taken from the biblical story of how death "passed over" the Israelite dwellings when slaying the Egyptian firstborn.

Patriarchal era   The generations of Abraham, Isaac and Jacob, the biblical ancestors ("patriarchs") of the Jewish people.

Patrilineal descent   According to a 1983 decision of the American Reform movement, children of a Jewish father should be accepted as Jewish even if the mother was not Jewish.

Pentateuch   Greek: "the five books [of Moses]"—the Torah.

Pesah   Hebrew: "Passover."

Peshat   Hebrew: "simple"—literal or contextual exegesis.

Pesher   Hebrew: "interpretation"—a genre of literature found at Qumran in which biblical texts are interpreted with reference to recent events or the specific history of the Qumran sect.

Pesiqta   Aramaic: "division"—midrashic expositions for "special" occasions, such as festivals and other days that are not part of the sequential cycle of readings from the Torah and Prophets.

Petihah/petihtah   Hebrew/Aramaic: "opening", "introduction"—a rhetorical structure for introducing midrashic homilies, especially by commencing with a verse from another part of the Bible, and developing a sermon that culminates with the beginning of the passage that is read that day in the synagogue.

Pharisees   From Hebrew: "separate"—a Second Temple movement that encouraged Torah scholarship as a religious value, and maintained strict standards of purity and dietary observance.

Pittsburg Platform   Policy statement of the American Reform movement in 1885, expressing strong opposition to Jewish peoplehood, ritual and other features of traditional Judaism.

Piyyut   Hebrew liturgical poetry.

Positive Historical Judaism   An evolutionary cultural conception of the Jewish religion advocated by Zacharias Frankel.

Practical Kabbalah   The use of kabbalistic principles in order to manipulate reality, a form of magic.

Priest   See "*kohen*."

Primordial Man (*Adam Kadmon*)   A form of kabbalistic symbolism according to which the *sefirot* are configured as limbs of a human form.

Psalms   A book in the *Ketuvim* section of the Bible consisting of poetic prayers, most of which are traditionally attributed to King David.

Pseudepigrapha   Ancient Jewish texts, many of them of an apocalyptic nature, that claimed to be written or revealed by biblical figures.

Purim   Hebrew: "[feast of] lots"—a holiday commemorating the events recounted in the book of Esther, when the Jews of the Persian empire were saved from Haman's plot to murder them. Also referred to as "the feast of Esther."

Purim-Shpils   Yiddish: "purim plays"—theatrical productions traditionally enacted on Purim.

Qorban   Hebrew: "sacrifice."

Qumran   An archeological site in the Judean desert near the Dead Sea where a library of manuscript scrolls was discovered from the Second Temple era. It is widely believed that Qumran was the site of an Essene community.

Ra'aya Meheimna   Aramaic: "faithful shepherd"—a kabbalistic work by an unknown Spanish author published in standard editions of the Zohar, and purporting to contain teachings of Moses (the shepherd), the prophet Elijah, and Simeon ben Yohai about the secret meanings of the commandments.

Rabbi   Hebrew: "my teacher"—the title given to a recognized authority on Jewish law. In modern times, the position is often perceived as a type of clergy.

Rabbinites   Jews who accept the authority of the rabbinic oral tradition; usually used as contrast to Karaites.

Rashi   Acronym for Rabbi Solomon ben Isaac (1041–1105) of Troyes, France, the foremost Jewish commentator on the Bible and Talmud.

Redemption of the firstborn   A ritual in which the firstborn son is redeemed from a *kohen* for five silver shekels in order to formally release him from his obligation to serve in the Temple. The ceremony is usually conducted when the boy is one month old.

Reform Judaism   The Jewish movement that advocated introducing changes into traditional Judaism in order to accommodate modern values and ideas, and to facilitate participation in post-Emancipation society.

Responsa   In Hebrew: "*she'elot utshuvot*" (questions and answers)—replies written by prominent rabbis to questions about Jewish law and other topics.

Resurrection   The belief that the dead will be restored to life in physical bodies.

Rishon le-Zion   Hebrew: "First to Zion" (Isaiah 41:27)—the official title given to the Sephardic Chief Rabbi of Israel.

Rosh Hashanah   The Jewish New Year, a biblical holiday celebrated on the first day of the seventh month (Tishri). It is portrayed as a solemn day of divine judgment.

Sabbath   Hebrew: "*shabbat*"—the weekly day of rest observed from sundown on Friday until Saturday night in commemoration of God's completing the six days of creation.

Sadducees   A Second Temple Jewish movement that upheld the ideals of the traditional Zadokite high priesthood.

Safed   A town overlooking the Sea of Galilee that became a preeminent center of kabbalistic activity in the sixteenth century.

Samael   In Jewish folklore and Kabbalah, the king of the evil demons.

Samaritans   A religious community who observe the Torah. According to the biblical account, they are descended from foreign peoples who were transferred by the Assyrians to Samaria after the exile of the northern Israelite kingdom.

Sandak   Probably from the Greek: "suntekos," "companion of child"—the person who holds the baby during the circumcision ceremony.

Sanhedrin, Syhedrion   Greek: "council"—a Jewish high court and rabbinical council during the Second Temple and rabbinic eras.

Satan   The angel charged with entrapping, accusing and punishing sinners.

Savora'im   The rabbis who were active in Babylonia between the end of the talmudic era and the beginning of the geonic era, sometime between 500 and 700 according to various calculations.

Scapegoat   In the Day of Atonement observances in the Temple, a goat was chosen by lot, then the high priest symbolically placed the sins of the people on its head and sent it to perish in the wilderness.

Scroll of Esther   The book of Esther handwritten on a parchment scroll, especially for liturgical reading on the holiday of Purim. See "*Megillah.*"

Second Commonwealth   The era in Jewish history extending from the return of the Babylonian exiles until the destruction of the second Temple of Jerusalem, roughly 530 BCE–70 CE.

Second Temple Era   Equivalent to "Second Commonwealth," viewed from a religious perspective.

Seder   Hebrew: "order"

- One of the six main topical divisions of the Mishnah
- The procedures for the ceremonial meal on the first night of Passover; or by extension, the meal itself.

Sefer Ḥasidim   Hebrew: "the book of the pious"—an important compendium of lore from the *Ḥasidut Ashkenaz* movement of the twelfth and thirteenth centuries.

Sefer Yeẓirah   Hebrew: "the Book of Creation"—a short and enigmatic treatise describing how God created the world by means of combinations of the ten decimal numbers and the twenty-two letters of the Hebrew alphabet.

Sefirah (singular), *Sefirot* (plural)   Ten emanated powers of God symbolically identified with divine attributes, according to the central doctrine of the Kabbalsh.

Seliḥot   Hebrew: "forgiveness"—penitential prayers recited during the Rosh Hashanah season, on fast days and other occasions.

Semites   Supposed descendants of Shem son of Noah, identified as the Middle Eastern peoples. The term is used most accurately as the name of the language family to which Hebrew, Aramaic and Arabic belong.

Sepharad   Hebrew: Spain.
Sephardic   Adjective referring to:

- Jews of medieval Spain.
- Jewish communities of Arabic and Islamic lands.
- Jewish refugees from Iberia since the time of the Inquisition.

Septuagint   Greek: "seventy"—the old Alexandrian Greek translation of the Torah (and the rest of the Bible). According to legend it was composed by seventy Jewish elders.

Seventeenth of Tammuz   A fast day held in the summer commemorating the breach of the walls of Jerusalem by the Babylonians as well as other national catastrophes.

Shabbat   See "Sabbath."

Shabbateans   Followers of the seventeenth-century messianic pretender Shabbetai Zevi.

Shalom   Hebrew: "peace."

Shas   An Israeli political party representing a Sephardic Haredi constitutency.

Shavuot   Hebrew: "(feast of) weeks"—a biblical pilgrimage festival observed fifty days after the beginning of Passover. The Torah depicts it as a time of agricultural thanksgiving, and the rabbinic tradition identified it as the anniversary of the revelation of the Torah at Mount Sinai.

Sheḥitah   Ritual slaughter of animals or fowl.

Shekhinah   The divine presence in the world.

Sheloshim   Hebrew: "thirty"—the first thirty days of mourning.

Shemaʿ (or *Shemaʿ Yisraʾel*)   A central component of the daily liturgy, containing Deuteronomy 6:4–9, 11:13–21, and Numbers 15:37–41, embedded in a framework of blessings. The Hebrew name consists of the opening words, "Hear O Israel . . ."

Shemini Aẓeret   Hebrew: "eighth day of assembly"—the day following the feast of Tabernacles (Sukkot), which is celebrated as a separate holiday.

Sheva berakhot   Hebrew: "seven blessings"—seven blessings, several of them poetic celebrations of marriage, that are recited at a Jewish wedding and during the subsequent week of festivities.

Shivah   Hebrew: "seven"—the first week of mourning, when the mourners remain at home and are consoled by the community.

Sho'ah   Hebrew: "destruction"—used to designate the murder of six million Jews by the Nazis and their collaborators; an alternative term for "Holocaust."

Shofar   A trumpet made from a ram's horn, sounded especially on Rosh Hashanah.

Shofarot   Hebrew: "trumpeting"—the third theme of the Additional (*Musaf*) service of Rosh Hashanah, dealing with diverse occasions of the sounding of the shofar.

Shulhan Arukh Hebrew: "set table"—an influential sixteenth-century codification of Jewish law by Rabbi Joseph Caro (with supplement by Rabbi Moses Isserles).

Sh'virat ha-kelim See "breaking of the vessels."

Simḥat Torah Hebrew: "rejoicing of the Torah"—a celebration of the completion of the cycle of reading the Torah and the commencement of a new cycle. It is standardly observed on the second day of Shemini Aẓeret (the day that is added in diaspora communities).

Sinai The mountain on which the Torah was revealed to Israel through Moses, according to the biblical account. By extension, the name may be applied to the event itself.

Song of Songs A book in the *Ketuvum* division of the Bible consisting of sensuous love poetry. Traditionally, it is understood as an allegory for the relationship between God and Israel. It is ascribed to King Solomon, and hence is often referred to as the Song of Solomon. Its Hebrew title is *Shir ha-Shirim*.

Special cherub See "Holy cherub."

Sukkah Hebrew: "tabernacle," "booth"—the temporary dwelling in which one lives during the feast of Tabernacles, in commemoration of the wanderings of the Israelites in the desert after the exodus from Egypt.

Sukkot A seven-day pilgrimage festival held in the fall (commencing on the fifteenth of Tishri) commemorating the ingathering of the crops and the sojourn of the ancient Israelites in the Sinai wilderness

Synagogue Greek: "assembly"—a place where Jews assemble for the reading of scripture, prayer and other religious and communal functions.

Tabernacles, feast of See "Sukkot."

Taharah Hebrew: "purification"—especially the cleansing and preparation of a corpse for burial.

Talmud One of two (Israeli and Babylonian) collective interpretations of the Mishnah composed between the third and seventh centuries, consisting largely of intricate debates and analysis on technical issues of religious law.

Talmud Torah Study of the Torah, as a religious activity and value. The term is also used to designate a Jewish elementary school.

Tamid Hebrew: "continual offering"—sacrifices offered every morning and evening on behalf of the community.

TaNaKh An acronym for the three divisions of the Hebrew Bible: Torah, *Nevi'im* and *Ketuvim*.

Tanhuma A family of aggadic midrash known for the frequency of the introductory formula "Thus began R. Tanḥuma"; and for its propensity for fashioning the individual statements of earlier traditions into continuous narratives and homilies.

Tanna (singular), *tannaim* (plural), **tannaitic** (English adjective) Aramaic: "recite from memory"

- A functionary in the amoraic schools responsible for memorizing and reciting earlier traditions.
- A sage whose views are cited in the Mishnah or other works from the first to early third centuries.

Targum   Hebrew: "translation"—the Aramaic translation that used to accompany the liturgical scriptural reading in the synagogue, for the benefit of those who were not fluent in Hebrew.

Teacher of righteousness   A revered figure mentioned in the Qumran scrolls, who is widely assumed to be the founder of the sect.

Tefillah   Hebrew: "prayer"—the term is used to designate prayer in general; or as the standard Hebrew designation for the Eighteen Benedictions/*Amidah*.

Ten days of repentance   The period extending from Rosh Hashanah to the Day of Atonement, when Jews repent their sins with a view to attaining divine forgiveness.

Ten lost tribes   The tribes of the northern kingdom of Israel during the era of the divided monarchy, who were conquered and exiled by the Assyrians, and subsequently lost to Judaism.

Tenth of Tevet   A minor fast day observed in the winter to commemorate the beginning of the siege of Jerusalem by the Babylonians.

Terumah   Hebrew: "that which is taken up," "heave offering"—a proportion of produce that is set aside for the priests, and must be consumed in a state of purity.

Tetragrammaton   The holy four-letter name of God that is not pronounced by Jews, and is usually replaced by an epithet meaning "Lord."

T'fillin   Passages from the Torah that are written on pieces of parchment and inserted in leather boxes that are strapped on the arm and forehead, in fulfillment of the biblical precept "it shall be for a sign for you upon your hand, and for a memorial between your eyes."

Tiferet   Hebrew: "beauty," "glory"—in Kabbalah, the central *sefirah* that embodies the perfect balance of justice and mercy.

Torah   Hebrew: "teaching," "guidance," "instruction"

- The first five books of the Hebrew Bible, believed to have been revealed by God through Moses.
- More generally, the teachings of Judaism, or some portion thereof.

Torah im Derekh Erez   Hebrew: "Torah with worldly culture"—the ideology advocated by Rabbi Samson Raphael Hirsch of integrating traditional Jewish belief and observance with involvement in secular culture.

Tosafot   Hebrew: "supplements"—critical comments to the Talmud, especially those produced in medieval France and Germany.

Tosefta   Aramaic: "supplement"—a tannaitic collection organized like the Mishnah and containing alternative or explanatory traditions.

Usha   A village in the Galilee that was a center of rabbinic leadership in the mid-second century CE.

Wissenschaft des Judentums German: "Science of Judaism"—the scientific or academic study of Judaism, especially as it developed in eighteenth- and nineteenth-century Germany.

Yahrtzeit German: "anniversary"—the anniversary of the death of a loved one, commemorated through the recitation of Kaddish and other observances.

Yavneh A coastal town in Judea that was the center of rabbinic leadership during the generations following the destruction of the second Temple. By extension, the term is applied to those generations (c. 70–135 CE).

Yeshivah An institution for advanced talmudic studies.

Yezirah Hebrew: "formation"—the third of the four worlds according to the Kabbalah; the realm of the lower angels, the souls and of Paradise.

Yiddish The vernacular language of Ashkenazic Jewry, consisting chiefly of a German dialect (written in Hebrew letters), with elements of Hebrew, Aramaic and other languages absorbed in the course of the community's migrations.

Yishuv Hebrew: "settlement"—a Jewish community in the land of Israel.

Yizkor Hebrew: "May God remember"—title and opening word of the memorial prayer for the dead, recited on some Jewish holidays.

Yom ha-Azma'ut Israeli Independence Day, celebrated on the fifth of Iyyar (in April or May).

Yom ha-Sho'ah Memorial day for the Holocaust.

Yom Kippur/*Yom ha-Kippurim* See "Day of Atonement."

Yom Yerushalayim Hebrew: "Jerusalem Unification Day"—Annual commemoration of the reunification of Jerusalem on 28 Iyyar (June 7) 1967.

Zaddik Hebrew: "righteous one"; a charismatic leader embodying the values of Hasidism.

Zadok High priest appointed by David, and the ancestor of the dynasty ("Zadokites") that occupied the high priesthood until the Hasmonean era.

Zealots A Jewish group committed to violent resistance against the Romans, motivated by their conviction that their sole allegiance should be to God.

Zikhronot Hebrew: "remembrance"—the theme of the second section of the Additional Service for Rosh Hashanah, stressing the theme that God recalls and judges all the deeds of his creatures.

Zimzum Hebrew: "contraction"—in the kabbalistic doctrines of Rabbi Isaac Luria, the idea that God intentionally withdrew himself from a part of the universe in order to enable the existence of something other than himself on which he could bestow his blessings.

Zion The name of a mountain in Jerusalem; by extension, an epithet for Jerusalem.

Zionism Political movement, founded by Theodor Herzl in the late nineteenth century that advocated the establishment of a national home for the Jewish people in its historic homelands.

Ẓiẓit   Hebrew: "tassle," "fringe"—knotted strings attached to the corners of a garment as a reminder of the commandments, in fulfillment of Numbers 15:38.

Zohar   Hebrew: "brilliance"—the name of the most influential compendium of kabbalistic teachings; composed in thirteenth-century Spain in the style of a rabbinic midrash whose central figure is Rabbi Simeon ben Yohai.

Notes

Introduction

1 My presentation of this question, as well as my location of the relevant texts, draws heavily on the masterful study by Jacob Katz. "Alterations in the Time of the Evening Service (Ma'ariv): An Example of the Interrelationship between Religious Customs and their Social Background." In *Divine Law in Human Hands: Case Studies in Halakhic Flexibility*, 88–127. Jerusalem: Magnes Press, 1998.

1 Prayers and liturgical texts

1 Translated from: Yechezkel Luger. *Weekday Amidah in the Cairo Genizah*. Jerusalem: Orḥot, 2001 (Hebrew).
2 Translated from: Israel Davidson, Simha Assaf, and Issachar Joel, eds. *Siddur R. Se'adyah Gaon: Kitab Gami' Altsalavat Va'altasabiḥ*. Sixth edition. Jerusalem: Meḳitse Nirdamim, 2000 (Hebrew).
3 Translated from: Rabinowitz, Zvi Meir, ed. *The Liturgical Poems of Rabbi Yannai according to the Triennial Cycle of the Pentateuch and the Holidays: Critical Edition with Introductions and Commentary*. Vol. 1. 2 vols. Jerusalem: Bialik Institute and the Hayyim Rosenberg Institute for Jewish Studies of Tel-Aviv University, 1985 (Hebrew).
4 Translated from: *Sha"S Teḥinnah Haḥadashah*. New York: Hebrew Publishing Company, 1916 (Yiddish and Hebrew).

2 Aggadah and Midrash

1 Translated from: S. Horovitz and I. A Rabin, eds. *Mechilta D'Rabbi Ismael cum variis lectionibus et adnotationibus*. Jerusalem: Wahrmann, 1970 (Hebrew); Jacob Zallel Lauterbach, ed. *Mekilta de-Rabbi Ishmael*. 3 vols. Paperback. The Schiff Library of Jewish Classics. Philadelphia: Jewish Publication Society of America, 1976 (Hebrew and English).
2 Translated from: S. Horovitz and I. A. Rabin, eds. *Mechilta D'Rabbi Ismael cum variis lectionibus et adnotationibus*. Jerusalem: Wahrmann, 1970 (Hebrew); Jacob Zallel Lauterbach, ed. *Mekilta de-Rabbi Ishmael*. 3 vols. Paperback. The Schiff Library of Jewish Classics. Philadelphia: Jewish Publication Society of America, 1976 (Hebrew and English).
3 Translated from: Bernard Mandelbaum, ed. *Pesikta De-Rav Kahana*. 2 vols. New York: Jewish Theological Seminary of America, 1987 (Hebrew).

4 Based on: Eliezer Segal. *The Babylonian Esther Midrash: A Critical Commentary*. 3 vols. Brown Judaic studies no. 291–293. Atlanta: Scholars Press, 1994.

3 The literature of halakhic discourse

1 Translated from: E. D. Goldschmidt. ed. *Seder Rav 'Amram Ga'on*. Jerusalem: Mossad Harav Kook, 1971 (Hebrew).
2 Translated from: Israel Davidson, Simha Assaf, and Issachar Joel, eds. *Siddur R. Se'adyah Gaon: Kitab Gami' Altsalavat Va'altasabih*. Sixth edition. Jerusalem: Meḳitse Nirdamim, 2000 (Hebrew).
3 Translated from: Benjamin Manasseh Lewin. *Otzar Ha-Gaonim: Thesaurus of the Gaonic Responsa and Commentaries following the order of the Talmudic Tractates*. Vol. 1. Haifa, 1928 [Hebrew].

4 Jewish bible commentaries

1 Translated from: Asher Weiser, ed. *Perushe Ha-Torah Le-Rabbenu Avraham Ibn Ezra*. Vol. 1. 3 vols. Jerusalem: Mosad Harav Kook, 1976 (Hebrew).
2 Translated from: David Rosin, and Abraham Isaac Bromberg, eds. *Perush Ha-Torah La-RaSHBaM*. (Jerusalem?): s.n, 1964 (Hebrew).
3 Translated from: *Perush Ha-Torah*. Vol. 2. 2 vols. Jerusalem: Mossad Harav Kook, 1959 (Hebrew).

5 Philosophy and rational theology

1 Translated from: Joseph Kafiḥ, trans. *Sefer Ha-Nivḥar Ba-'Emunot Uva-De'ot Le-Rabbenu Sa'adiah ben Yosef Fayyumi: Maqor Ve-Targum*. Jerusalem: Sura Institute of Yeshiva University, 1970 (Hebrew and Judeo-Arabic).
2 Translated from: Joseph Kafiḥ, trans. *Torat Ḥovot Ha-Levavot LeRabbenu Bah ya ben Yosef ben Paquda ZṢ"L*. Jerusalem, 1973 (Hebrew and Judeo-Arabic); with extensive use of: Edwin Collins, trans. *The Duties of the Heart by Rabbi Bachye*. Wisdom of the East. E. P. Dutton and Company, 1909.
3 Translated from: Moses Maimonides. *Mishneh Torah; Hu Ha-Yad Ha-Ḥazaqah (Sefer Ha-Mada')*. Edited by Jacob ben Eliezer Cohen and Moshe Hayim Katzenelenbogen. Jerusalem: Mosad Harav Kook, 1964 (Hebrew).
4 Translated from: Moses Maimonides. *Moreh Ha-Nevukhim*. 3 vols. Jerusalem: Mosad Harav Kook, 1972 (Hebrew and Judeo-Arabic); with particular reliance on: Moses Maimonides. *Moreh Nevukhim*. Translated by Michael Schwarz. 3 vols. Tel-Aviv: Tel Aviv University, The Lester and Sally Entin Faculty of Humanities, The Chaim Rosenberg School of Jewish Studies, 1996 (Hebrew).
5 Translated from: David Baneth and Haggai Ben Shammai, eds. *Kitab al-radd wa'l-dalil fi al-din al-dhalil, The Book of Refutation and Proof on the Despised Faith (The Book of the Khazars)*. Jerusalem: Magnes, 1977.

6 Esoteric, mystical and kabbalistic texts

1 Translated from: Saul Lieberman, ed. *Tosefta*. New York: Jewish Theological Seminary of America, 1955 (Hebrew).
2 Translated from: Peter Schäfer, Margarete Schüter, and Hans Georg von Mutius, eds. *Synopse zur Hekhalot – Literatur*. Texte und Studien zum Antiken Judentum 2. Tübingen: Mohr Siebeck, 1981.
3 Translated from: Reuben Margulies, ed. *Sefer Ha-Bahir*. Jerusalem: Mosad Harav Kook, 1950 (Hebrew).

4 Translated from: Reuben Margulies, ed. *Sefer Ha-Zohar*. 3 vols. Jerusalem: Mosad Harav Kook, 1964 (Aramaic and Hebrew).
5 Translated from: Reuben Margulies, ed. *Sefer Ha-Zohar*. 3 vols. Jerusalem: Mosad Harav Kook, 1964.
6 Translated from: Gershom Gerhard Scholem. *Ha-ḳabalah Shel Sefer Ha-Temunah Ve-Shel Avraham Abul'afyah*. Yerushalayim: Aḳademon, 1965 (Hebrew).

7 Moralistic and ethical writings

1 Translated from: Judah ben Samuel. *Sefer Ḥasidim*. Edited by Jehuda Wistinetzki and Jakob Freimann. 2nd edn. Frankfurt am Main: Wahrmann, 1924 (Hebrew).
2 Translated from: Chava Turniansky, ed. *Gliḳl: Zikhronot, 1691–1719*. Jerusalem: Zalman Shazar Center for Jewish History and the Ben-Zion Dinur Center for Research in Jewish History, 2006 (Yiddish and Hebrew).
3 Translated from: Dob Baer ben Samuel. *Shivḥe Ha-Beshṭ*. Edited by Samuel A. Horodezky. Tel-Aviv: Dvir, 1947 (Hebrew).
4 Translated from: Gedaiyah Nigal, ed. *No'am Elimelekh le-Rabbi 'Elimelekh mi Lizensḳ*. Jerusalem: Mosad Harav Kook, 1978 (Hebrew).

Bibliography of Jewish religious texts in English

General

Alexander, Philip S. *Textual Sources for the Study of Judaism*. Chicago: University of Chicago Press, 1990.

Holtz, Barry W., ed. *Back to the Sources: Reading the Classic Jewish Texts*. New York: Summit Books, 1984.

Singer, Ellen, and Bernard M. Zlotowitz. *Our Sacred Texts: Discovering the Jewish Classics*. New York, NY: UAHC Press, 1992.

Prayer and liturgy

Daily prayer book

Aigen, Ronald S. *[Ḥadesh Yameinu =] Renew Our Days: A Book of Jewish Prayer and Meditation*. Hampstead, Quebec: Congregation Dorshei Emet, 1996.

Birnbaum, Philip. *Ha-Sidur Ha-Shalem. Meturgam U-Meforash Be-Tosefet Mavo*. New York: Hebrew Publishing Company, 1969.

Bokser, Ben Zion. *The Prayer Book: Weekday, Sabbath, and Festival*. New York: Behrman House, 1983.

Sacks, Jonathan. *[Sidur Ḳoren] = The Koren Siddur*. Jerusalem: Koren Publishers, 2009.

Sabbath and festivals

Birnbaum, Philip. *Sidur Le-Shabat Ve-Yom Ṭov*. New York: Hebrew Publishing Company, 1950.

Greenberg, Sidney, and Jonathan D. Levine. *Siddur Ḥadash: Worship, Study, and Song: For Sabbath and Festival Mornings [= Sidur Ḥadash: Le-Shabat Ve-Yom Ṭov]*. Prelim. edn. New York: Prayer Book Press/Media Judaica, 1991.

Harlow, Jules. *Siddur Sim Shalom: For Shabbat and Festivals*. New York City: Rabbinical Assembly, 1998.

Kaplan, Mordecai Menahem. *High Holiday Prayer Book, with Supplementary Prayers and Readings and with a New English Translation*. New York: Jewish Reconstructionist Foundation, 1948.

Scherman, Nosson, and Meir Zlotowitz. *[Sidur Ets Ḥayim: Ḥol/Shabat/Shalosh Regalim =] The Complete ArtScroll Siddur: Weekday/Sabbath/Festival: A New*

Translation and Anthologized Commentary. ArtScroll mesorah series. Brooklyn, NY: Mesorah Publications in cooperation with Eitz Chaim Foundation, 1985.

Scherman, Nosson, Benjamin Yudin, and Sheah Brander. *[Mahzor Zikhron Avraham: Rosh Ha-Shanah =] ArtScroll Transliterated Linear Machzor: Rosh Hashanah: Based on The Complete ArtScroll Machzor.* The ArtScroll Series. Brooklyn, NY: Mesorah Publications in conjunction with the Orthodox Union, 2000.

Scherman, Nosson, Benjamin Yudin, and Sheah Brander. *[Mahzor Zikhron Avraham: Yom Kipur =] ArtScroll Transliterated Linear Machzor: Yom Kippur: Based on The Complete ArtScroll Machzor.* The ArtScroll series. Brooklyn, NY: Mesorah Publications in conjunction with the Orthodox Union, 1999.

Scherman, Nosson, Benjamin Yudin, and Sheah Brander. *[Sidur ḳol Ya'aḳov: Ḥol/ Shabat/Shalosh Regalim =] The Complete ArtScroll Siddur: Weekday/Sabbath/ Festival: A New Translation and Anthologized Commentary.* 3rd edn. ArtScroll mesorah series. Brooklyn, NY: Mesorah Publications, 1990.

Silverman, Morris. *Mahzor Le-Rosh Ha-Shanah Ule-Yom Ha-Kipurim. High Holiday Prayer Book.* Hartford: Prayer Book Press, 1951.

Union of Liberal and Progressive Synagogues (Great Britain). *[Petah Teshuvah] Gate of Repentance; Services for the High Holydays.* London: Union of Liberal and Progressive Synagogues, 1973.

Passover haggadah

Birnbaum, Philip. *Seder Hagadah Shel Pesaḥ.* New York: Hebrew Publishing Company, 1953.

Cohen, Jonathan. *[Hagadah Shel Pesaḥ: Lefi Minhage Ha-Sefaradim Ṿa-'adot Ha-Mizraḥ =] The Sephardi Haggadah: With Translation, Commentary, and Complete Guide to the Laws of Pesah and the Seder.* Jerusalem: Feldheim, 1988.

Freedman, Jacob. *Polychrome Historical Haggadah for Passover. [Hagadah "Me'ir 'enayim"].* Springfield, MA: Jacob Freedman Liturgy Research Foundation, 1974.

Glatzer, Nahum N. *The Passover Haggadah.* 3rd edn. New York: Schocken, 1979.

Kaplan, Mordecai Menahem, Eugene Kohn, and Ira Eisenstein. *The New Haggadah for the Pesah Seder [= Hagadah Shel Pesaḥ: Seder Ḥadash].* Rev. edn. New York: Behrman House, 1942.

Raphael, Chaim. *A Feast of History; the Drama of Passover Through the Ages.* London: Weidenfeld and Nicolson, 1972.

Wiesel, Elie. *[Hagadah Shel Pesaḥ =] A Passover Haggadah.* New York: Simon & Schuster, 1993.

Yerushalmi, Yosef Hayim. *Haggadah and History: A Panorama in Facsimile of Five Centuries of the Printed Haggadah from the Collections of Harvard University and the Jewish Theological Seminary of America.* Philadelphia: Jewish Publication Society of America, 1974.

Piyyut

Heinemann, Joseph, and Jakob Josef Petuchowski. *Literature of the Synagogue.* Piscataway, NJ: Gorgias Press, 2006.

Lieber, Laura Suzanne. *Yannai on Genesis: An Invitation to Piyyut.* Cincinnati: Hebrew Union College Press, 2010.

Rosenfeld, Abraham. *Tisha b'Av Compendium: Including Kinot for the Ninth of Av, Prayers for the Evening, Morning, and Afternoon Services, Reading of the Law and the Blessing of the New Moon According to the Ashkenazic Rite: Also Two Elegies on the York Massacres and a Special Elegy in Memory of Our Six Million Martyrs Who Perished During the Nazi Regime*. New York: Judaica Press, 1983.

Women's prayer

Kay, Devra. *Seyder Tkhines: The Forgotten Book of Common Prayer for Jewish Women*. Philadelphia: The Jewish Publication Society, 2004.
Neuda, Fanny. *Hours of Devotion: Fanny Neuda's Book of Prayers for Jewish Women*. Edited by Dinah Berland. New York: Schocken Books, 2007.
Tarnor, Norman. *A Book of Jewish Women's Prayers: Translations from the Yiddish*. Northvale, NJ: Jason Aronson, 1995.
Weissler, Chava. *Voices of the Matriarchs: Listening to the Prayers of Early Modern Jewish Women*. Boston, MA: Beacon Press, 1998.

Midrash and Aggadah

Halakhic Midrash

Basser, Herbert W. *In the Margins of the Midrash: Sifre Ha'azinu Texts, Commentaries, and Reflections*. Atlanta, GA: Scholars Press, 1990.
Basser, Herbert W. *Midrashic Interpretations of the Song of Moses*. American University Studies v. 2. New York: P. Lang, 1984.
Fraade, Steven D. *From Tradition to Commentary: Torah and Its Interpretation in the Midrash Sifre to Deuteronomy*. SUNY Series in Judaica. Albany: State University of New York Press, 1991.
Hammer, Reuven. *The Classic Midrash: Tannaitic Commentaries on the Bible*. Classics of Western Spirituality. New York: Paulist Press, 1995.
Hammer, Reuven. *Sifre: A Tannaitic Commentary on the Book of Deuteronomy*. New Haven: Yale University Press, 1986.
Kadushin, Max. *A Conceptual Approach to the Mekilta*. New York: Published by J. David for the Jewish Theological Seminary of America, 1969.
Lauterbach, Jacob Z., ed. *Mekilta De-Rabbi Ishmael*. Philadelphia: Jewish Publication Society of America, 1933.
Levertoff, Paul P. *Midrash Sifre on Numbers; Selections from Early Rabbinic Scriptural Interpretations*. London: Society for Promoting Christian Knowledge, 1926.
Montefiore, C. G., and H. M. J. Loewe. *A Rabbinic Anthology*. New York: Schocken Books, 1974.
Neusner, Jacob. *Sifre Zutta to Numbers*. Lanham, MD: University Press of America, 2009.
Neusner, Jacob. *Sifré to Numbers: An American Translation and Explanation*. Atlanta, GA: Scholars Press, 1986.

Aggadic Midrash

Braude, William G. *Pesikta Rabbati; Discourses for Feasts, Fasts, and Special Sabbaths*. Yale Judaica Series v. 18. New Haven, CT: Yale University Press, 1968.

Braude, William Gordon. *The Midrash on Psalms*. Yale Judaica series v. 13. New Haven, CT: Yale University Press, 1959.

Braude, William G., and Israel J. Kapstein. *Pěsiḳta Dě-Rab Kahǎna: R. Kahana's Compilation of Discourses for Sabbaths and Festal Days*. 2nd ed. Philadephia, Pa: Jewish Publication Society, 2002.

Braude, William G., and Israel G. Kapstein. *[Tanna Děbe Eliyyahu =] The Lore of the School of Elijah*. Philadelphia: Jewish Publication Society of America, 1981.

Freedman, H. *The Soncino Midrash Rabbah*. Edited by Isidore Epstein. The CD-ROM Judaic classics library. Chicago, IL: Davka, 1995.

Freedman, H. *Midrash Rabbah*. Edited by Maurice Simon. London: Soncino Press, 1939.

Friedlander, Gerald. *Pirke De Rabbi Eliezer (The Chapters of Rabbi Eliezer the Great) According to the Text of the Manuscript Belonging to Abraham Epstein of Vienna*. 2nd edn. New York: Hermon Press, 1965.

Neusner, Jacob. *Genesis Rabbah: The Judaic Commentary to the Book of Genesis: A New American Translation*. Brown Judaic Studies no. 104–106. Atlanta, GA: Scholars Press, 1985.

Segal, Eliezer. *From Sermon to Commentary: Expounding the Bible in Talmudic Babylonia*. Waterloo, ON: published for the Canadian Corporation for Studies in Religion/Corporation canadienne des sciences religieuses by Wilfrid Laurier University Press, 2005.

Segal, Eliezer. *The Babylonian Esther Midrash: A Critical Commentary*. Brown Judaic studies no. 291–293. Atlanta, GA: Scholars Press, 1994.

Biblical interpretation

Benyowitz, Allan R. *Translation of Ibn Ezra's Commentary on the Pentateuch*. Jerusalem: s.n., 2006.

Block, Richard A. *Ibn Ezra's Commentary on the Song of Songs = [Perush Ibn 'Ezra' al Shir Ha-Shirim]*. Cincinnati, OH: Hebrew Union College-Jewish Institute of Religion, 1982.

Chavel, Charles Ber, ed. *Ramban: Commentary on the Torah*. New York: Shilo, 1971.

Cohen, A., ed. *The Soncino Chumash; the Five Books of Moses, with Haphtaroth*. Soncino Books of the Bible. London: The Soncino Press, 1956.

Gruber, Mayer I. *Rashi's Commentary on Psalms*. South Florida studies in the history of Judaism no. 161. Atlanta, GA: Scholars Press, 1998.

Hirsch, Samson Raphael. *The Hirsch Chumash: The Five Books of Torah*. Translated by Daniel Haberman. Jerusalem: Feldheim, 2000.

Hirsch, Samson Raphael. *The Pentateuch*. Translated by Isaac Levy. 2nd edn. Gateshead: Judaica Press, 1982.

Jacobs, Louis. *Jewish Biblical Exegesis*. New York: Behrman House, 1973.

Japhet, Sara. *The Commentary of R. Samuel Ben Meir, Rashbam, on Qoheleth*. Translated by Robert B. Salters. Jerusalem: Magnes Press, Hebrew University, 1985.

Lancaster, Irene. *Deconstructing the Bible: Abraham Ibn Ezra's Introduction to the Torah*. RoutledgeCurzon Jewish philosophy series. London: RoutledgeCurzon, 2003.

Leibowitz, Nehama. *Studies in Bamidbar (Numbers)*. Translated by Aryeh Newman. Jerusalem: World Zionist Organization, Dept. for Torah Education and Culture in the Diaspora, 1980.

Leibowitz, Nehama. *Studies in Devarim (Deuteronomy)*. Translated by Aryeh Newman. Jerusalem: World Zionist Organization, Dept. for Torah Education and Culture in the Diaspora, 1980.

Leibowitz, Nehama. *Studies in Vayikra (Leviticus)*. Translated by Aryeh Newman. Jerusalem: World Zionist Organization, Dept. for Torah Education and Culture in the Diaspora, 1980.

Leibowitz, Nehama. *Studies in Shemot: The Book of Exodus*. Jerusalem: World Zionist Organization, Dept. for Torah Education and Culture in the Diaspora, 1976.

Leibowitz, Nehama. *Studies in the Book of Genesis in the Context of Ancient and Modern Jewish Bible Commentary*. Jerusalem: World Zionist Organization, Dept. for Torah Education and Culture, 1972.

Leibowitz, Nehama. *Studies in the Weekly Sidra*. Jerusalem: World Zionist Organisation, Dept. for Torah Education and Culture in the Diaspora, 1958.

Lockshin, Martin I. *Rashbam's Commentary on Deuteronomy: An Annotated Translation*. Brown Judaic studies no. 340. Providence, RI: Brown Judaic Studies, 2004.

Lockshin, Martin I. *Rashbam's Commentary on Leviticus and Numbers: An Annotated Translation*. Brown Judaic studies no. 330. Providence, RI: Brown Judaic Studies, 2001.

Lockshin, Martin I. *Rashbam's Commentary on Exodus: An Annotated Translation*. Brown Judaic studies no. 310. Atlanta, GA: Scholars Press, 1997.

Lockshin, Martin I. *Rabbi Samuel Ben Meir's Commentary on Genesis: An Annotated Translation*. Lewiston, NY: E. Mellen Press, 1989.

Pearl, Chaim. *Rashi, Commentaries on the Pentateuch*. New York: Norton, 1970.

Rosenau, William. *Jewish Biblical Commentators*. Baltimore, MD: The Lord Baltimore Press, 1906.

Shachter, Jay F. *The Commentary of Abraham Ibn Ezra on the Pentateuch*. Hoboken, NJ: Ktav Pub. House, 1986.

Simon, Uriel. *Four Approaches to the Book of Psalms: From Saadiah Gaon to Abraham Ibn Ezra*. SUNY series in Judaica. Albany: State University of New York Press, 1991.

Strickman, H. Norman. *Rabbi Abraham Ibn Ezra's Commentary on the First Two Books of Psalms*. Brighton, MA: Academic Studies Press, 2009.

Strickman, H. Norman, and Arthur M. Silver. *Ibn Ezra's Commentary on the Pentateuch*. New York: Menorah, 1988.

Halakhic literature

Mishnah and Tosefta

Blackman, Philip, ed. *Mishnayoth*. London: Mishna Press, 1951.

Danby, Herbert. *The Mishnah*. London: Oxford University Press, H. Milford, 1938.

Neusner, Jacob. *The Law of Agriculture in the Mishnah and the Tosefta: Translation, Commentary, Theology*. Leiden: Brill, 2005.

Neusner, Jacob. *The Tosefta*. South Florida studies in the history of Judaism no. 214–216. Atlanta, GA: Scholars Press, 1999.

Neusner, Jacob. *The Mishnah: Introduction and Reader*. Philadelphia: Trinity Press International, 1992.

Neusner, Jacob. *The Mishnah: A New Translation*. New Haven, CT: Yale University Press, 1988.

Neusner, Jacob. *Learn Mishnah*. New York: Behrman House, 1978.

Talmuds

Epstein, Isidore, ed. *The Babylonian Talmud*. London: Soncino Press, 1935.

Guggenheimer, Heinrich W. *The Jerusalem Talmud [= Talmud Yerushalmi]*. Berlin: Walter de Gruyter, 2000.

Neusner, Jacob. *The Babylonian Talmud: A Translation and Commentary*. 22 vols. Peabody, MA: Hendrickson Publishers, 2005.

Neusner, Jacob. *The Talmud: Introduction and Reader*. Atlanta, GA: Scholars Press, 1995.

Neusner, Jacob, ed. *The Talmud of the Land of Israel: A Preliminary Translation and Explanation*. Chicago Studies in the History of Judaism. Chicago: University of Chicago Press, 1982.

Schorr, Yisroel Simcha, and Chaim Malinowitz. *The Gemara: The Classic Vilna Edition, with an Annotated, Interpretive Elucidation*. The ArtScroll Series. Brooklyn, NY: Mesorah Publications, 1992.

Steinsaltz, Adin. *The Talmud [= Talmud Bavli]: The Steinsaltz Edition*. 1st edn. New York: Random House, 1989.

The Talmud: With English Translation and Commentary. Jerusalem: El-'Am, 1965.

Codes

Kadushin, J. L. *Jewish Code of Jurisprudence. Talmudical Law Decisions, Civil, Criminal and Social*. 4th edn. New Rochelle, NY: The Jewish Jurisprudence Co, 1917.

Kadushin, J. L. *Jewish Code of Jurisprudence*. 2nd edn. New York: The author, 1915.

Kagan, Israel Meir. *Mishnah Berurah: The Classic Commentary to Shulchan Aruch Orach Chayim, Comprising the Laws of Daily Jewish Conduct*. Edited by Aharon Feldman and Aviel Orenstein. Hebrew-English edn. Jerusalem: Pisgah Foundation, 1989.

Kaplan, Aryeh. *The Laws of Chanukah from the Shulchan Arukh*. New York: Moznaim, 1977.

Karo, Joseph ben Ephraim, and Stephen M. Passamaneck. *The Traditional Jewish Law of Sale: Shulḥan Arukh, Hoshen Mishpat, Chapters 189–240*. Monographs of the Hebrew Union College no. 9. Cincinnati: Hebrew Union College Press, 1983.

Karo, Joseph ben Ephraim. *The Kosher Code of the Orthodox Jew, Being a Literal Translation of That Portion of the Sixteenth-Century Codification of the Babylonian Talmud Which Describes Such Deficiencies as Render Animals Unfit for Food (Hilkot Ṭerefot, Shulḥan 'aruk); to Which Is Appended a Discussion of Talmudic Anatomy in the Light of the Science of Its Day and of the Present Time*. Edited by Solomon Isaac Levin and Edward A. Boyden. New York: Hermon Press, 1969.

Maimonides, Moses. *The Guide of the Perplexed of Maimonides*. Translated by Michael Friedländer. London: Trübner, 1981.

Maimonides, Moses. *The Guide of the Perplexed*. Edited by Shlomo Pines. Chicago: University of Chicago Press, 1963.

Maimonides, Moses. *The Guide of the Perplexed*. Translated by Julius Guttmann. Philosophia Judaica. London: East and West Library, 1952.

Maimonides, Moses. *The Code of Maimonides*. New Haven, CT: Yale University Press, 1949.

Quint, Emanuel B. *A Restatement of Rabbinic Civil Law*. Northvale, NJ: J. Aronson, 1990.

Russell, H. M, and J. Weinberg, eds. *The Book of Knowledge: From the Mishneh Torah of Maimonides*. New York: Ktav, 1983.

Touger, Eliyahu, ed. *[Hilchot Yesodei HaTorah =] The Laws (which Are) the Foundations of the Torah*. New York: Moznaim, 750.

Touger, Eliyahu, ed. *[Hilchot Tefilah, II, and Birkat Kohanim =] The Laws of Prayer and the Priestly Blessing: A New Translation with Commentaries, Notes, and Diagrams*. New York (4304 12th Ave., Brooklyn 11219): Moznaim, 749.

Touger, Eliyahu, ed. *[Hilchot Melachim U'milchamoteihem =] The Laws of Kings and Their Wars: A New Translation with Commentaries, Notes, Illustrations, and Index*. New York: Moznaim Pub. Corp, 747.

Touger, Eliyahu, ed. *[Hilchos Bais Habechirah =] The Laws of (Go-D's) Chosen House: A New Translation with Commentaries, Notes, Tables, Charts, and Index*. New York: Moznaim, 746.

Townsend, John T. *Midrash Tanḥuma*. Hoboken, NJ: Ktav, 1989.

Twersky, Isadore. *A Maimonides Reader*. New York: Behrman House, 1972.

Responsa

Bazak, Jacob, and Stephen M. Passamaneck. *Jewish Law and Jewish Life: Selected Rabbinical Responsa*. New York: Union of American Hebrew Congregations, 1979.

Feinstein, Moses. *Responsa of Rav Moshe Feinstein: Translation and Commentary*. Edited by Moshe David Tendler. Hoboken, NJ: KTAV Pub. House, 1996.

Freehof, Solomon Bennett. *New Reform Responsa*. Cincinnati, OH: Hebrew Union College Press, 1980.

Freehof, Solomon Bennett. *The Responsa Literature and A Treasury of Responsa*. New York: KTAV Pub. House, 1973.

Freehof, Solomon Bennett. *A Treasury of Responsa*. Philadelphia: Jewish Publication Society of America, 1963.

Ginzberg, Louis. *The Responsa of Professor Louis Ginzberg*. Edited by David Golinkin. Moreshet series v. 16. New York: Jewish Theological Seminary of America, 1996.

Golinkin, David. *An Index of Conservative Responsa and Practical Halakhic Studies, 1917–1990*. New York: Rabbinical Assembly, 1992.

Jacob, Walter. *American Reform Responsa: Collected Responsa of the Central Conference of American Rabbis, 1889–1983*. New York: Central Conference of American Rabbis, 1983.

Kirschner, Robert. *Rabbinic Responsa of the Holocaust Era*. New York: Schocken, 1985.

Schwarz, Jacob D. *Responsa of the Central Conference of American Rabbis Contained in Its Yearbook, Vols. I–LX, 1890–1950*. New York: Union of Amerian Hebrew Congregations, 1954.

Philosophy

Baḥya ben Joseph ibn Paḳuda. *The Duties of the Heart*. Edited by Yaakov Feldman. Northvale, NJ: J. Aronson, 1996.

Bokser, Ben Zion. *The Essential Writings of Abraham Isaac Kook*. Teaneck, NJ: Ben Yehuda Press, 2006.

Bokser, Ben Zion. *Abraham Isaac Kook: The Lights of Penitence, The Moral Principles, Lights of Holiness, Essays, Letters, and Poems*. The Classics of Western Spirituality. New York: Paulist Press, 1978.

Feldman, Tzvi, ed. *Rav A.Y. Kook: Selected Letters*. Ma'aleh Adumim, Israel: Ma'aliot Publications of Yeshivat Birkat Moshe, 1986.

Halevi, Judah. *The Kuzari: In Defense of the Despised Faith*. Edited by N. Daniel Korobkin. Jerusalem: Feldheim, 2009.

Halevi, Judah. *[Sefer Ha-Kuzari =] Book of Kuzari*. Edited by Joshua Bloch. Translated by Hartwig Hirschfeld. New York: Pardes Pub. House, 1946.

Kook, Abraham. *Orot*. Translated by Betsal'el Na'or. Northvale, NJ: Jason Aronson, 1993.

Kook, Abraham. *Rabbi Kook's Philosophy of Repentance: A Translation of "Orot Ha-Teshuvah"*. 2nd edn. Studies in Torah Judaism 11. New York: Yeshiva University Press, Dept. of Special Publications, 1978.

Lewy, Hans, Alexander Altmann, and Isaak Heinemann, trans. *Three Jewish Philosophers: Philo, Saadya Gaon, Jehuda Halevi*. New York: Meridian Books, 1960.

Na'or, Betsal'el, ed. *Of Societies Perfect and Imperfect: Selected Readings from Eyn Ayah, Rav Kook's Commentary to Eyn Yaakov Legends of the Talmud*. Brooklyn, NY: Sepher-Hermon Press, 1995.

Sa'adia ben Joseph. *The Book of Doctrines and Beliefs*. Edited by Alexander Altmann and Daniel H Frank. Indianapolis: Hackett Pub. Co, 2002.

Sa'adia ben Joseph. *The Book of Beliefs and Opinions*. Edited by Samuel Rosenblatt. New Haven, CT: Yale University Press, 1976.

Samson, David, and Tzvi Fishman. *War and Peace: The Teachings of HaRav Avraham Yitzhak HaCohen Kook*. Lights on Orot v. 2. Jerusalem: Torat Eretz Yisrael Publications, 5757.

Samson, David, and Tzvi Fishman. *Eretz Yisrael: The Teachings of HaRav Avraham Yitzhak HaCohen Kook*. Lights on OROT 1. Jerusalem: Torat Eretz Yisrael Publications, 5756.

Twersky, Isadore. *A Maimonides Reader*. New York: Behrman House, 1972.

Mysticism and kabbalah

Ben Zion, Raphael. *An Anthology of Jewish Mysticism*. New York: Judaica Press, 1981.

Blumenthal, David R. *Understanding Jewish Mysticism: A Source Reader*. The Library of Judaic learning v. 2, 4. New York: KTAV, 1978.

Jacobs, Louis. *The Schocken Book of Jewish Mystical Testimonies*. New York: Schocken Books, 1997.

Matt, Daniel Chanan. *The Essential Kabbalah: The Heart of Jewish Mysticism*. San Francisco, CA: HarperSanFrancisco, 1995.

Bahir and early kabbalah

Dan, Joseph, and Ronald C Kiener. *The Early Kabbalah*. The Classics of Western Spirituality. New York: Paulist Press, 1986.

Kaplan, Aryeh, ed. *The Bahir: An Ancient Kabbalistic Text Attributed to Rabbi Nehuniah Ben HaKana, First Century*, CE. New York: S. Weiser, 1979.

Zohar

Ashlag, Yehudah. *The Zohar: Parashat Pinḥas*. Edited by Philip S Berg. Rev. edn. New York: Research Centre of Kabbalah, 1994.

Englander, Lawrence A., and Herbert W. Basser. *The Mystical Study of Ruth: Midrash HaNe'elam of the Zohar to the Book of Ruth*. Atlanta, GA: Scholars Press, 1993.

Giller, Pinchas. *Reading the Zohar: The Sacred Text of the Kabbalah*. New York: Oxford University Press, 2001.

Lachower, Yeruḥam Fishel, and Isaiah Tishby. *The Wisdom of the Zohar: An Anthology of Texts*. Translated by David Goldstein. Oxford: For the Littman Library by Oxford University Press, 1989.

Matt, Daniel Chanan. *The Zohar [= Sefer Ha-Zohar]*. Pritzker edn. Stanford, CA: Stanford University Press, 2004.

Matt, Daniel Chanan. *Zohar: Annotated & Explained*. SkyLight illuminations. Woodstock, VT: SkyLight Paths Publishing, 2002.

Matt, Daniel Chanan. *Zohar, the Book of Enlightenment*. The Classics of Western Spirituality. New York: Paulist Press, 1983.

Scholem, Gershom Gerhard. *Zohar, the Book of Splendor*. New York: Schocken Books, 1963.

Sperling, Harry. *The Zohar*. Edited by Maurice Simon. 2nd edn. London: New York, 1984.

Zohar, and Dagobert David Runes. *The Wisdom of the Kabbalah*. New York: Philosophical Library, 1957.

Lurianic kabbalah

Dunn, James David, and Nathan Snyder. *Window of the Soul: The Kabbalah of Rabbi Isaac Luria (1534–1572): Selections from Chayyim Vital*. San Francisco, CA: Weiserbooks, 2008.

Gordon, Hirsch L. *The Maggid of Caro; the Mystic Life of the Eminent Codifier Joseph Caro as Revealed in His Secret Diary*. New York: Pardes, 1949.

Moralistic and ethical works

Abrahams, Israel. *Hebrew Ethical Wills*. Facsimile of original 1926 edn. JPS Library of Jewish Classics. Philadelphia: Jewish Publication Society of America, 1976.

Bahya ben Joseph ibn Pakuda. *The Duties of the Heart*. Edited by Yaakov Feldman. Northvale, NJ: J. Aronson, 1996.

Glueckel. *The Memoirs of Glückel of Hameln*. Edited by Marvin Lowenthal. New York and London: Harper & Brothers, 1932.

Goldberg, Hillel. *Musar Anthology*. 1st edn. Hyde Park, MA: Harwich Lithograph, 1972.

Judah ben Samuel. *Sefer Chasidim: The Book of the Pious*. Edited by Avraham Yaakov Finkel. Northvale, NJ: Jason Aronson, 1997.

Judah ben Samuel. *Medieval Jewish Mysticism. Book of the Pious*. Northbrook, IL: Whitehall Co, 1971.

Luzzatto, Moshe Hayyim. *Derekh H*. Edited by Aryeh Kaplan and Gershon Robinson. 5th edn. Torah Classics Library. Jerusalem: Feldheim Publishers, 1997.

Luzzatto, Moshe Hayyim. *The Path of the Just*. Edited by Yaakov Feldman. Northvale, NJ: Jason Aronson, 1996.

Luzzatto, Moshe Hayyim. *The Path of the Upright = Mesillat Yesharim*. Translated by Mordecai Menahem Kaplan. Northvale, NJ: Jason Aronson, 1995.

Luzzatto, Moshe Hayyim. *[Mesillat Yesharim =] The Path of the Just*. Translated by Shraga Silverstein. 3rd edn. The Torah Classics Library. Jerusalem: Feldheim, 1990.

Riemer, Jack, and Nathaniel Stampfer, eds. *Ethical Wills: A Modern Jewish Treasury*. New York: Schocken Books, 1983.

Rosenblatt, Samuel, ed. *The High Ways to Perfection of Abraham Maimonides*. Columbia University Oriental Studies v. 27. New York: Columbia University Press, 1927.

Salanter, Israel, and Isaac Blaser. *Ohr Yisrael: The Classic Writings of Rav Yisrael Salanter and His Disciple Rav Yitzchak Blazer*. Edited by Zvi Miller and Eli Linas. Southfield, MI: Targum, 2004.

Singer, Sholom A. *Sefer Hasidim (Book of the Pious): A Translation with Notes and Introduction*. (n.p, n.d).

Avot

Bunim, Irving M. *Ethics from Sinai: A Wide-Ranging Commentary on Pirkei Avos*. Jerusalem: Feldheim Publishers, 2000.

Goldin, Judah, ed. *The Fathers According to Rabbi Nathan*. New York: Schocken Books, 1974.

Goldin, Judah. *The Living Talmud; the Wisdom of the Fathers and Its Classical Commentaries*. Chicago: University of Chicago Press, 1958.

Herford, Robert Travers, ed. *Pirke Aboth. The Ethics of the Talmud: Sayings of the Fathers*. New York: Schocken Books, 1962.

Neusner, Jacob. *Torah from Our Sages: A New American Translation and Explanation [= Pirke Avot]*. 1st edn. Chappaqua, NY: Rossel Books, 1984.

Hasidism

Buber, Martin. *Martin Buber's Ten Rungs: Collected Hasidic Sayings*. Secaucus, NJ: Carol Pub. Group, 1995.

Eliach, Yaffa. *Hasidic Tales of the Holocaust*. New York: Oxford University Press, 1982.

Green, Arthur, and Barry W. Holtz. *Your Word Is Fire: The Hasidic Masters on Contemplative Prayer*. New York: Schocken Books, 1987.

Handler, Andrew, Albert Neumann, József Patai, and Lajos Szabolcsi. *Rabbi Eizik: Hasidic Stories About the Zaddik of Kallo*. Rutherford: Fairleigh Dickinson University Press, 1978.

Levin, Meyer. *Classic Hassidic Tales: Marvellous Tales of Rabbi Israel Baal Shem and of His Great-Grandson, Rabbi Nachman, Retold from Hebrew, Yiddish, and German Sources*. New York: Penguin Books, 1975.

Newman, Louis I. *The Hasidic Anthology; Tales and Teachings of the Hasidim*. New York: Schocken Books, 1963.

Schneersohn, Dov Baer. *Tract on Ecstacy*. Edited by Louis Jacobs. London: Vallentine Mitchell, 2006.

Ba'al Shem Tov

Ben-Amos, Dan, and Jerome R. Mintz. *In Praise of the Baal-Shem Tov: The Earliest Collection of Legends About the Founder of Hasidism [= Shivhei Ha-Besht]*. New York: Schocken Books, 1984.

Buber, Martin. *The Legend of the Baal-Shem*. New York: Schocken Books, 1969.

Klapholz, Israel Jacob. *Tales of the Baal Shem Tov: A Collection of Stories and Biographical Sketches Taken from Reliable Sources*. [Bnei Brak: Klapholz], 1973.

Schneersohn, Dov Baer. *Tract on Ecstacy*. Edited by Louis Jacobs. London: Vallentine Mitchell, 2006.

Schochet, Jacob Immanuel. *The Testament of Rabbi Israel Baal Shem Tov*. Brooklyn, NY: Kehot Publication Society, 1998.

Rabbi Nahman

Buber, Martin. *The Tales of Rabbi Nachman*. London: Souvenir Press, 1974.

Kaplan, Aryeh. *Gems of Rabbi Nachman*. Monsey, NY: Breslov Research Institute, 1980.

Rabbi Nachman's Stories: The Stories of Rabbi Nachman of Breslov [= Sippurey Ma'asioth]. Brooklyn, NY (3100 Brighton 3rd St., Brooklyn 11235): Breslov Research Institute, 1983.

Steinsaltz, Adin. *The Tales of Rabbi Nachman of Bratslav*. Northvale, NJ: Jason Aronson, 1993.

Steinsaltz, Adin. *Beggars and Prayers: Adin Steinsaltz Retells the Tales of Rabbi Nachman of Bratslav*. Edited by Jonathan Ober-Man. Translated by Yehuda Hanegbi. New York: Basic Books, 1979.

Sternharz, Nathan. *Rabbi Nachman's Wisdom: Shevachay haRan, Sichos haRan*. Brooklyn, 1973.

Index

A

Aaron 26–29, 56, 172, 173
Aaron of Karlin 185
Abrabanel, Don Isaac 103, 104, 108, 191
Abraham 11, 20, 25, 28, 46
absolute intellect 125
Abulafia, Abraham 154
account of the chariot 7, 130–137, 142, 182
account of the creation 130
active intellect 124, 125, 154
Adam and Eve 20, 35, 152
Additional Service (Musaf) 16–18
afterlife 134, 163 see also world to come, resurrection
aggadah 5, 21–24, 36, 43, 49, 69, 162
Ahasuerus 50–52
Akiva, Rabbi 24, 36, 133, 134
Alfasi, Isaac 68–71, 78, 81, 171
allegory 121
America 85
Amora, Amora'im 56, 79, 191
Amram Gaon 65
angels 12, 33, 52, 90, 103, 105, 125, 131–133, 136, 155, 156, 159, 160
anthropomorphism 92, 119, 124, 126, 144
apocalypse 2, 156
apostates 14
Arabic 4, 6, 94, 110, 113, 114
Aramaic 4, 22, 57, 98, 144, 148, 149
archeology 3
Aristotelianism 7, 8, 115, 122, 125
Aristotle 110, 112, 114, 120–122
astrology 103–105
attributes 110, 116–120
attributes of action 117–120
Avot, Mishnah tractate (Ethics of the Fathers) 8, 162–164, 176, 178

B

Ba'al Shem Tov, Israel 178, 180, 188, 191
Babylonian Talmud 56, 71, 72, 133, 170
Bahir 7, 137, 140, 142–144, 190
Baḥya Ibn Paquda 113, 114, 165–167
Balaam 89–109
Balak 89, 90, 92–95, 100–108
Baraita 53, 56–65, 68–70, 78, 79, 87, 90, 91
Ben Azzai 133, 134, 163, 190
Ben Zoma 24, 25, 133, 134, 162
Bible commentaries 6, 8, 89, 171
blessings 10–14, 16, 19–21, 25, 29, 33, 40, 41, 55, 65–67, 73, 74, 77–79, 81, 85–87, 90, 104, 107, 108, 145, 146, 149, 151, 175, 179, 187–189
Book of the Pious [Sefer Ḥasidim] 168–171

C

Cairo Genizah 10, 25
Caro, Joseph 81, 160, 161, 191 see also Maggid Meisharim; Shulḥan 'Arukh
celestial academy 161
Christians 14, 166
circumcision 20
commandments 1, 4, 19, 34, 37–39, 41, 55, 67, 110, 113, 123–126, 151, 158, 163, 165, 186, 188, 189

covenant 1, 19, 20, 45, 139
creation out of nothingness 147
curriculum 8, 152, 154, 168, 170,
  180
curses 55, 89, 90, 92, 95, 97–102, 104,
  106–109, 188, 189

D

Daniel (biblical book) 2
Darwin, Charles 121, 127
David (biblical king) 15, 48, 168, 169
de Leon, Moses 144 *see also Zohar*
demons 71–73
Dov Baer of Mezhirech 185

E

Ecclesiastes 2, 108, 133, 141, 166, 167,
  175
Eden, garden of 7, 20, 21, 133, 134,
  152
education 8, 168–170 *see also*
  curriculum
Eighteen Blessings 10–13, 25, 66, 67,
  87 *see also* Tefillah
Ein Sof 7, 127, 157, 158
Elijah (prophet) 2, 113, 152
Elimelech of Lyzhansk 186–189, 191
Elisha ben Abuya (Aḥer) 133, 134,
  179, 180
erotic and sexual imagery in Kabbalah
  139
eschatology 10, 32, 48, 127, 153,
  188
Essenes 4
Esther 49–53
eternity of the universe 120–122
evil 46, 47, 93, 95, 101, 104, 128,
  151–153, 158, 160, 180, 182
evolution 127
exile 1, 13, 14, 16, 17, 21, 23, 48, 49,
  124, 129, 139, 151–153, 184
Ezekiel 12, 29, 97, 98, 130, 136,
  151, 156

G

Gabriel, angel 51, 52, 124, 125, 136
Gehenna 170
Geonim 64, 65, 69, 78–80, 94, 95, 97,
  110
German Pietism [Ḥasidut Ashkenaz]
  168

gezerah shavah 41, 42, 47
Ginzberg, Louis 63, 64
Glueckel of Hameln 174

H

Haggadah for Passover 21–24
Hai Gaon 66–68, 72
halakhah 5, 6, 8, 36, 54, 55, 64, 65, 67,
  69, 77, 79–83, 85–88, 162
Halevi, Judah 6, 122–125
Haman 50–53
Ḥananel 78
hand-washing, ritual 179
Hasdai Ibn Shaprut 122
Ḥasidism 178, 180, 186–189
Hasmoneans 1
Havdalah 79, 85
heave-offering (terumah) 55–58, 61, 63,
  65, 69, 70
heavenly court 160, 179
Hebrew Bible 3
Heikhalot 134, 137
heretics 14, 123
Hezekiah ben Manoah 98–100
Hillel the Elder 36, 164
humility 136, 176, 177

I

Ibn Ezra, Abraham 11, 20, 25, 27, 28,
  45, 46, 55, 94–98, 101, 131, 132,
  154, 190
incest 38, 130
incorporeality of God 110, 112, 121,
  122, 125, 139
Isaac 11, 20
Isaac of Dampierre 76
Ishmael, Rabbi 36–37, 134, 135,
  137, 190
Islam 123, 166
Isserlein, Israel 80, 82, 191
Isserles, Moses 80–82, 191

J

Jacob 11, 145
Jephthah's daughter 47
Jerusalem 1, 5, 11, 15, 21, 58
Jerusalem Talmud 68, 71
Josephus Flavius 3
Judah ben Samuel of Regensburg 168
Judeo-Arabic 4, 111
justice 14, 139, 142, 143, 158

K

Kabbalah 7–9, 83, 100, 108, 127, 130,
  137–140, 142–144, 146–148, 150,
  151, 153, 157, 159, 160, 175, 178,
  179, 184
Kabbalah, Lurianic 9, 157, 159, 179,
  184, 188
Kagan, Israel Meir 86, 191
Kalam 110
Karaites 4, 94, 110
Katz, Jacob 87, 88
Khazars 122
kinnah (elegy) 30, 31
kohen, kohanim see priests
Kook, Abraham Isaac Hakohen
  126–129, 191

L

levirate marriage 38
Lilith 152, 153
Lipschutz, Israel 82–86, 191
Luria, Isaac 7, 137, 157, 158, 179, 191
  see also Kabbalah, Lurianic
Luzzatto, Moses Hayyim 175, 176, 191

M

maggid 160, 161
Maggid Meisharim 160, 161 *see also*
  Caro, Joseph
Maimonides, Moses 7, 70, 71, 78, 81,
  101, 114–116, 119, 120, 122, 125,
  154, 174, 190
manna 123, 149, 150
maror (bitter herbs eaten on Passover) 23
Meir (ben Baruch) of Rothenburg 78
Meir Ha-Kohen of Rothenburg 78, 80,
  191
Mekhilta 37–43
Meklenburg, Jacob Zevi 108, 191
Mendelssohn, Moses 3, 113
menstruation 152, 171
mercy 14–16, 118–120, 139, 151
messiah 24, 46, 48, 49, 152, 163, 176,
  180, 185 *see also* eschatology;
  redemption
Metatron 156
Midian 89–93, 95, 99
midrash 2, 3, 5, 9, 20, 22, 25, 26,
  35–37, 41–47, 49, 50, 52, 53, 55, 92,
  93, 98, 101, 103, 108, 137, 139–141,
  143, 144, 151, 173

Minḥah (afternoon service) 66, 74–76
miracles 12, 16, 26, 37, 111, 113, 121,
  123, 124, 133, 178
Miriam 172, 173
Mishnah 4, 7, 8, 22, 23, 33, 55–58, 60,
  61, 63, 64, 68–77, 79, 82–87, 91,
  130, 131, 134, 140, 152, 160–164,
  170, 190
Mishneh Torah (by Moses
  Maimonides) 70, 71
Moab 89–91, 93, 95, 99, 105, 109
Mordecai 50, 51
Moses 1, 26–29, 37, 45, 46, 49, 96,
  111, 116, 117, 119, 120, 123–125,
  152, 153, 172, 173

N

Naḥman of Bratslav 180, 185
Naḥmanides, Moses (Ramban)
  100–103, 108, 190
nationalism 128, 129
Nazarenes 14
Nehunya ben ha-Kanah 140
Neoplatonism 7, 8, 113, 114, 165
Nissim ben Reuben of Gerona 171,
  173, 174
Nothingness 147

O

oral Torah 2, 5, 10, 62, 94, 108, 162

P

Pappa 91, 190
parables 39, 40, 134, 141, 143, 144,
  155, 188, 189
pardes 134
Passover 21–24, 44
peace 13, 16, 21, 90, 99, 116
Pesiqta 44
petiḥa or *petiḥta* 44, 49
Pharisees 2, 12, 38
Philo Judaeus of Alexandria 3, 7
philosophy 3, 4, 6–8, 65, 70, 94,
  110, 112–115, 119, 120,
  122–127, 147, 154, 165, 166
piety 2, 7, 14, 33, 82, 87, 113,
  119, 142, 153, 165, 167–172,
  178, 186
piyyuṭ (liturgical poetry) 5, 9, 25–30,
  171
Plato 110

prayer 5, 6, 8, 10–13, 15–19, 21,
    25–27, 29, 32–35, 55, 65–68, 71–77,
    79, 80, 82–84, 86, 87, 119, 150,151,
    154, 156, 165, 178
prayer leader 10, 12, 16, 27
priestly blessing 16
priests (kohen / kohanim) 55–58, 60,
    61, 63–65, 69, 70, 79, 128
Primordial Man 158
prophecy 1, 2, 104, 105, 111, 123–125,
    154, 172–174
prophets 1, 2, 12, 30, 31, 36, 45, 89, 90,
    102–106, 108, 111, 112, 115, 118,
    121, 123–126, 130, 139, 148, 152,
    154, 156, 165, 166, 170–174, 176
Provence 68, 87
purity and impurity 5, 8, 56, 64, 69,
    128, 136, 151–153, 171, 177

Q

Qumran (Dead Sea scrolls) 4, 36, 38

R

Ra'aya Meheimana 151, 153
rabbinic Judaism 2, 4
rain 12, 13, 29, 148
Rashbam *see* Samuel ben Meir
Rashi (Rabbi Solomon ben Isaac) 9, 20,
    25, 26, 36, 43, 44, 46, 49, 50, 53,
    55, 60, 71–73, 75, 77, 78, 91–96, 98,
    101, 103, 108, 134, 137, 139–141,
    143, 144, 151, 173
redemption 11, 13, 18, 25, 45–49,
    65–68, 73, 74, 79, 87, 127, 151–154,
    163, 180, 185, 188
reincarnation 180
repentance 12, 151, 153, 179, 180, 188
responsa 5, 66, 80, 88, 171
Restoration (Tiqqun) 157, 158, 179,
    180
resurrection 11, 12, 29, 128, 155, 163
revelation 1, 6, 18, 37, 112, 124, 125
Rome 14, 30, 46, 48, 49, 134, 137,
    139, 143
Rosh Hashanah 17–19

S

Saadiah Gaon 7, 16, 17, 65, 94,
    110–113
Sabbath 17, 25, 33–35, 37–41, 43, 44,
    49, 58, 60, 62, 64, 69, 71, 76, 77,

    79, 83–86, 123, 152, 160, 162, 165,
    171, 187
sacrifice 17, 22, 38, 69, 74
Samael 160
Samuel ben Hofni 94
Samuel ben Meir (Rashbam) 96–98
Satan 160, 179
seder (Passover meal) 21
sefirot 7, 9, 137–140, 142–150, 153,
    157–159, 184
separate intelligences 125
Shaharit (morning service) 66
Shattering of the Vessels 157–159
Shavuot 82, 83
Shekhinah 139, 140, 143–148, 150,
    153, 159, 184, 186
Shema' 6, 24, 25, 55–58, 60, 63–81,
    83, 84, 86, 87
Shimshai 51, 52
Shivhei Ha-Besht 178
Shulhan 'Arukh by Joseph Caro 81, 82,
    86, 160
Simeon ben Yohai 144, 148, 151
simsum (Lurianic doctrine of divine
    self-contraction) 157, 158
Sinai 37, 41, 89, 107, 124, 125, 132
Solomon 166
Solomon ben Isaac *see* Rashi
Song of Songs 44–49, 133, 139, 145,
    161, 166, 168
soul 54, 56, 113, 114, 124, 125, 141,
    142, 144, 155, 179
Spain 55, 68, 81, 87, 94, 100, 108,
    113, 114, 122, 144, 151, 154,
    174
speech 37, 39, 114, 125, 126, 145–147,
    156, 160, 166, 167
Spinoza, Baruch 120
standard of justice and standard of
    mercy 139
Sufism 113
sukkah 165

T

t'khinnes 5, 32–35
talismans 104
Talmud 2, 5, 6, 8, 10, 11, 18, 22,
    49–79, 81–83, 85, 87, 90–94, 96,
    100, 101, 103, 104, 108, 110, 113,
    130, 131, 133, 134, 136, 139–142,
    145, 148, 153, 161, 169–171, 180,
    186, 190 *see also* Babylonian
    Talmud; Jerusalem Talmud

Tam, Jacob ben Meir 73, 75–80, 86, 96, 190
Tanna, Tannaim 55, 62, 63, 76, 79
Targum 98
tassels (ṣiṣit) 38, 39, 82–84, 86, 165
Tefillah 65–68, 71, 73–75, 77–79, 83, 84, 87 *see also* Eighteen Blessings
tefillin (phylacteries) 154, 156
Temple of Jerusalem 1, 12, 15–17, 22, 23, 30–32, 34–36, 38, 46, 52, 56, 64, 69, 74, 139
Ten Commandments 37, 41, 123–126, 186
Ten Imperial Martyrs 137
Torah 1, 5, 7, 10, 12, 16–18, 21, 22, 24, 32, 34–44, 49, 54–56, 62, 65, 67, 68, 72, 73, 77, 83, 86, 92, 94, 96–98, 100, 101, 103, 108–110, 112–115, 120, 121, 123, 124, 126, 129, 134, 139, 140, 142–145, 147, 148, 151, 153, 156, 158, 160–162, 164, 165, 170, 171, 179, 186
Tosafot 73–79, 96
Tosefta 133
Tree of Good and Evil 151, 152
Tree of Life 151–153

U

unleavened bread (matzah) 22, 23

V

Vital, Ḥayyim 157–159, 191

W

wedding 20, 21
women 2, 32–34, 112, 118, 152, 167, 171, 174
world to come 66, 73, 161, 163

Y

Yannai 25–30
Yavneh 134, 164, 190
Yiddish 4, 5, 33, 174, 180
Yoḥanan ben Zakkai 139, 140, 191

Z

ẓaddik (ḥasidic leader) 185, 188
Zohar 7, 137, 144–151, 153, 157